Studies in Contemporary and Historical Archaeology 4

Contemporary and Historical Archaeology in Theory

Papers from the 2003 and 2004 CHAT conferences

Edited by

Laura McAtackney
Matthew Palus
Angela Piccini

BAR International Series 1677
2007

Published in 2016 by
BAR Publishing, Oxford

BAR International Series 1677

Studies in Contemporary and Historical Archaeology 4
Contemporary and Historical Archaeology in Theory

ISBN 978 1 4073 0115 0

BAR Publishing is the trading name of British Archaeological Reports (Oxford) Ltd.
British Archaeological Reports was first incorporated in 1974 to publish the BAR
Series, International and British. In 1992 Hadrian Books Ltd became part of the BAR
group. This volume was originally published by Archaeopress in conjunction with
British Archaeological Reports (Oxford) Ltd / Hadrian Books Ltd, the Series principal
publisher, in 2007. This present volume is published by BAR Publishing, 2016.

Printed in England

BAR
PUBLISHING

BAR titles are available from:

BAR Publishing
122 Banbury Rd, Oxford, OX2 7BP, UK
EMAIL   info@barpublishing.com
PHONE   +44 (0)1865 310431
FAX   +44 (0)1865 316916
www.barpublishing.com

FOREWORD
STUDIES IN CONTEMPORARY AND HISTORICAL ARCHAEOLOGY

Studies in Contemporary and Historical Archaeology is a new series of edited and single-authored volumes intended to make available current work on the archaeology of the recent and contemporary past. The series brings together contributions from academic historical archaeologists, professional archaeologists and practitioners from cognate disciplines who are engaged with archaeological material and practices. The series will include work from traditions of historical and contemporary archaeology, and material culture studies, from Europe, North America, Australia and elsewhere around the world. It will promote innovative and creative approaches to later historical archaeology, showcasing this increasingly vibrant and global field, and celebrating its diversity, through extended and theoretically engaged case studies.

Proposals are invited from emerging and established scholars interested in publishing in or editing for the series. Further details are available from the series editors: Email Dan.Hicks@bristol.ac.uk or Joshua. Pollard@bristol.ac.uk

In this, the fourth volume in the series, Laura McAtackney, Matthew Palus and Angela Piccini bring together contributions from established and emerging scholars in historical archaeology and contemporary archaeology, based in the United Kingdom and North America across 17 chapters. The volume brings together papers that were read at the first two meetings of the CHAT (Contemporary and Historical Archaeology in Theory) conference group, which were held at the University of Bristol in November 2003 (convened by Dan Hicks and Angela Piccini) and at Leicester University in November 2004 (convened by Sarah Tarlow and Marilyn Palmer).

As the editors explain in their introduction, the papers address a number of themes - from colonialism and conflict to heritage, performance and practice - from a range of different perspectives. The volume includes 15 innovative and detailed archaeological studies of the modern period, with studies that range from the 16th-century Rose Theatre in London to 19th-century clove plantations in Zanzibar, the colonial mapping of British Columbia, an abandoned city street in Malta, public archaeology in Annapolis, Maryland, and an early 21st-century out-of-town shopping centre in south Wales.

These 15 chapters are complemented by a preface and an afterword from two leading thinkers in the field - Mary Beaudry (Boston University) and Victor Buchli (UCL).Based on their keynote papers at the inaugural CHAT meeting in Bristol, these two major statements reflect upon current developments in historical and contemporary archaeology. Taken together, this landmark volume captures much of the energy and diversity of contemporary and historical archaeology, presenting substantive and compelling case studies that are combined with theoretically sophisticated reflections upon historical and contemporary archaeology.

Dan Hicks and Joshua Pollard (University of Bristol)

Series Editors

TABLE OF CONTENTS

LIST OF FIGURES

LIST OF TABLES

LIST OF CONTRIBUTORS

Mary C. Beaudry is Professor of Archaeology and Anthropology at Boston University

Julian Bowsher is Senior Archaeologist at the Museum of London Archaeology Service.

Victor Buchli is Reader in Material Culture in the Department of Anthropology, at University College London.

John Carman is Birmingham University Research Fellow in Heritage Valuation and is co-Director of the Bloody Meadows Project.

Patricia Carman is co-Director of the Bloody Meadows Project.

Sarah Croucher is Assistant Professor in Anthropology at Wesleyan University.

Graham Fairclough is Head of Characterisation at English Heritage

Brian W Gohacki is a Ph.D. Candidate in the Department of Anthropology, at Brown University.

Paul Graves-Brown is a freelance archaeologist working in Wales.

David Harvey is Senior Lecturer in Historical Cultural Geography in the Department of Geography, at University of Exeter.

Martin Locock is an Archivist at the National Library of Wales

Laura McAtackney is a Ph.D. Candidate in the Department of Archaeology and Anthropology, at the University of Bristol

Christopher Matthews is Associate Professor of Anthropology at Hofstra University.

Emily Morrissey is a freelance archaeologist, based in Somerset.

Martin Newman works for the National Monuments Register, at English Heritage.

Jeff Oliver is a Research Assistant in the Department of Archaeology, at the University of Sheffield

Matthew Palus is a Ph.D. Candidate in the Department of Anthropology at Columbia University

Krysta Ryzewski is a Ph.D. Candidate in the Department of Anthropology, at Brown University

John Schofield works for the English Heritage Chracterisation Team and is Research Fellow in Archaeology at the University of Bristol

Andrew Tierney is Visiting Lecturer at the School of Art History and Cultural Policy at University College, Dublin.

ACKNOWLEDGEMENTS

There are many people who, individually, we would like to thank in the construction of this volume, as it has at times been a long and arduous task. However, we will use this space to thank only those who were imperative to the successful completion of this volume. We express our special appreciation to Joshua Pollard and Dan Hicks for their guidance and input throughout the editing process. We would also like to thank all the contributors to this volume for creating their interesting and exciting papers, as well as for their patience and fortitude in waiting for the production of the book. Lastly, we would like to thank Brent Fortenberry for his swift and meticulous proofreading.

LM, MP & AP, April 2007.

Preface: Historical Archaeology with Canon on the Side, Please

Mary C. Beaudry

I am privileged to be part of the excitement that CHAT is generating, by promoting innovative and theoretically informed studies of the recent and contemporary past. I suspect, however, that some North American historical archaeologists' reaction to the notion of 'contemporary historical archaeology' would be, 'what's the big deal? We've been doing this sort of thing for decades!'

It is true that historical archaeology has been practiced in the US and Canada for some time; since the 1960s it has even been considered a respectable pursuit though not nearly as worthwhile as other sorts of archaeology. From the initial stages of the development of North American historical archaeology, researchers have unabashedly turned their attention to archaeology of the contemporary or very recent past; in 1962, for instance, Bernard Fontana and colleagues published a monograph on a late nineteenth-/early twentieth-century ranch in Arizona (Fontana *et al* 1962; Fontana 1967), ushering in the era of 'tin can archaeology' (Ascher 1974). In the 1970s, William Hampton Adams conducted a multidisciplinary research project on the early twentieth-century town of Silcott in the US state of Washington, publishing in 1975 an article titled 'Archaeology of the Recent Past' in *Northwest Anthropology Research Notes*. Adams defined his research as *ethnoarchaeology* because he employed what he termed a 'synergistic approach' that combined archaeological and documentary research with oral histories from people who had once lived in Silcott (Adams 1977).

Publications on Johnny Ward's Ranch (Fontana *et al* 1962) and Silcott (Adams *et al* 1975; Adams 1977) focused, however, on identifying the mysterious artifacts, often strangely familiar yet nevertheless unrecognized, from these sites. Indeed, Adams's analysis of the finds from Silcott focused not on what the people of Silcott did with the material culture he unearthed from their dumps, privies, and houses but on the sources and systems of supply for the isolated community (eg, Adams and Riordan 1985). This initiated a long-term devotion to the study of 'consumer choice' among US historical archaeologists. Initially the approach focused on the global supply systems that provided goods, such as bottled patent medicines, to far-flung 'frontiers'. Interest in 'commodity flows' and supply networks often overrode any concern for the contents of such bottles and what they meant to the people who used them and what this in turn could tell us about those people (for a different approach see Jones 1981; 1983). Eventually, consumer choice studies aimed to delineate

the 'socio-economic status' and, sometimes, ethnicity of households based on goods, chiefly ceramics and glass, excavated from a wide range of sites (eg, Spencer-Wood 1987).

Silcott and Johnny Ward's Ranch are examples of early studies in 'contemporary archaeology' that serve as illustrations of the intellectual conservatism that characterizes US historical archaeology. A field that has existed for less than a half-century has a pretty tenuous claim to maturity (Beaudry 1995; Hicks 2003) and, one would think, would not have developed a fixed set of intellectual precepts. Both Fontana and Adams advocated an integrated approach to historical archaeology that combined humanistic — specifically ethnological and ethnographic— with scientific approaches (Fontana 1965; Adams 1980). Despite these early efforts to convince historical archaeologists of the value of an open-ended, integrative approach that draws on diverse influences from many fields, US historical archaeology has been characterized by a limited range of theoretical perspectives and by recurrent efforts on the part of one or another of the major figures in the field to develop and promulgate a consensus approach to the way historical archaeology is done.

In other words, there has been a fairly constant effort to establish some sort of canon for both theory and practice, and since the late 1970s US historical archaeology has entertained little in the way of debate about the direction the field should take. Instead we have been treated to a series of pronouncements that it should be one thing or another: we are told that we should all employ the same theoretical armature and the mode of practice it informs if we are to be taken seriously (eg, Deetz 1989; Leone and Potter 1999; Paynter 2000; Orser 1996; South 1977). Many US historical archaeologists continue to espouse the principles of the 'New Archaeology' (processualism) first embraced in the 1970s, or have adopted other totalizing explanatory schemes; the resulting distinct and strongly delineated schools of thought are resistant to influences from contemporary social theory. This is why I see US historical archaeology as conservative at its core.

Under the processualist program, we were encouraged to be truly scientific and to search for patterns in archaeological data that would, in turn, lead to law-like generalizations about culture. The person whose work is most strongly associated with this approach in historical archaeology is Stanley South, whose 1977 book, *Method and Theory in Historical Archaeology*, was wildly influential in the late 1970s and throughout the 1980s. It found special favor among prehistorians who found themselves forced by cultural resource legislation to address historical sites even though they preferred not to. In part this was because South's program eschewed historical sources as overly particularistic, and hence far too unscientific to be trusted. His aim was to develop statistically based formulae that would permit archaeologists to dig historical sites without having to mess about with documents. In other words, his aim was to make historical archaeology as much like prehistory as possible. 'Southian' processualist studies have predominated in the US Southeast and Caribbean (eg, Deagan 1983; Ewen 1991; Otto 1984), but South's approach was also embraced by many who worked in CRM archaeology as an easy means of 'processing' data without having to think about it very much — though the stated rationale for employing the approach continues to be that South's rigidly defined artifact groupings and statistically based pattern analysis allow for ready comparability of sites and assemblages (eg, Cheek and Seifert 1994) . Pattern analysis paired up very nicely with consumer choice studies that had already found a strong following among historical archaeologists (eg, Klein and LeeDecker 1991; Spencer-Wood 1987).

While UK archaeologists may justifiably congratulate themselves on having escaped from what must be some of the worst and most pernicious evocations of the processualist program ever promulgated—for example, studies of ceramic patterning, at military sites to 'prove' that officers had higher status than enlisted men (Turnbaugh and Turnbaugh 1977), at southern plantations to 'prove' that masters and overseers had higher status and better pots than enslaved Africans (Otto 1984), in urban dumps to define a statistically based 'holiday behavior pattern' (Dickens and Bowen 1980)—conservatism in US historical archaeology means that many archaeologists, especially those working in the US Southeast and in what we call contract archaeology, still practice 'Southian' pattern analysis, mainly because they have always done so (eg, Seifert and Balicki 2005). For a time the state of California *mandated* that all archaeological projects, including those involving historical sites, should follow the hypothetico-deductive approach. Only after intense lobbying on the part of what we would now think of as post-processualist archaeologists was this requirement modified to allow for alternative theoretical perspectives, if the investigator provided sufficient justification for his or her divergence from the 'canon'. The current guidelines for preparing archaeological reports for review by the office of the California State Archaeologist nevertheless require that archaeologists must 'present testable hypotheses', stating that any 'useful theoretical approach should be capable of generating testable hypotheses' and that archaeologists must 'identify the test implications of the hypotheses' (California Office of Historic Preservation 1990: 9). Such requirements constitute a clear effort to restrict the intellectual breadth of archaeology conducted under the purview of the state's historic preservation office by requiring that archaeologists report research results according to a processualist, one-size-fits-all format; perhaps it is apt, then, that the acronym for California's Archaeological Resource Management Report guidelines is ARMR!

By the late 1970s, other theoretical programs were advanced by US historical archaeologists as alternatives to processualism, with greater or lesser impact on the field. Among them is Deetz's structuralist approach (Deetz 1977). Deetz's students seldom embraced structuralism in an outright way (eg, Yentsch 1991) but many were influenced by his notion of mindsets, mental templates, and world view. In *In Small Things Forgotten* Deetz (1977) posited that English immigrants arrived with a 'medieval' mindse, which eventually became Georgian; on the other hand, African Americans maintained a distinctly African mindset. Deetz viewed these mindsets as beginning with a blueprint that immigrants brought with them for recreating the life that they had left behind; mindsets were transformed into new cultural orders that would then define America. The ideas put forth by Deetz in his seminal volume influenced historical archaeology's focus on how cultural worlds were reconstructed through objects, on ethnogenesis, quotidian practices, 'small things', and disenfranchised peoples in colonial contexts (eg, Purser 1995; Stewart-Abernathy 1992).

Both the South and Deetz programs have as their primary aim the 'recovery' or 'discovery' of sweeping, totalizing generalizations about cultural processes, offering rather little in the way of explanation for cultural change or even for how culture is constituted in the first place. Leone's critical theory approach and his insistence that historical archaeology is the study of capitalism is really not all that different in ultimate aim; it merely offers a different explanatory mechanism, that is, a Marxist perspective, on American culture (Leone 1995; Leone *et al* 1987). It, too, is a universalizing approach that seeks similar explanations for disparate phenomena. In the 'archaeology of capitalism' material culture plays an anecdotal role as illustration of the ways in which capitalism has affected all aspects of human life for the past several centuries. Artifacts may be seen to 'act back' in ways that control and shape human behavior (usually negatively, by creating false consciousness), but the interpretations of material culture offered by Leone and his followers tend to be as lacking in subtlety and nuance as the other approaches I have described.

By addressing subtle differences in the deployment of material culture, however, historical archaeology gains its own subversive power. For me, an interpretive approach first establishes a local framework for interpretation, standing in contrast to decontextualized comparisons that force the researcher to argue backwards towards context only after he or she perceives some seeming anomaly in the data (Beaudry 1996: 490).

Interpretive scholars are aware that the intersubjective space of cultural transactions can be constructed through deliberate manipulation of material culture in ways that produce multiplicities of meanings. This awareness leads interpretive historical archaeologists to seek ways of comprehending ubiquitous items such as ceramics, glass bottles, and a plethora of small finds not as parts of closed cultural 'systems' or as universal reflections of monolithic 'total institutions'. Rather, artifacts and the cultural 'transcripts' in which they figured can be examined as potentially multivalent props employed in colonial and post-colonial discourses (see, eg, Barrett 1988; Beaudry *et al* 1991; De Cunzo 1996; Hall 2000).

My approach, which I identify loosely as interpretivist, allows me to pursue my interest in how objects become highly charged with import and send messages that seem confusing because they are saying more than we expect them to say. The message for the archaeologist may be equally confusing because documentary examples that enable the construction of complex and polyvalent cultural fields for interpreting material culture underscore the weakness of analytical frameworks that aim to disambiguate artifact interpretation by slotting objects into grand narratives and systemic programs that have as their aim the delineation of fixed 'meanings of things'. Such frameworks overlook the role individuals play in the negotiation of personal identity and the role of symbols in social and cultural life. Any object can be symbolically mobilized in service to the ambitions of an individual as well as to the enforcement of rules and mores of the collectivity. Even humble or seemingly inconsequential objects figured prominently in the construction and negotiation of identity, and it is our task to work at understanding not the true meaning of material culture in some universal sense but, to the extent that we can, possible, potential meanings that they have and may have had. Therefore, I see interpretive archaeologies as distinct not just from processualism, but also from structuralist and Marxist or Marxian archaeologies (*contra* Hicks 2005; Thomas 2000), as separate from any rigidly delimited 'school' of archaeological thought that at its core is programmatic and canonical. Interpretive historical archaeology is one of many projects in postmodern cultural studies through which researchers aim to 'gain an understanding of the context because the context itself has in part already been constructed by theory, or at least by cultural practices and alliances' (Grossberg 1997: 262); in this sense, theory itself is contingent, not a paradigmatic construct that provides us with the answers in advance: 'Theory and context are mutually constituted' (Grossberg 1997: 262).

Through the diversity of research 'outputs' generated by interpretive archaeologists — conventional publications but also experimental narrative, fiction, and performance — as well as through events such as CHAT, historical archaeology is continuously reinvented as an open-ended, transdisciplinary pursuit that operates beyond the bounds of any single theoretical program. Practitioners of contemporary historical archaeology do not question the validity of archaeological studies that incorporate bold forays into the worlds of documentary analysis or material culture studies; we reject the sadly still too prevalent notion that archaeology is 'only dirt, only excavation' (Beaudry 1996: 480). The purposeful combination of multiple approaches and theoretical perspectives that interpretivists employ, which certain critics labeled sneeringly as eclecticism, has not brought about a state of ritual impurity in the field but in fact represents a way of experimenting and even playing with archaeological data, much as musicians in creating what falls loosely under the rubric of 'world music' practice a kind of reckless eclecticism that results in new and engaging forms of music. Hybridity and eclecticism, both in archaeological theory and practice, are creative and far from reckless ways of challenging totalizing schemes and can only strengthen the field.

Interpretive historical archaeologists in the US (eg, De Cunzo 1996, 2004; King 1996; Praetzellis and Praetzellis 2004; Wilkie 2000, 2003; Yamin 1998, 2005) and elsewhere (eg, Hicks 2005; Lawrence 2000; Symonds 2000; Turgeon 2004) are gently nibbling at the edges of canonical practice(s) in historical archaeology, but we still face knee-jerk negative reactions to much of our work. For instance that we are unable to 'prove' anything — as if that were desirable — and that we trivialize archaeology as a discipline by taking up as subjects of archaeological inquiry any and all cultural productions, including contemporary and recent ones, and also that by adopting empathetic approaches we seek unjustifiably to 'speak for' people in the past, and so forth. That is why I am very pleased to be a part of the CHAT grouping, in which historical archaeology is truly being reinvented by a diverse group of people who are not bound by any established canon. I am heartened by Victor Buchli's argument that it is in the superfluities and pluralities of experience, practice, and interpretation that contemporary historical archaeology will find its strength (Buchli 2000: 7). I am privileged to be a part of this emerging and wholly non-canonical reformulation of historical archaeology, and I look forward to bearing witness to the continued and continuous reinvention of contemporary historical archaeology.

References

Adams, W.H. 1975. Archaeology of the recent past: Silcott, Washington, 1900–1930. *Northwest Anthropology Research Notes* 9 (1), 156–65.

Adams, W.H. 1977. *Silcott, Washington: Ethnoarchaeology of a rural American community. Reports of Investigations* 54. Pullman, WA: Washington State University.

Adams, W.H. 1980. Historical archaeology: science and humanism. *North American Archaeologist* 1(1), 85–96.

Adams, W.H., Gaw, L.P. and Leonhardy, F.C. 1975. *Archaeological Excavations at Silcott, Washington: The Data Inventory*. Pullman, WA: Laboratory of Anthropology, Washington State University.

Adams, W.H., with Riordan, T.B. 1985. Commodity flows and national market access. *Historical Archaeology* 19 (2), 5–18.

Ascher, R. 1974. Tin*Can archaeology. *Historical Archaeology* 8, 7–16.

Barrett, J.C. 1988. Fields of discourse: reconstituting a social archaeology. *Critique of Anthropology* 7 (3), 5–16.

Beaudry, M.C. 1995. Review-article: Coming of age: historical archaeology in the Chesapeake. *Antiquity* 69 (262), 192–96.

Beaudry, M.C. 1996. Reinventing Historical Archaeology. In L. A. De Cunzo and B. L. Herman (eds), *Historical Archaeology and the Study of American Culture*, 473–97. Knoxville: University of Tennessee Press.

Beaudry, M.C., Cook, L.J., and Mrozowski, S.A. 1991. Artifacts and Active Voices: Material Culture as Social Discourse. In R. Paynter and R. McGuire (eds.), *The Archaeology of Inequality*, 150–191. Oxford: Blackwell.

Buchli, V. 2000. *An Archaeology of Socialism*. Oxford: Berg.

California Office of Historic Preservation. 1990. *Archaeological Resource Management Reports (ARMR): Recommend Contents and Format*. Sacramento: California Office of Historic Preservation. Available at www.ohp.parks.ca.gov/pages/1054/files/armr.pdf (11 August 2005).

Cheek, C.D. and Seifert, D.J. 1994. Neighborhoods and Household Types in Nineteenth-Century Washington, D.C.: Fannie Hill and Mary McNamara in Hooker's Division. In P. Shackel and B.J. Little (eds), *Historical Archaeology of the Chesapeake*, 267–81. Washington, DC: Smithsonian Institution Press.

Deagan, K. 1983. *Spanish St. Augustine: The Archaeology of a Colonial Creole Community*. New York: Academic Press.

De Cunzo, L.A. 1996. Introduction: People, Material Culture, Context, and Culture in Historical Archaeology. In L.A. De Cunzo and B.L. Herman (eds), *Historical Archaeology and the Study of American Culture*, 1–18. Knoxville: University of Tennessee Press.

De Cunzo, L.A. 2004. *A Historical Archaeology of Delaware: People, Contexts, and the Cultures of Agriculture*. Knoxville: University of Tennessee Press.

Deetz, J. 1977. *In Small Things Forgotten: An Archaeology of Early American Life*. New York: Anchor Books.

Deetz, J. 1989. Archaeography, archaeology, or archeology? *American Journal of Archaeology* 93 (3), 429–35.

Dickens, R.S., Jr. and Bowen, W.R. 1980. Problems and promises in urban historical archaeology: The MARTA Project. *Historical Archaeology* 14, 42–57.

Ewen, C.R. 1991. *From Spaniard to Creole: The Archaeology of Cultural Formation at Puerto Real, Haiti*. Tuscaloosa: University of Alabama Press.

Fontana, B.L. 1965. The tale of a nail: On the ethnological interpretation of historic artifacts. *The Florida Anthropologist* 18 (3, part 2), 85–101.

Fontana, B.L. 1967. The archaeology of post-18th century ranches in the United States. *Historical Archaeology* 1, 60–63.

Fontana, B.L., Greenleaf, J.C., Ferguson, C.W., Wright, R.A. and Frederick, D. 1962. Johnny Ward's Ranch: A study in historic archaeology. *The Kiva* 28 (1/2), 1–115. Tucson: Arizona Archaeological and Historical Society.

Grossberg, L. 1997. Cultural studies: What's in a name? (One more time). In *Bringing It All Back Home: Essays in Cultural Studies*, 245–271. Durham, North Carolina: Duke University Press.

Hall, M. 2000. *Archaeology and the Modern World: Colonial Transcripts in South Africa and the Chesapeake*. London: Routledge.

Hicks, D. 2003. Archaeology unfolding: diversity and the loss of isolation. *Oxford Journal of Archaeology* 22 (3), 215–29.

Hicks, D. 2005. 'Places for thinking' from Annapolis to Bristol: Situations and symmetries in 'world historical archaeologies'. *World Archaeology* 37 (3), 373–91.

Jones, O.R. 1981. Essence of peppermint: A history of the medicine and its bottle. *Historical Archaeology* 15 (2), 1–57.

Jones, O.R. 1983. London mustard bottles. *Historical Archaeology* 17 (1), 69–84.

INTRODUCTION

Laura McAtackney and Matthew Palus

This volume assembles some of the contributions to the first two annual meetings of the Contemporary and Historical Archaeology in Theory ('CHAT') conferences, held at Bristol University in November 2003 and Leicester University in November 2004. Bringing together a wide range of archaeological practitioners from higher education and from professional archaeology, these contributions explore the potential of archaeological studies of the recent and contemporary past from a range of perspectives. Included are studies that focus on a range of themes, and whilst diverse they are united by an awareness of archaeology as a contemporary practice, and of the radical potential for the extension of archaeological perspectives into the recent past and the contemporary world.

In this brief introduction, we want to explore some of the themes that emerge from the papers collected here. The themes we choose to explore include, but are not limited to, archaeological studies of colonialism, conflict, heritage and performance and practice. We want to underline that such themes are intertwined, and how complexity and diversity contribute to the vibrancy of current research in contemporary and historical archaeology. We shall conclude with some final thoughts about this field of study.

Colonialism

The study of colonial and postcolonial worlds is an important emerging theme in historical archaeology (Orser, 1996; Gosden 2004; Lawrence and Shepherd, 2006). Several contributors to this volume exemplify our ability to interrogate colonialism as a mode of engagement with cultural and ecological settings around the world. Chapters by Andrew Tierney, David Harvey, and Jeff Oliver examine aspects of British colonial history in locations that have been little examined in postcolonial perspective by archaeologists: British Columbia, Ireland, and the British Isles itself. Moreover, Sarah Croucher presents an important counterpoint to conventional Eurocentric archaeologies of colonialism by examining the archaeology of slavery on clove plantations in 19th-century Zanzibar.

This association of archaeology with colony and empire is emphasized by Andrew Tierney, who examines Irish oral traditions in which the existence of castles was translated into tenure in land, and therefore legitimate claims to rule between competing chiefly lineages in the sixteenth and seventeenth century. Association with these castles have been the subject of ongoing negotiation. Initially they were usurped for colonialist discourses and identities, were later abandoned by Irish nationalist historians and now find their role within a confident, contemporary Irish society subject to reappraisal. David Harvey in his contribution submits that this same project is also a colonial one, and that the intelligibility of these monuments is rendered simultaneously through scientific and imperial modes. Just as race was central to nation-building in the New World, Harvey describes the importance of racialization to the construction of imperial British identities, specifically through the inscription of ancient monuments such as Avebury, Co. Wilshire, England, and Newgrange, Co. Meath, Ireland as sources of cultural power, emerging imperial identities and desires.

Jeff Oliver appraises the language of progress in the history of colonial expansion, particularly in the tangible and very material drama of land survey and cadastral mapping. In the territorial survey of British Columbia, the abutting of technologies for making progress – basic mapping and survey infrastructure – and contexts of wilderness reflects the partiality or failure of cartographies superimposed onto British Columbia wilderness. Contradictory outcomes of mapping on-the-ground undermine the very purposes of colonization: the sale and (re)settlement of land (cf. Byrne, 2003; Mrozowski, 1999).

Land is the original colonial desire, and that landscape should emerge as an important mode for interpreting colonialism and its alternatives may offer a particular archaeological approach to this issue. Harvey does not disarticulate landscape, as a particularly material domain for colonialism, from the discourse on identity more familiar from postcolonial studies. He reminds us that empire is about more than land, but land itself is more than simple territory. This suggests approaches that begin to consider land's materiality and see it as a component of the colonial project equal in gravity to politicized identity projects, a vision that Jeff Oliver begins to fulfill.

Croucher observes not only the invisibility of colonialism in the archaeology of Zanzibar, but the near-complete absence of 19th-century archaeology in the region. The outcome is an awkward tourist fantasy elaborated upon clove plantations, at once exotic and quintessentially Oriental for their production of spices and their association with Omani merchants. Croucher explores how archaeology can be used not only to enlighten historical narratives but to provide alternative stories of the past, and her essay has great relevance for understanding the contemporary political economies and the consequences and conflicts resulting from colonialism and empire-building throughout East Africa.

Conflict

The archaeological manifestations of both blunt and subtle forms of conflict can also be most effectively explored within the context of contemporary and historical archaeology. Research into conflict in the historical archaeological record crosses a wide spectrum of activities (see Schofield, 2002) and can cover such manifestations as warfare (Carman, 1997) as well the greater subtlety of class conflict (Leone, 2005) Most prominently in this volume, John and Patricia Carman focus on the much-needed development of theoretical understandings of battlefield archaeology with the 'Bloody Meadows' project, however, this is but one form of conflict to be found in the archaeological record.

Less obvious manifestations of conflict, through class conflict or political action, can also be found through conducting historical and contemporary archaeologies. This is due to the existence of a greater survival and range of archaeological remains from the recent past and the existence of supporting, often documentary, evidence that allows archaeologists to be able to investigate greater subtlety of conflict within the archaeological record. This documentary evidence covers institutional and governmental records, which attempt to record the workings of society, to the personal letters and diaries of the most lowly. The range of documents relating to any site can, like their archaeological remains, vary wildly in the state of their survival between different periods, locations and people. Furthermore, the conditions of modernity has created circumstances in which new forms of conflict have arisen, in particular Marxist archaeologists highlight the growth of capitalism as the impetus to class consciousness and conflict (eg Leone and Potter, 1999). Of course, there are difficulties with this approach in that it tends to focus on the archaeology of the recent past and on western ideas of what is significant. Explorations of conflict away from North American and European contexts, such as Croucher's archaeological work on Zanzibar, are therefore especially welcome.

The forms of politics and conflict that can be expected to arise in such an archaeological context will, of course, include the traditional concern with and interest in the archaeology of warfare. In particular, the changes and impacts of mass warfare in the twentieth century are of great concern to many archaeologists, particularly in Europe with the investigations of the battlefields and remnants of World Wars I and II. However, the growth of nationalism from the nineteenth century onwards have also precipitated, particularly within Europe, Africa, and Asia, many physical manifestations of ongoing civil conflict that have had a lasting impact on the cultural landscapes of many lands. For example, the security infrastructure associated with 'the Troubles' in Northern Ireland are of increasing interest. As the peace process appears to be a permanent fixture there is growing concern with what we do with these long standing remains of conflict. With much of the fortified police stations and army bases disappearing over night, with little trace of what once stood there, should we be preserving, or at least recording, these manifestation of internecine conflict or is it more productive for society to attempt to forget periods of unrest? As with much investigation into the recent historical and contemporary archaeological record, there is no easy answer.

Archaeologists are increasingly attempting to engage with less obvious manifestations of the conflicts encountered in everyday life, especially through archaeologies of class conflict, the manifestations of capitalism and 'the impact of industrialisation upon those who make up what is known as the working classes'. In this vein, Martin Locock's contribution to this volume explores the physical remains connected to early capitalist ventures in the buildings industry through his case-study of Castle Bromwich Hall, Warwickshire, UK. As in his paper, often we find that the signs of politics and conflict are not as obvious as those of mass civil unrest but it is possible to locate the subversion and sabotage used by those who are considered powerless to show their discontent. As James Scott (1985) famously argued, small subversions can help to empower those who appear superficially weak. Archaeologies of the recent past can often identify the traces of such small subversions.

Heritage

There has been a huge growth in recent years of interest in the field of heritage as both a concept (Skeates, 2002) and as a practice (Cooper et al, 1995). The treatment of the remains of the very recent past as heritage is also a major emerging field of current debate in archaeology (Bradley et al 2004, Penrose forthcoming) and a number of papers in this volume engage with the concept of the recent past as a potential heritage resource. Graham Fairclough's paper (this volume), in particular, uses the English Heritage document, *Change and Creation: historic landscape character 1950-2000*, (Bradley et al, 2004) as a means to provide suggestions for how the public can interact with, and appreciate, the recent additions to the contemporary British landscape. Of most interest is Fairclough's contention that there should be a move towards accepting that the British landscape is, and always has been, changing and evolving and there is a need to use heritage issues and contemporary archaeology to reflect on archaeological practices in general.

Martin Newman's discussion of the digitisation and organisation of archaeological materials in this volume is also poignant and timely in regard to the public's relationship with archaeology. Newman's paper focuses on archaeological data that is available to the public through the internet and, although it is obviously positive that such data is now more freely available to those who ultimately pay for it, he does highlight the problem of accessibility. He points to the potential problems of social exclusivity, in particular, as archaeological material often continues to be presented in an élitest way with interested members of the public frequently discouraged through the use of overly academic and specialist language. However, he does show that despite theoretical problems of physical and academic access there are a number of high-profile initiatives that are attempting to break these barriers down.

The relationship between archaeology and the heritage industry is often difficult. Contemporary and historical archaeologies can prompt us to explore issues of what becomes heritage and why. What aspects of our past and present are officially selected for commemorations and which areas are rejected? Brian Gohacki in his investigation of the treatment of shipwrecks off the North American coast (this volume) explores the interface between archaeology and the heritage industry and highlights some potential causes for concern, as well as possible opportunities for a more fruitful relationship. The relationship between official and unofficial heritage is of particular concern, for as Ashworth and Graham (2005: 5) have shown, despite heritage often being officially directed, the public will not always interact with it as expected or designated. Official heritage can, and is, subverted by the public at will. Such themes are explored by Matthew Palus and Christopher Matthews (this volume), in their ongoing work in the City of Annapolis. They especially concentrate on the continued, possibly racially related, rejection of one neighbourhood's significant heritage value with preference to the more mainstream Founding Fathers heritage of Annapolis's historic district, and thereby address the often murky realities of heritage selection/creation.

Performance and Practice

The archaeological study of performance - including performance in the past, the performative qualities of things, and even the 'performance' of archaeology itself - has become an important area for archaeological focus in recent years (Pearson and Shanks, 2001; Shanks, 2004). In their discussion of their 'Bloody Meadows' battlefield archaeology project, John and Patricia Carman (this volume) explore:

> the often slow and deliberate movements of bodies of troops across the space of a battlefield frequently in defiance of a natural desire to avoid danger ... Accordingly, gaining a feeling for the place as a place and focussing on how one moves through it in performance, one can perhaps gain a sense of what a particular historic battlefield represents in terms of experience and meaning.'

Julian Bowsher examines the archaeology of theatrical performance in his chapter on the archaeology of the Rose Theatre, London. Whilst focusing on the physical traces of the performance of the theatregoers he highlights the wear at the front of the stage, the dress accessories found under the stage area, and items discarded by the audience such as hazelnut shells, counting tokens and drinking vessels. He then delves further by considering the performance of the archaeologists, in this arena of past performance, as they excavate the remains of the theatre. John Schofield and Emily Morrissey's chapter on the archaeology of Strait Street in Valetta, Malta, engages with performance insofar as it examines the deliberately hidden material remains of ephemeral moments in the street's former bars and brothels. Their study is of particular interest in that Strait Street is now largely derelict in comparison to its previous life as a vibrant and alive, if seedy, section of Valetta, which would have been the focus of numerous nightly 'performances' of consumption, forceful interactions and lust. Schofield and Morrissey now explore it, during daylight hours, as a largely ignored series of street that, by its very existence, continues to contradict the city's aspiring image of World Heritage respectability.

Some of the studies collected in this volume aim to reveal hidden practices, which were performed, but in secret. Krysta Ryzewski's archaeological study of the consumption of patent medicines in different social contexts in New England during the nineteenth century (this volume) explores how respectability ensured that higher social status ensured more covert use of patent medicines, however, in reality their usage was similar in quantity and type throughout the social spectrum. Within the more working class contexts the archaeological discovery of medicine bottles secreted around privies, dating from a time when the consumption of alcohol was forbidden, hidden consumption of patent medicines can be interpreted as a small but important act of defiance.

The material dimensions of contemporary practices are explored in Paul Graves-Brown's unconventional study of the control of access for walkers to a contemporary shopping mall in South Wales (cf. Graves-Brown, 2000). Through his own performative engagement with the landscapes, he explores how the space is walked, how people often reject the planned pathways and subvert the careful created spaces by establishing their own paths, which they found more suitable to their needs. Graves-Brown's use of J.G. Ballard in his explorations of these attempts to control movement – and more importantly the articulation of pedestrian and automobile ways – makes chilling reading for those who usually are unconscious of the control of space by such, seemingly benign, corporations.

***

The essays by Mary Beaudry and Victor Buchli, which begin and end the collection, highlight the development of archaeologies of the recent and contemporary past,

and some of the issues we need to grapple with when conducting these archaeologies. Moreover, they raise many new themes with which archaeologists can work. Many chapters fall across, rather than within, the themes discussed in this introduction - for example, John Schofield and Emily Morrissey's chapter on Strait Street not only explores past performances, but illuminates the tensions between the darker heritage of Strait Street in Valetta and the city's status as a World Heritage site. A number of the papers discussed under the theme of colonialism above contribute equally to the archaeological study of conflict. Indeed, although the contributions to this volume focus on different geographical locations, as well as different aspects of past and contemporary experience, many papers use archaeology as a tool to unearth contradictions, complexities and alternative narratives rather than to supplement existing histories, or to contribute to single disciplinary themes. At the same time, many of the papers consciously interact with their studies as contemporary as well as historical concerns. In this way, they seek to contribute to what Cornelius Holtorf has described as one of the principal aspects of all archaeology - its role as a field that 'offers a perspective from which the past and its remains can be experienced and understood in the light of our present' (Holtorf, 2005: 15).

References

Ashworth, G.J. and B. Graham (eds) 2005. *Senses of Place: Senses of Time*. Aldershot: Ashgate.

Bradley, A., V. Buchli, G. Fairclough, D. Hicks, J. Miller and J. Schofield 2004. *Change and Creation: the later 20th century contribution to England's landscape. An English Heritage manifesto on historic landscape character from the period 1950-2000*. London: English Heritage.

Byrne, D. R. 2003. Nervous Landscapes: Race and space in Australia. *Journal of Social Archaeology* 3(2): 169-193.

Carman, J. 1997. *Material Harm: archaeological studies of war and violence*. Glasgow: Cruithne Press.

Cooper, M. A. Firth, J. Carman and D Wheatley (eds). 1995. *Managing Archaeology*. London: Routledge.

Gosden, C. 2004. *Archaeology and Colonialism*. Cambridge: Cambridge University Press.

Graves-Brown, P. 2000. *Always Crashing the Same Car*. In P. Graves-Brown (ed.) *Always Crashing the Same Car*. London: Routledge, pp. 156-165.

Holtorf, C. 2005. *From Stonehenge to Las Vegas: Archaeology as Popular Culture*. Oxford: Altamira Press.

Lawrence, S. and N. Shepherd 2006. *Historical Archaeology and Colonialism*. In D. Hicks and M.C. Beaudry (eds) *The Cambridge Companion to Historical Archaeology*. Cambridge: Cambridge University Press, pp. 69-86.

Leone, M. 2005. *The archaeology of liberty in an American capital: excavations in Annapolis*. London: University of California Press.

Leone, M. and P. B. Potter, Jr. 1999. *Historical Archaeologies of Capitalism*. New York: Kluwer Academic/Plenum Publishers.

Mrozowski, S. A. 1999. *Colonization and the Commodification of Nature. International Journal of Historical Archaeology* 3(3):153-166.

Orser, C. E., Jr. 1996. *A Historical Archaeology of the Modern World*. New York: Plenum Press.

Pearson, M. and M. Shanks 2001. Theatre/Archaeology. London: Routledge.

Penrose, S. forthcoming. *Images of Change*. Swindon: English Heritage.

Schofield, J. and W.G. Johnson 2006. *Archaeology, Heritage and the Recent and Contemporary Past.* In D. Hicks and M.C. Beaudry (eds) *The Cambridge Companion to Historical Archaeology.* Cambridge: Cambridge University Press, pp.104-122.

Schofield, J., W.G. Johnston and C.M. Beck. 2002. *Matériel culture: the archaeology of twentieth century conflict.* London: Routledge.

Scott, J.C. 1985. *Weapons of the Weak: Everyday forms of peasant resistance.* New Haven: Yale University Press.

Shanks, M. 2004. *Three Rooms: Archaeology and Performance. Journal of Social Archaeology 4*: 147-180.

Skeates, R. 2002. *Debating the Archaeological Heritage.* London: Duckworth.

SIGNIFICANCE, VALUE, AND PROPERTY IN THE PUBLIC FACE OF ARCHAEOLOGY

Matthew M. Palus And Christopher N. Matthews

Introduction

Over four summers from 2001 to 2004, field school students from the University of Maryland conducted excavations in a neighborhood in the city of Annapolis that is located outside of and adjacent to – or perhaps most appropriately *on the margins of* – the historic district of the city. The neighborhood is called Eastport and was named in the late 1880s after the hometown of a local promoter and entrepreneur, who brought a glass factory to the area that faced Annapolis from Eastport's waterfront. Annapolis is a peninsular city extending into the Severn river in Maryland, and Eastport was established as a speculative venture on the next peninsula south of what is today the historic district of Annapolis. In 1868, a group of investors formed the Mutual Building Association of Annapolis and purchased a 100-some acre tract on the peninsula. They laid out 256 small home sites on a grid of streets, and this plan matches the layout of the neighborhood today (Figure 1). Though most lots have been subdivided and rearranged, they have not fundamentally been reassembled into larger packages except for condominium developments on the waterfront facing the downtown. The interior of the peninsula is, for lack of a better word, intact, and resembles the condition of the neighborhood during the early twentieth century: small, wood-frame dwellings stand individually or as duplexes on lots of a quarter-acre or less. Archaeology in Annapolis, the long-term project behind the University of Maryland's field school, developed archaeological research in Eastport that approached the twentieth-century history of the city – a city that has literally attacked its twentieth-century fabric, for instance dismantling neon signage and overhead utilities that are considered a blight by preservationists – and we have aimed for an archaeology that has relevance to the community. This chapter discusses our approach to identifying that relevance. The public to which this public archaeology is addressed is that which resides in Eastport.

A key question for public archaeology is what immediate and local benefits derive from having archaeologists working in a community? We might ask a more preliminary question. How have we arrived at the position of being able to provide an archaeology to a community, to consider ourselves as its authors? Our point is not so much to survey those answers that have already been submitted in the public archaeology literature. Rather, we outline a methodology for asking the question in a productive way, to ask, as Foucault does in his 1984 essay 'What is an author', who we are when we write, and how do writing and similar practices connect us to the social world in which we are affective as professionals. If archaeologists have acquired the entitlement to disseminate information of importance – for instance, in public discourses on heritage – we might ask how that was accomplished discursively, and how those social powers were derived. Further, and this is the key issue that will be treated in this paper, what is the shape of that larger discourse within which archaeologists have carved out an authoritative position, and within which archaeological discourses also circulate?

What contains it, and who else inhabits it? For it is certainly inhabited, and through their desires, projects, and agendas its *other* inhabitants contribute to the positioning of archaeologists and their works. Following numerous scholars before us (Bender 1998; Hall 1994; 1999; 2001; Dongoske *et al* 2000; Potter 1994) we acknowledge that we cannot understand what a particular archaeology is without closely investigating the discourses that subsume archaeological research. This entails mapping archaeology into the larger domain of heritage, which we suggest both contains and gives shape to archaeological discourses. Thus the ethnographic consideration of archaeology conducted in specific places, and the ways it is appropriated or simply borrowed, dissembled or reformulated, exploited for profit, etc, becomes an objective of field research.

How might our projects make space for these social processes in our interpretation of archaeological remains? How do our projects make room for those social relations that allow archaeologists to claim the legitimacy of what they do within the non-archaeological world that has made space for us? For instance, in Eastport we must establish the contingency of our social positions as experts within a certain prescribed system that allows for, if not desires, the existence of experts. We must examine this space, how it was formed, and what we (and others) now do to sustain it, especially in our interpretations of the past. Then we must critically evaluate and incorporate these *public* interests into the foundations of our interpretative projects. We emphasize these as public issues because we feel that the term 'public archaeology' is fast losing any stable useful meaning. In particular we are concerned that the public stands now for interest groups who are objectively distinct from archaeology and archaeologists. The public in this sense may be served by an independent archaeology, while that formulation of archaeology as free from social interests is at best a fiction.

In this sense we are tracking the same patterns that Joyce (2002) discusses regarding the 'language of archaeology,' but we are engaged here in creating a revised notion of the 'public face' or the 'community' for archaeology. Joyce adopts Bakhtin's (1981) focus on dialogism to analyze archaeological writing so that we may capture the 'total contexts' of authorship as part of the way that archaeological research is produced as a communicative act. Bahktin's dialogics characterizes any text, including archaeological reports or their productive contents – such as stratigraphic profiles or artifact descriptions – as dialogue rather than monolog. Dialogics is thus as concerned with knowing the other who is being written for, as it is with the author and matters being written about. In this light, the decisions that create archaeological truths are always seen as dialogues held between active and subjective voices.

We see this process as active specifically in the manner in which archaeology is locally situated. Ours is not a process of simply doing archaeology, or in a metaphorically spatial sense, 'putting' archaeology in the world. Archaeology is

Figure 1. Plate of Eastport neighbourhood made for the Mutual Building Association by Surveyor John Duvall, 1868 (Source: Anne Arundel County Land Records Office).

overdetermined by the substantial contexts of site access, political agendas and connections, or research interests of archaeology and its publics. Archaeologists are not free agents who bring archaeology to the world. To be archaeologists specific persons are already engaged with multiple discourses – including the interests and values of private property, cultural heritage, and professional status – whose boundaries restrict the possibilities of archaeological work. By this we mean the already-established public discourse about archaeology that makes our presence in the world as archaeologists meaningful, regardless of what we say about why we are there. This heteroglossia is the public face we are considering here.

We think this is an especially vital approach, for it brings to the surface the ruptures in, or caused by, the social process of archaeology that are often smoothed over in our writing and practices as we assemble our work as *an* archaeology, a consolidated production. If we assume that 'what we do' is archaeology then we silence the contexts for our works, making it impossible to know which archaeology actually emerges from the field in the end. Nor can we know who the authors actually are because instead we just say who they are. This is not to suggest that there is a programmatical step taken in each arrangement, of denial or suppression. Rather, we wish to describe a more sincere investigation of the politically charged

situations that sustain archaeological research and public interest in archaeology. In this way we think the dialogics of archaeology may be brought to light in a manner that allows these relationships and assumptions in turn to be made available for archaeological investigation. We illustrate this process by considering the specific dialogic relations that fuel the archaeological results from this four-year research project in Eastport.

Our success in seeing other authors, in identifying these dialogues and in approaching and contacting community values, has been partial, and for the purposes of this essay we will select one value that has had relevance for our project: the notion of property. In particular, we address this issue by articulating the idea of property and, especially, homeownership. All of the land available for our excavations in Eastport was privately owned, and we required the permission and cooperation of homeowners to begin excavations. We approached this work home-by-home, family-by-family, taking opportunities to excavate as they appeared and scheduling several home sites for investigation each summer. The welcome we received was uneven. Eastport today is a biracial community. The racial geography of the neighborhood, a site of ferocious gentrification since preservation efforts in the adjacent historic district achieved some successes, is such that home sites associated historically with African Americans were made available to our field school by their contemporary white owners, while the relatively limited area that is still occupied by African Americans was closed to us. This situation did not improve despite outreach carried on through appeals to cultural and spiritual leaders within the African American community, contiguous with a larger community extending throughout Annapolis and the surrounding county. The response to our research would best be described as impassive disinterest among all but a very few black Eastporters: we could and should have learned more from Carol McDavid's experiences at Levi Jordon Plantation (see McDavid 1997).

The profile of those who did cooperate with our research was fairly consistent, comprised of families who had come to reside within the community recently and who owned their homes; their similarity to us was undeniable and unsurprising. As such – and like us – most of our hosts had yet to establish their 'residency' in the sense that they might become 'Eastporters.' Many communities have the sort of social criteria for residency that we witnessed in Eastport, where working-class roots and ties to the water extended residency to those who had family of four or even five generations on the peninsula, and to a few who had in the course of their lifetimes become 'honorary' residents.

Beyond the seeming narrow demographic appeal of our project, there was a particular case that struck us as important in the context of our potential impact on residents' understandings and uses of the neighborhood. One homeowner was forthright regarding his objectives for our excavation, and those were to show that his house was the oldest on his block. In fact, based on discussions with neighbors about who had built his home and when, he concluded that his home preceded most others on the peninsula with a construction date of 1855, more than ten years before the neighborhood had been platted. His house resembled other two-story wooden homes in Eastport and, after researching the title to the house, we concluded that it had probably been constructed during the 1890s. Beyond this, after two summers we failed to find anything deposited on the property predating the late nineteenth century. So based on this category of evidence it was not likely that the parcel had been settled earlier. This homeowner had researched the title to his house himself when he purchased it. He saw documentation on the purchase of his lot from the original land speculators towards the turn of the century, and (it seemed to us) implausibly maintained his early date for the construction of the house, with all of the same information that was available to the field school. We may not agree, and we may find his steadfastness implausible, but he has installed his 1855 date in the permanent land records of the county, allowing him to throw our opinions back at us. We do not respond here with ridicule, but rather appreciate this illustration of the push-and-pull over different issues that went on between ourselves and homeowners everywhere in Eastport. That he can maintain his statements against ready evidence is confounding to archaeology, which, more often, is given greater evidential authority, and it betrays a tactics relevant to our consideration of heritage and homeownership in this community. The fact that we had no impact on his ideas about his own house after working on his property for two summers was discouraging, but what we learn from this is that he and other Eastport homeowners understand the functional power of inscription, and are capable of weighing the social power we felt entitled to apply to the situation against that of the documents he had installed in appropriate repositories.

As stated, while we intended to undertake an archaeology that was based in support from within the community and that addressed salient issues deriving from these interactions, support for our project was strong, but only from a partial, if not in fact quite narrow, representation of the community. This prompted the methodological question of how we might have garnered wider support and acceptance, but in the context of our essay we also want to understand why we received any support at all. This is especially pressing when one considers the inevitable disruption and expense that our excavations entailed and the number of home sites that contained no dramatic discoveries, or nothing traditionally recognized as significant by historical archaeologists in the Chesapeake. In other words, why would anyone in Eastport allow us to dig at her or his home in the first place? We assume that there is a reason, and that people do not participate for no other reason than because they are asked. Were we simply underwriting the advancing gentrification and ballooning of property values in the neighborhood, with the prestige and archaeological value-added that our work sometimes provides to homes as well as neighborhoods? That answer comes to us immediately, and seems to be almost too facile a criticism. While it cannot be set aside because it is facile, we can acknowledge that it could obscure something else at work regarding the relationship between discourses on heritage and living in a place that 'has' heritage (this fetishization of heritage is also facile but, we believe, useful in the following discussion).

~~Candlelight~~ Cannibal Tours of Annapolis

We now want to consider 'home' in another context. Just as in Dennis O'Rourke's film *Cannibal Tours*, discussed so cogently by Dean MacCannell (1992), some homeowners in Annapolis open up their homes to tourists in a coordinated performance of heritage stewardship. The domains of heritage and homeownership overlap considerably in Annapolis. Much of the historic district of the city is zoned for residences, and the local engine for preservation claims wide support among private homeowners. By far the majority of buildings contributing to the nationally recognized historic district are residences, with a few important exceptions that include five Georgian mansions now operated as house museums or offices, several shopping streets, and some civic architecture as well. We want to present a parallel case from the historic district of Annapolis, whereby the premier preservation advocacy group in the city has formed important partnerships with homeowners in one particular neighborhood. The purpose here is to problematize the overlap that exists in Annapolis between heritage and homeownership, and learn something of value for our project in Eastport.

Every autumn, Annapolis homeowners are enlisted in a fundraising scheme that extends to the beginnings of historic preservation activism in the city with the founding of the Historic Annapolis Foundation (HAF) in 1952, known then as Historic Annapolis, Inc. HAF sells tickets for candlelight tours of private homes selected for their architectural significance and excellent renovation work, but they are also utilized due to the willingness of homeowners to participate and open their homes so that HAF can raise funds to support its activities. Exclusive VIP tours that include peeks into details of construction in cellars and attics are also available. VIPs pay significantly more for the privilege of receiving a tour from an architectural historian employed by HAF than those guided by volunteer-docents through the spotlessly-clean-but-cozy spaces designated by homeowners for the candlelight tours.

Most of these homeowners have been recognized by HAF with historic markers to display on their homes, which are color-coded to indicate the period and style of the structure. They receive the recognition that this entails, and during the tours they receive further recognition for dramatizing homeownership and, perhaps more importantly, dramatizing good-faith stewardship. Again, the notion of gentrification occurs to us. However, historic preservation has had a much more complicated role to play in the twentieth-century development of the city than to be considered synonymous with gentrification. Preservation arrived in Annapolis as a viable alternative, if not a counter-movement, to urban renewal and the location in which HAF first settled was a neighborhood very much like those cleared block-by-block in other parts of the city during the 1960s. The neighborhood was predominantly, but not exclusively, comprised of African Americans, many of whom rented their homes. The result of preservation was not dissimilar to that of urban renewal; however, what we want to highlight is that in Annapolis – and we believe many American cities – the two were contemporaneous and comparable strategies for cities to shift populations and re-designate or repurpose whole neighborhoods, and were supported by many of the same people as a means of returning economic vitality to the city. In fact, both activities were supported by the same pool of money made available by the Department of Housing and Urban Development (HUD). This refers to Federal money made available to the states through housing reform laws passed during the 1950s and then allocated to local authorities to administer at the municipal level. Critics of urban renewal have almost universally pointed to the fact that control over vast monies introduced by urban renewal legislation was obtained locally and with minimal oversight or control at higher levels of government. Once a municipality established a workable plan for renewal and an authority to execute it, very little could deter the authority from making dramatic and sweeping changes to the built environment if not the social fabric of the community (Saunders and Shackelford 1998; Wilson 1966; Schuyler 2002; Colborn 1963; Foard and Fefferman 1966).

HUD money built public housing projects in one part of Annapolis, and HUD money also purchased the William Paca house and garden and a dozen other buildings in the neighborhood in which HAF made its headquarters (what was once Pinkney-Fleet Street, southeast of the State Capitol Building). Both were part of the same project, and both entailed complicated rationales and discourses that enabled each process to advance on underdeveloped portions of the city. These candlelight tours obviate the need to consider the long-term strategies that were put in place in order to recover this neighborhood for these good stewards. They do so in part because this project of historic preservation was successful in Annapolis. The neighborhoods that HAF took an interest in starting in the 1960s, and Eastport for that matter, are underdeveloped areas of the city that were not redeveloped when the opportunity existed, and that is a significant part of their historical trajectory.

Antagonism

Historic markers on homes in Annapolis are an interesting way to view the power that preservationists have to ascribe, by designating what is valuable in the standing architecture of the city. What is also interesting and telling is the criterion under which individual homeowners have applied for markers (again, administered by HAF, a private advocacy group) and failed to qualify. Two homeowners in the Eastport neighborhood applied for house markers during the 1980s, and one was considered eligible. The terms of the single proffered rejection were:

Figure 2. 2003 Advertisement for the Annual Tug of War between Eastport and the Historic District of Annapolis: 'The Slaughter Over the Water' (courtesy of the Maritime Republic of Eastport, http://themre.org/tug2003/index.htm)

HA plaques are awarded to buildings that represent distinguished architecture in their period. Such buildings usually combine construction characteristics representative of their era and features that display an exceptional sense of design... The house [on] Chesapeake Avenue is described by HA's consultants in historical architecture as: 'Another example of the Annapolis Federal vernacular that is so common in the city. While this particular version has better than normal sawn trim on the porch, it is still vernacular in style.' In sum, the residence reflects the typical building style of the era rather that the exceptional. Buildings such as this provide an important part of the background for the city's high styled buildings in that, through their small size and wooden construction they provide the attractive ambiance which is now associated with Annapolis (Letter dated 19 October 1984, on file, Historic Annapolis Foundation Archive).

This is followed with an apology, as well as an affirmation that the neighborhood has significant interest and ambiance, and that there are plans being drawn to survey the neighborhood, etc. Meanwhile, HAF was simultaneously deciding whether it was its responsibility to evaluate and designate worthwhile historic buildings like those in the Eastport neighborhood that were outside of the established historic district, and whether it would one day have a plaque designated for 'environmental' architecture that contributes to the feel of a neighborhood without itself excelling in any way.

Figure 3. The Tug of War from the Eastport Side in November of 2003. Photograph: Matthew Palus.

This rejection may appear capricious, but it was based on a systematic evaluation of architecture in Eastport that took place almost ten years before this application was lodged. An architectural historian working for HAF surveyed Eastport and evaluated each house, and HAF still has these records, including photographs of the façade of each Eastport home that was standing at the time. Across the board, Eastport homes received the lowest marks possible: they were consistently only 'worthy of mention.' So, while Eastport (and arguably other neighborhoods in the city) is excluded from the entitlement of historic home markers, it is an exclusion that is also an inclusion. The neighborhood seems to have been enclosed by the apparatus designed by preservationists for the purposes of rejection.

Conclusion

This brief departure and criticism of historic preservation in Annapolis must also be a criticism of Archaeology in Annapolis, as a project that has been defined by its partnership with preservationists in the city, and a project in which we have both played a part. We see a trajectory of antagonism between preservationists in Annapolis and residents and business owners in Eastport, and as historical archaeologists we are guilty of underwriting the tacit valuation of older-as-better, even though we reject it in daily practice and in the conduct of fieldwork in Eastport.

One Eastport resident showed us how to do this by rejecting the social powers we had established working at archaeological sites in the historic district of Annapolis. 'My deed says 1855,' is what he asserted again and again, and this document, this date is conceptually equal to any we might try to connect to his home. This conforms to Richard Handler's essay 'On having a culture', and his central statement, derived from an analysis of the relationship between nationalism and cultural patrimony in the Province of Quebec, that *we are a nation because we have a culture* (Handler 1985). The key to this phrase is not culture, it is the infinitive *to have*. Handler described the identification of culture as objects that a collectivity

can and must possess in order to have a culture, and his analysis is elegant. However, he writes as if the discourses themselves were transparent, and that the basic necessity to have was not challenged. 'My deed says 1855.' I suggested earlier that this statement demonstrated a facility in manipulating the specific social powers at work, in judging between competing truths: archaeological discoveries versus records administered by the municipality under a different regime of authorship. Eastporters have expressed the same facility in dealing with the historic district of the city, approaching it through satirical performances and parody directed at the emphasis on colonial history in the downtown, with its patron signers of the Declaration of Independence. This amounts to an insurrection against the criterion applied to them from outside of the community by preservationists. They have identified the terms of this discursive engagement with heritage and simply set them aside, provoking a sort of 'scandal' (Casteñeda 1996). The content of the parody includes: a Declaration of Independence *from the City of Annapolis* in 1998, read by costumed militia halfway across the bridge spanning Spa Creek between Eastport and the historic district, and, amazingly, the firing of brussels sprouts from cannons and muskets at the historic district. The flag of the City of Annapolis was also stolen from the front of City Hall under cover of night. Thus in 1998 was established the Maritime Republic of Eastport, essentially a civic association that promotes the interests of Eastport businesses and residents, similar in nature to the Conch Republic in Key West, Florida. The Declaration of Independence has become an annual event, the hurling of brussels sprouts having been replaced by a tug of war across Spa Creek involving residents, business owners and sponsored teams (Figures 2 and 3). The Maritime Republic describes the 1,700-foot rope used in this enterprise on its web site: 'With a replacement value [in 1998 US dollars] of $23,488.50, it is one of MRE's most valuable capital assets' (www.theMRE. org/tug2003/rope.htm 20 November 2003). Witness also the slogan of the Maritime Republic, 'We like it this way,' and that of the Eastport Business Association, to us even more compelling: 'What I do in Eastport is my business'.

The possibilities for cooperation between heritage professionals and homeowners, as well as the differences and divisiveness that textures relationships between these two neighborhoods of Annapolis, constitute a context in which home-ownership should be approached and understood in Eastport as a domain that impacts our interaction with homeowners. It includes categorizations and hierarchies, histories of exclusionary practices, apparatuses for preservation and so forth. It also entails resistances – sometimes dramatic struggles – and local projects of emancipation from exactly those discourses, and also from our own. Assembling this contextual material is necessary for a critical dialogical approach to our own project and for considering what might comprise 'community archaeology' in this very specific setting.

References

Bakhtin, M.M. 1981. *The Dialogic Imagination*. Austin: University of Texas Press.

Bender, B. 1998. *Stonehenge: Making Space*. Oxford: Berg.

Casteñeda, Q.E. 1996. *In the Museum of Maya Culture: Touring Chichén Itzá*. Minneapolis: University of Minnesota Press.

Colborn, F.M. 1963. *The Neighborhood and Urban Renewal*. New York: National Federation of Settlements and Neighborhood Centers.

Dongoske, K.E., Martin, D.L. and Ferguson, T.J. 2000. Critique of the claim of cannibalism at Cowboy Wash. *American Antiquity* 65, 179–90.

Foard, A.A. and Fefferman, H. 1966. Federal Urban Renewal Legislation. In J.Q. Wilson (ed.), *Urban Renewal*: The Record and the Controversy, 71–125. Cambridge: MIT Press.

Foucault, M. 1984. What is an Author? In P. Rabinow (ed.), *The Foucault Reader*, 101–20. New York: Pantheon Books.

Hall, M. 1994. Lifting the Veil of Popular History: Archaeology and Politics in Urban Cape Town. In G.C. Bond and A. Gilliam (eds), *Social Construction of the Past: Representation as Power*, 167–84. London: Routledge.

Hall, M. 1999. Virtual colonization. *Material Culture* 4, 39–55.

Hall, M. 2001. Social archaeology and the theaters of memory. *Journal of Social Archaeology* 1, 50–61.

Handler, R. 1985. On Having a Culture: Nationalism and the Preservation of Quebec's Patrimoine. In G.W. Stocking, Jr (ed.), *Objects and Others: Essays on Museums and Material Culture*, 192–217. Madison: University of Wisconsin Press.

Joyce, R.A. 2002. *The Languages of Archaeology*. London: Blackwell.

MacCannell, D. 1992. *Empty Meeting Grounds*: The Tourist Papers. London: Routledge.

McDavid, C. 1997. Descendants, Decisions, and Power: the Public Interpretation of the Archaeology of the Levi Jordan Plantation. *Historical Archaeology* 31, 114–31.

Potter, P.B., Jr. 1994. *Public Archaeology in Annapolis: A Critical Approach to History in Maryland's Ancient City*. Washington, DC: Smithsonian Institution Press.

Saunders, J.R. and Shackelford, R.N. 1998. *Urban Renewal and the End of Black Culture in Charlottesville, Virginia*. Jefferson, North Carolina: McFarland and Co.

Schuyler, D. 2002. *A City Transformed: Redevelopment, Race, and Suburbanization in Lancaster, Pennsylvania, 1940–1980*. University Park, Pennsylvania: Pennsylvania University Press.

Wilson, J.Q. (ed.) 1966. *Urban Renewal: The Record and the Controversy*. Cambridge: MIT Press.

Epidemic of Medicine:
an Archaeological Dose of Popular Culture

Krysta Ryzewski

In 1871, J.C. Ayer's patent medicine factory in Lowell, Massachusetts was producing 630,000 doses a day. Ayer's remedies were advertised as cure-alls that would treat everything from anxiety to arthritis in a single product. The company claimed that the annual output of its 12 million advertising pamphlets would stand at a height of a mile and a quarter, and that the circulation of its almanac was second only to that of the Bible (Steward 1993: 10). The Ayer Company's productivity was not exceptional but characteristic of the boom in the patent medicine industry, which lasted from the mid-nineteenth until the early twentieth century. Across North America, medicinal advertisements surfaced in all conceivable forms of media. Images and testimonials were plastered everywhere from the sides of urban factory buildings to billboards along country roads, and from the recently deforested land in Yosemite to the cliffs of Niagara Falls (Helfand 2002). Historians refer to this period of explosive, transformative, and ubiquitous marketing as the 'Age of Disfigurement' (Young 1960: 120).

This chapter examines the patent medicine boom as a relic of nineteenth-century popular culture, thus prompting a critical discussion about what popular culture might have been in the past and providing an example of how to interpret it archaeologically. Patent medicine consumption prospered in the increasingly global and industrialized world of the late nineteenth century. In the United States, patent medicines were among the very first standardized, brand-name products marketed and consumed on a national scale. Medicinal advertising shaped peoples' perceptions of well being and their senses of familiar landscapes. In this period predating modern medical practices, consumers self-medicated with non-prescription patent medicines, many of which contained sizeable quantities of addictive drugs and alcohol.

If the patent medicine boom represents a form of past popular culture, then significance lies in understanding how everyday, mundane medicine consumption became elevated to a more symbolic status among users. By examining the phenomenon of patent medicine usage in a broader context of communication, it may be possible to understand relationships between the production and reception of advertisements, medicine consumption and use, and the active negotiation of personal tastes, identities, and concerns.

Understandings of the overlapping and discursive reality of these processes, as gathered through the following contextual analysis, provide insight into historical health concerns, but also into less accessible and under-theorized perceptions of the body, individual constructions of self image, ideas of pain relief, and social expectations (Beaudry *et al* 1991; Loren 2001; Meskell 2000: 20).

Patent medicines

Patent medicines were non-prescription, brand-name remedies concocted with plant extracts and heavy doses of alcohol, drugs, or caffeine. In an era predating modern medical science, patent medicine producers marketed homemade remedies to soothe every imaginable ailment. Although the term 'patent' was applied by nearly all producers to invoke some sort of tangible authenticity, most medicines of the late nineteenth century did not actually have government-issued patents (American Medical Association 1912: 9).

The social conditions of the late nineteenth century enabled patent medicines to spread rapidly. The introduction of inexpensive newspapers, the growth of urban populations, unhealthy eating habits characterized by starchy diets, and emerging discourses on health and hygiene created an untapped market, especially among the urban poor, who represented millions of potential customers (Leiss *et al* 1986: 74). The scale of patent medicine consumption is impressive; the number of medicines advertised as 'patented' increased from 15,000 in 1850 to 50,000 by 1905 (Young 1974: 94). In the United States, the growth in patent medicine popularity coincided with a utopian climate of institutional reform, temperance campaigns, and suffrage movements. The democratic spirit of the 1840s supported the popular and traditional belief that everyone could be his or her own physician. In effect, advertisements informed consumers of what ailments should be medicated and which medicines should be used (Helfand 2002; Figure 4).

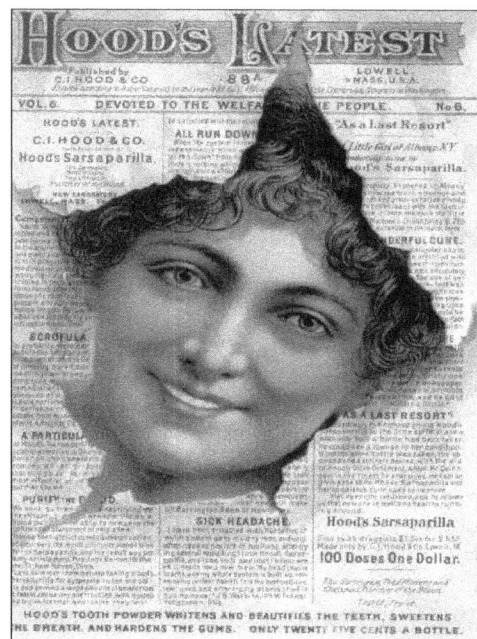

Figure 4. Trade card advertisement for Hood's Sarsaparilla. By kind permission of Victorian Trade Cards Collection, Miami University Library, Oxford Ohio. Digital collection viewable online at www.digital.lib.muohio.edu/tradecards

The turn-of-the century exposés of muckraking journalists and Progressive Era temperance crusaders portrayed the patent medicine boom as an epidemic that prospered by creating drug addicts out of consumers. In 1905, Samuel Hopkins Adams' compositional tests revealed that many of the best-selling patent medicines included intoxicating amounts of alcohol and sizeable doses of narcotics such as cocaine, cannabis, morphine, and opium (Adams 1905: 10–12). Adams published his findings with *Collier's Weekly* in a series of essays entitled 'The Great American Fraud'. In one essay Adams warned that in 1905, '[America would] swallow huge quantities of alcohol, an appalling amount of opiates and narcotics, and a wide assortment of drugs ranging from powerful and dangerous heart depressants to insidious liver stimulants, and far in excess of all other ingredients, undiluted fraud' (Young 1960: 219). These exposés provided the impetus for the swift passage of the Food and Drug Administration's (FDA) Pure Food and Drug Act in 1906.

Typical of the period, American manufacturers did not usually disclose ingredients on their bottle labels, which critics viewed as intentional manipulation of consumers' trust. In advertisements, however, many manufacturers made no effort to hide narcotic substances or stimulants; they often stressed their presence by promoting their reliable and invigorating properties (Spillane 2000: 74–75; Figure 5). Even though the feel-good ingredients in patent medicines may have only masked rather than cured some ailments, consumers relished in their powers, familiarity, and satisfying performance.

Popular culture

> 'No class escapes them – from the poor man's pay, the nostrum takes no trifling part away.' (Crabbe in A.M.A. 1912: i)

Popular culture emerged as an idea during the Enlightenment era among intellectual circles who aimed to set apart the culture of the people, which was considered the more primitive culture, from the high, learned culture of intellectuals (Burke 1978: 9; Browne 1991: 2). By the nineteenth century popular culture was commonly associated with mass-produced culture, particularly those items made for and consumed by working classes (Traube 1996: 131). Today this association persists, especially in the scholarly tendency to analyze material culture using binary (high vs low) classifications in which popular culture objects are understood as analogous to low culture. Glass medicine bottles from three distinct New England settlements confirm that patent medicine usage transcended conventional and structured socio-economic categories. This complexity signals a more ambiguous dimension that forces us to reexamine the 'popular' in popular culture.

A challenge exists for historical and contemporary archaeological theory in how to recognize and grasp past popular culture. A review of the literature on popular culture reveals that archaeologists have rarely attempted to define or apply the topic in relation to material culture research (see Gould and Schiffer 1981; Shanks and Tilley 1987; Browne 1991; Little 1991; Buchli and Lucas 2001). Rather than conducting contextual analyses, the predominant tendency of archaeologists working with items of popular culture, especially mass produced goods, is to analyze them in Marxist-inspired frameworks. Consequently, artifacts of popular culture are usually interpreted as reflecting relationships of dominance and resistance, and as being particular to lower social classes (Shackel 1991: 36).

The aim here is to reexamine interpretations for material remains of popular culture by exploring possibilities that account for the complexity of human agency within culturally and temporally-specific social phenomena (Gramsci 1971: 7; Hall 1981: 239: Bennett 1986: 6–21; Barker 1989: 261; Beaudry *et al* 1991: 159–65; Traube 1996: 133). In understanding these complexities, it is necessary to move beyond straightforward analyses of objects and their dissemination, and, as Kaplan suggests, shift attention to the diverse ways that objects of popular culture were 'by accident and by design' perceived, used, and transformed (1984: 2). Approaches that consider dialogues between individuals and cultural texts are most

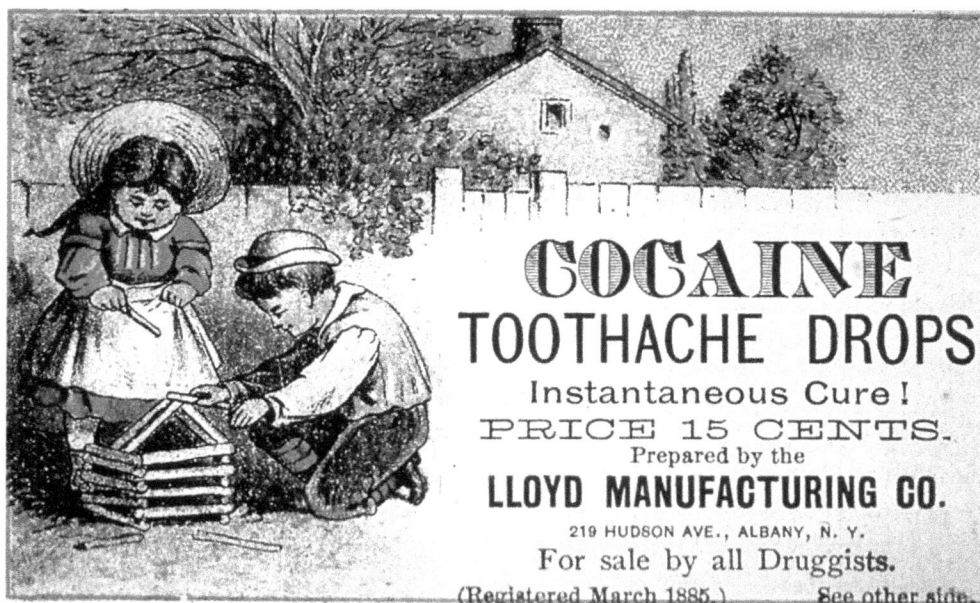

Figure 5. Cocaine praised for its curative powers, 1885. (National Library of Medicine, History of Medicine Collections)

applicable, especially for broaching less exotic topics that were once hallmarks of daily life in a diverse community ie, conceptions of well-being, health concerns, body image, pain relief, and even addictions (Abu-Lughod 1991: 130; Hall 2000; Ortner 1991: 163–89; Thomas 1991: 3). One influential approach is Martin Barker's notion of 'contract', which simply states that texts communicate to people in ways that they will recognize. The resulting dialogues succeed insofar as they have elements that are relevant to values in the readers' lives (Barker 1989: 261).

The ability of people to recognize and find relevance in a medicinal advertisement or patent medicine product can be further understood as operating within the framework of Bourdieu's *habitus*, in which structure and agency are mediated, reproduced, and transformed by both individuals and social circumstances (Bourdieu 1977: 72–79). The concept of *habitus* offers a critical link between the social contexts of patent medicine popularity, advertising, and the meaningful experiences of individuals negotiating these broader social structures. This perspective provides the ability to contextualize individuals within lived experiences of the patent medicine boom. Most importantly, their lived experiences embody the many motivations, strategies, and tastes that factored into decisions to consume patent medicines. These theoretical underpinnings stress the need to recognize artifacts of popular culture for their complexity. Patent medicine bottles and advertisements can only be understood as objects infused with multiple meanings and situated within individual cultural negotiations.

As the following archaeological evidence illustrates, the same brands of patent medicines were consumed by all classes. The widespread trend of patent medicine consumption does not mean, however, that people had the same concerns for the same reasons. In this case, the failure of class to act as a structure for interpreting meaning signals the presence of more complex concerns located at the individual level. Central to Barker's idea of 'contract' is the need to recognize ideology as dialogical, contextually dependent, and enormously variable, with reasons for consumption rooted in explanations that can be rational, emotional, private, public, harmless, and harmful (Barker 1989: 261). These manifold possibilities for consumption demonstrate that a clear relationship does not exist between treatments of the body, advertising representations, material culture, and landscape. Rather, the relationship between medicine consumption and the user's behavior is supported by archaeological contextual associations, which sometimes signal regular use inside the home, but sometimes clandestine use elsewhere. The very act of 'medicating' in a particular place is tied to conscious decisions of the consumer. These decisions are further mediated by culturally constructed discourses concerning the body and a perceived need for medicine. All of these elements are inextricably linked in a way that can inform constructions of identity in relation to particular episodes of consumption (Meskell 2000: 13).

The wide range of media outlets containing patent medicine advertisements, both in print and on the landscape, provide part of a cultural text for recovering meanings about how medicines were received, experienced, and incorporated as part of the users' realms of acceptable treatment possibilities at a given moment (Beaudry *et al* 1991: 165; Brumfiel 2000: 249). The advertisements should not, however, be viewed as literal displays of late nineteenth-century social realities. Instead, they should be recognized for their intrinsic ideological constructs, which reflect social relationships, identities, and ideals concerning health, hygiene, and morality (Fisher and Loren 2003: 227). The phenomenon of patent medicines and their advertisements documents a widespread popular culture

of consumption that traversed the American population. Through careful contextual analysis, the complexity of the dialogue between people and these cultural texts sheds valuable light onto the unfolding of social relationships and individuals' very personal concerns.

Advertisements

Advertisements were the flexible mechanism that allowed patent medicines to appear respectable and acceptable. Depending on the media in which they appeared, the images used, and their embedded ideological constructs, patent medicines thrived as a form of popular culture that capitalized on and overlapped realms of high, low, and folk cultures. Advertisements flourished in all types of magazines, newspapers and literature, at tourist attractions, and along railroad routes. All of these media had manifestations favored by working and upper classes (Traube 1996: 140). The urban working classes were likely to encounter advertisements in public spaces, at amusement parks, and in the penny press. These public activities were routinely frowned upon by the long-established upper class, which related to advertisements that catered to their more refined values, as they traveled along railroad routes or read intellectual publications. The character of advertisements simultaneously catered to and redefined identities by targeting social expectations and familiar cultural concerns. With such an overwhelming and rapid saturation of media in their daily environments, it is likely that peoples' senses of time, space, routine, and self were somewhat altered (Kasson 1978; Strinati 2000: 242).

Advertisements had as profound an effect on the landscape as they did in shaping how people treated and understood their bodies in the late nineteenth century. By notifying and sometimes alarming the public about health concerns, advertisers created new social realities of the body that were not necessarily accurate medically. Some products were advertised to treat entirely unrelated ailments in one dose. For example, Atlas' Baby Syrup claimed 'to facilitate teething and regulate bowels' at the same time, while Cooper's Quick Relief offered the 'three minute cure of deafness and stiffened joints' (Fike 1987: 145; Baldwin 1973: 128).

Manufacturers contributed significantly to social conceptions of disease by publicizing names of illnesses, outlining their symptoms, and explaining both with biological and medical language. By suggesting a common frame of reference for how people thought about and talked about bodily concerns, these new notions of medicine and illnesses likely superceded many traditional and cultural understandings of disease. To a degree, the public displays of advertising created a collective social memory that was greater than an individual experience, yet simultaneously allowed for the individual to reflect on his or her own identity (Fisher and Loren 2003: 227; Joyce 1998). Whether or not individuals paid close attention to 'medical' information in advertisements, at the very least advertisements urged individuals to dose with medicine when they did not feel well. For the consumer who might not be sure what was wrong or which product to buy, an endless array of all-in-one products existed. Medicines, such as Fahrney's Celebrated Blood Cleanser, Davis' Depurative, Daniels' Electric Oil, and Colton's Tonic Elixir, promised simply to 'cure everything' (Baldwin 1973: 141).

The magnitude of advertising and its implications for reshaping cultural and physical landscapes, as well as social and individual bodies, should not be understated. In effect, people were literally surrounded by advertisements at every turn. In 1893, Ayer's patent medicine varieties, originating from Lowell, were advertised in 6,900 publications. One of these, the *Ayer's Almanac*, sold 18 million copies in 31 languages ranging from Swedish to Hawaiian. Advertisers catered to every imaginable audience. Medicines appeared on trading cards, puzzles, in children's storybooks, and in the housewife's *Preserve Book, Book of Emergencies, and Book of Pies and Puddings* (Steward 1993: 42). Each publication was sure to contain at least one reference per page to an Ayer's patent medicine variety, reminding users at all stages of life where to turn when they felt ill.

Advertisers recognized that pain and vanity had the strongest psychological appeal to consumers (Fishbein 1932: 328). Some patent medicine manufacturers used personal testimonials to market their product. Manufacturers from Raymond & Co., the maker of Raymond's Pectoral Plasters ('the positive cure for whooping-coughs, bronchitis, etc.'), combed through local newspapers to target potential customers. In a superficial attempt at humanitarian outreach, Raymond & Co. located a Sunday school superintendent in Virginia and furnished him with the following note, which was later published in advertisements:

> Dear Sir: We noticed in the _____ Journal that Whooping Cough is interfering with the attendance of your school and are of the opinion that Raymond's Pectoral Plasters are not known in your vicinity, or this would not be the case. We wish you would hand the one enclosed to the mother of one of the little ones affected, that she may see for herself what they ACCOMPLISH. Then advise us, on the enclosed card the name of the merchant in _____ who sells medicines of any kind that we may take up with him the sale of these Pectoral Plasters in your community. (American Medical Association 1912: 689)

Manufacturers used especially clever marketing strategies to promote their patent medicines. The assortment of meaningful and provocative imagery in advertisements communicated to all classes, ethnicities, genders, and ages. Advertisers transformed traditional symbolic meanings by pairing patent medicines with mixes of artistic imagery, patriotic heroes, historical events, and cultural references. Ultimately there were no limits to the tactics that advertisers

used to gain public appeal except, of course, images of ill people, who were conspicuous by their absence from medicine advertisements. Many products were named after doctors, presumably with the intention of adding a measure of medical legitimacy to the remedy. Native Americans also frequently appeared in product names and imagery, invoking special healing powers along with the charm of the noble savage (Helfand 2002; Figure 6)

Other advertising tactics involved partial descriptions in Latin, which were likely to appeal to more educated audiences. Often, patent medicines implied worldliness in their depictions of foreign, remote, and mythological places (Orser 1994). By utilizing these exotic destinations, advertisers marketed patent medicines as the ticket to paradise. Most common, however, were images of children (see Figures 5 and 6), due to their associations with universal and romanticized ideals of innocence and purity: children symbolized the vitality that the sick, unpleasant, and tired consumers hoped to regain through taking patent medicines (cf. Figure 7).

Archaeological examples

An initial attempt to tease out the complex interrelationships between advertising, the popularity of patent medications, and their uses is explored in analyses of patent medicine bottle assemblages from excavations at three contrasting properties in Massachusetts: the urban upper-middle-class Kirk Street Agents' House in Lowell; the working-class Boott Mills boardinghouses also in Lowell; and the rural upper-middle-class Spencer-Peirce-Little Farm in Newburyport. The embossing, manufacturing techniques, and style of glass medicine bottles provide highly diagnostic information on product date and type (Toulouse 1970: 50). Contextual associations reveal much about the social circumstances surrounding the bottles' deposition and reasons for use.

Excavations conducted by Boston University over the past two decades situate the Spencer-Peirce-Little farm as the seat of Newburyport merchant elite from 1670–1827, and as the residence of upper-middle class farmers for the remainder of the nineteenth century (Benes 1986: 13; Beaudry 1995: 19). The excavated deposits document three distinct periods of occupational history; glass bottle

Figure 6. A late nineteenth-century advertisement featuring a combination of imagery. By kind permission of National Library of Medicine, History of Medicine Collections.

Figure 7. Advertisement for teething syrup with an active ingredient of morphine, 1887. Unlike American versions, British labels for this product had to be marked 'Poison' (Helfand 2002).

remains reflect a clear transition in consumption from homemade and locally produced remedies in the earlier years to a full scale and frequent consumption of patent medications during the later half of the nineteenth century. A minimum number of 64 medicine bottles were excavated and of these 58 bottles were manufactured in the later third of the nineteenth century. The increasing consumption of patent medicines is associated with the late nineteenth-century Little family occupation and two stratigraphic contexts, a wood house outbuilding and a fence-post construction. The deposits reveal an assortment of baby syrup, extracts, pectoral, frostilla, nervine, hair restorer, cocaine, sarsaparilla, and highly alcoholic bitters. Many of these products were locally produced examples from the Colton and Ayer Companies in Lowell, Massachusetts, while some indicated manufacturers as distant as Oregon (Ryzewski 2001: 56).

At first glance, the assemblage seems to depict an array of health concerns troubling the Little household. At least two different brands of hair restorer (Burnett's Cocaine and Ayer's Hair Vigor) were found in separate archaeological contexts. Perhaps a Little had seen the ad for Burnett's Cocaine that proclaimed:

> Premature loss of the hair, which is so common now-a-days, may be entirely prevented by the use of Burnett's Cocaine. It has been used in thousands of cases where the hair was coming out in handfuls, and has never failed to arrest its decay, and to promote a healthy and vigorous growth. It is, at the same time unrivaled as a dressing for the hair. A single application will render it soft and glossy for several days (Harper's Weekly 1861, cited in Wilson 1981: 65).

Or perhaps someone in the household had seen an advertisement for Burnett's Cocaine and was drawn to the product that claimed to be, 'The Best and Cheapest Hair Dressing in the World' (cited in Abodeely 1999: 12).

Viewed in light of the diseases they *claimed* to treat, the patent medicines at the Spencer-Peirce-Little Farm indicate that the Littles might have experienced an array of ailments including indigestion, constipation, chest congestion,

blood impurities, nausea, anxiety, pimples, balding and graying hair, female concerns, and teething – to name but a few (Fike 1987: 239; Bingham 1994: 151; Ryzewski 2001: 51). To infer specific health problems directly from the medicines present in the archaeological assemblage may be possible, but this inference risks masking the more complex connections between advertising, medicines, and individuals. As items of popular culture, these patent medicines must not immediately be viewed as literal indicators of the Littles' ailments, but rather as vehicles for interpreting how they perceived their bodies, their health, and the standards of well-being established in their broader social contexts.

Similar insight into the widespread popularity of patent medicines is gained from analyses of bottles from the Boott Mills in Lowell, Massachusetts. The Kirk St. Agents' House was constructed in 1845–46 to house the agents and their families from the Boott Mills and the Massachusetts Mills, which were two of the largest textile mills in Lowell. Located just one block away from the mills' boardinghouses, this impressive upper-middle class duplex stood in stark contrast to the workers' living conditions (Beaudry and Mrozowski 1987: 11).

In 2001, archaeological fieldwork in the Boott Mills agent's half of the private backyard uncovered a minimum of 16 patent medicine bottles in two strata of a single 1x1 meter unit, which dated to the late nineteenth century (Griswold 2003: 19–22). Such a high volume of patent medicine consumption excavated from this one area indicates a probable habit of frequent usage amongst the Boott Mills agents who, ironically, were notorious for their firm restrictions against workers' drunkenness (Mrozowski *et al* 1996: 72).

Despite such efforts to regulate workers' lives, earlier excavations at the Boott Mills workers' boardinghouses did uncover evidence of frequent medicine consumption, with minimum totals of 29 and 49 patent medicine bottles from two excavated areas. In total, medicinal bottles represented 50% and 49.5% of the total assemblages (Bond 1989: 124–27). The vast majority of these bottles date from 1880 to the early 1900s. With strict regulations and a negative stigma attached to alcohol consumption, complete medicine bottles excavated from a privy, under the floorboards of an outbuilding, and along regularly traversed backyard pathways provide important contextual associations. Kathleen Bond suggests that these contexts indicate clandestine drinking activities among the borders, which included a range of ethnic and immigrant groups. Whether or not these medicines were consumed with intentions to treat health concerns, it is noteworthy that a bottle of medicinal bitters, such as those found at the boardinghouses contained as much as 44% alcohol at a time when beer contained 5% alcohol (American Medical Association 1912: 16–21).

These diagnostic artifacts and their associated contents permit comparisons between household deposits and the social context of the patent medicine boom. The archaeological evidence from the Kirk Street Agents' House reveals that the Boott Mills agent's household was consuming many of the same locally produced brands as the Little family in Newburyport and the workers in the nearby Boott Mills boardinghouses. Bond noted that of the 29 medicine bottles excavated from one area of the boardinghouses 14 were local products from the Ayer and Hood Companies in Lowell, three were products from other Massachusetts companies, and the remaining 12 were from a variety of distant locales linked to Massachusetts by the transcontinental railroad (Bond 1989). This pattern mirrors the diversity in origins of the Little's and the Kirk Street agents' bottles (Ryzewski 2001).

Also intriguing is the deposition of intact or nearly intact glass bottles at each site (Mrozowski *et al* 1996: 73). The reluctance to recycle or redeem bottles for cash signals a degree of privacy, secrecy, or even shame about exposing one's health concerns, or drinking habits, to the boardinghouse keepers and general public. Whether dosing for disease, leisure, vanity, or addiction, it is likely that if these vulnerabilities were revealed, one would not measure up to the social standards of the late nineteenth century. Given the importance of maintaining a healthy and upstanding image, openness about the misuse of these medicines would not only discredit the product, but the immoral undertones of addiction, abuse, and indulgence would likely exclude the consumer from membership in Newburyport's social circles or in Lowell's community.

Interpretation

The patent medicine boom was both embraced and propelled by closely intertwined dialogues between media, medicines, social expectations, and individual identities. Several archaeologists and material culture scholars have discussed the role of advertising in relation to consumption, concluding that there is no direct relationship between advertisements and long-term consumer choice (Miller 1987: 169; Majewski and Schiffer 2001: 32). To treat consumers of patent medicine (and popular culture) as duped by misleading advertisements is to accept a deterministic perspective that ignores other aspects of culture and the consumer's active role in the decision making process.

It is clear from the archaeological evidence that patent medicines were popular. It is clear from the documentary evidence that advertisements of patent medicines were also popular. Yet a clear cause-and-effect relationship does not exist between advertisements and patent medicine consumption, or vice versa. Rather, the contexts of medicinal use and the content of advertising exist together as part of an intangible popular domain, which was only

materialized through the decisions of consumers. These individual experiences involved overlapping relationships to one's landscape of advertisement, material culture of patent medicines, bodily perceptions, motivations, and desired outcomes.

Historical archaeology can achieve more in-depth explorations of selection and consumption by recognizing what popular culture was, by viewing its processes in a larger framework of communication, and by using multiple strands of evidence in reconstructing the complex and sometimes discrete variables of selection (Bennett 1986; Miller 1987: 175; Spencer-Wood 1987; Barker 1989; Ashplant and Smyth 2001: 47; Majewski and Schiffer 2001: 27).

No matter how inexpensive or common the medicine, the consumer always aimed for a specific outcome, but not necessarily an outcome that was listed in an advertisement or on a medicine bottle's label. Perhaps an outcome would enhance a reputation, relieve stress, calm a crying baby, prevent balding, freshen breath, clear up a complexion, lessen female complaints, or intoxicate. These desired outcomes were always deeply rooted in non-medical social contexts. In one of the many testimonials for Hood's Sarsaparillas, the medicinal and non-medicinal uses of patent medicines are both praised. At 18% alcohol, Hood's could not freeze but, as advertised, could certainly 'cheer as it cured' (Holbrook 1959: 45). This 'cheer' might have been especially alluring for someone who sought to alleviate the stress of a long day, or for someone who needed a quick boost. In some situations, consumers may have hoped that the medicine's effects would give them abilities to gain access to different social groups by revealing and concealing different selves. Extending Fisher and Loren's notion that, through dressing, individuals have the ability to 'put on a social skin', perhaps patent medicines provided an outcome or feeling that empowered some weary individuals to 'face the day', and allowed others to 'save face' in demanding social situations (2003: 225).

However mundane or routine the concern appears, the aspired end result signifies a very individual concern related to the consumer's desire for group membership, individual identity, well being, and comfort. The wrong medicine selection or an unintended outcome could easily lead to frustration, embarrassment, and exclusion (Miller 1987: 171). Most importantly, however, the archaeological evidence surrounding the popularity of patent medicine consumption indicates that people really believed in their curative *and* their comforting powers and correspondingly purchased and dosed with medicines in epidemic proportions. This insight into individual concerns is facilitated within the mediating framework of *habitus* and by close contextual readings of the complex dialogues surrounding the patent medicines as popular culture.

The end?

> They can talk about Shakespeare, but in my opinion old Hostetter – and Ayer – had more influence on the national life than any of 'em. (Uncle Henry in *Collier's Weekly*, in Young 1960: Chapter 9)

Archaeological remains of patent medicine bottles coupled with documentary evidence from advertisements provide a clear example of the significance of past popular culture. The abundance of advertisements, which ostensibly offered consumers complete freedom of choice, did not actually articulate social reality. As structures within a broader cultural discourse, advertisements harnessed and organized ideological constructs, framing a limited set of possibilities for how users thought about, spoke about, and imagined how medicine should work. Consumers of patent medicines in the late nineteenth century were reminded through advertisements about new standards for well being, health and hygiene. Forced to negotiate and interpret these expectations in their daily lives, individuals undoubtedly experienced transformations relating to conceptions of their body, health, and identities. This may have been the case in Lowell where unmarried women workers found themselves newly detached from their nuclear families and where recent immigrants intermingled with each other in boardinghouses and mills. But it is also likely that such transformations occurred on more unpredictable and smaller scales, as might be captured in the momentary feeling of empowerment or relief that a worker experienced from covertly drinking intoxicating medicine behind a boardinghouse (Bond 1989: 121–27; Dobres and Robb 2000; Strinati 2000: 237). Historical archaeological approaches offer the opportunity to explore how individuals, living in the midst of mass-marketed discourses and waves of popular culture, successfully managed their identities through choices that reflected their individual health concerns, emotional stresses, and social aspirations (Root 1987: 44).

Advertising and the media publicly fueled the patent medicine boom of the late nineteenth century from its start to its demise in 1906. In retrospect, to think of a temperance crusader addicted to the narcotics in her bitters paints an amusing, scandalously historic, and even nostalgic picture of a seemingly passing fad. However, a comparison of the patent medicine boom of the late nineteenth century with the omnipresence of medicine commercials in today's American media forces a reconsideration of the patent medicine epidemic as a short-lived phenomenon.

In the US, popular historical memory accepts an end of the patent medicine boom as coinciding with the passage of the Pure Food and Drug Act in 1906. As marketing and advertising evidence demonstrates, and as archaeological evidence will likely confirm, the popularity of patent medicine consumption, (though now in the guise of over-the-counter and some prescription medicines), continues to thrive. Over the past century medical philosophy and social demands have changed in step with the influxes of trained doctors and medical advances (penicillin, vaccines, etc) (Steward 1993: 43). These changes have transformed medical practices, the medicine industry, and how individuals perceive their bodies. Yet a familiar historical continuity remains today in the persistence of similar health concerns and in the rhetorical and symbolic discourses present in the advertising and pharmaceutical industries (Helfand 2002).

Perhaps the practices and messages existing in present-day contexts of communication can be understood as part of a longer-term process spanning a century and a half of medicine consumption, during which late nineteenth-century patent medicines thrived as a unique episode of popular and material culture. This element of continuity exemplifies how *habitus* successfully reproduces structures that are maintained over time but are also constantly altered by transformations. Ultimately, these transformations are adopted into the daily praxis of individuals operating within broader structures (Bourdieu 1977: 72–79). Though several subtle contrasts or transformations exist between the medicinal practices of the nineteenth century and today, even a brief glimpse below the surface of modern FDA rules on disclosure and accountability reveals that quackery continues to flourish in various guises. (CNN 17 December 2004) New waves of medicinal popular culture, like Viagra and antidepressants, continuously emerge and

thrive, propelled by recurring promises of cheerful, stress-free and happier lives for a new generation of consumers.

References

Abodeely, J. 1999. *Medicine Bottles of the Spencer-Peirce-Little Farmstead in Newburyport, MA: An Analysis of Locus 33.* MS on file at Department of Archaeology, Boston University, Boston, Massachusetts.

Abu-Lughod, L. 1991. Writing Against Culture. In, R.G. Fox (ed.), *Recapturing Anthropology: Working in the Present*, 137–62. Santa Fe: School of American Research.

American Medical Association. 1912. *Nostrums and Quackery*. Chicago: The American Medical Association Press.

Adams, S.H. 1905. The Great American Fraud: Fraudulent claims and endorsements of patent medicines. *Collier's*, 28 October 1905.

Ashplant, T.G., and Smyth, G. (eds). 2001. *Explorations in Cultural History*. London: Pluto Press.

Barker, M. 1989. *Comics: Ideology, Power, and the Critics*. Manchester: Manchester University Press.

Baldwin, J.K. 1973. *A Collector's Guide to Patent and Proprietary Medicine Bottles of the Nineteenth Century.* Nashville: Thomas Nelson Inc.

Beaudry, M. 1995. Scratching the surface: seven seasons at the Spencer-Peirce-Little Farm, Newbury, Mass. *Northeast Historical Archaeology* 24, 19–50.

Beaudry, M.C., and Mrozowski, S.A. (eds). 1987. *Interdisciplinary Investigations of the Boott Mills, Lowell, Massachusetts. Vol. 2: The Kirk Street Agents' House*. Cultural Resources Management Study no. 19. Boston: National Park Service, North Atlantic Region.

Beaudry, M.C., Cook, L.J. and Mrozowski, S.A. 1991. Artifacts and Active Voices: Material Culture as Social Discourse. In R.H. McGuire and R. Paynter (eds), *The Archaeology of Inequality*, 150–91. Oxford: Blackwell.

Benes, P. 1986. *Old-Town and the Waterside: Two Hundred Years of Tradition and Change in Newbury, Newburyport, and West Newbury, 1635–1835.* Newburyport: Historical Society of Old Newbury.

Bennett, T. 1986. Introduction: Popular Culture and 'the Turn to Gramsci': the Politics of 'Popular Culture'. In T. Bennett, C. Mercer, and J. Woollacott (eds), *Popular Culture and Social Relations*, xi–xix; 6–21. Philadelphia: Open University Press.

Bingham, A. 1994. *The Snake-Oil Syndrome: Patent Medicine Advertising*. Hanover: Christopher Publishing House.

Bond, K. 1989. The Medicine, Alcohol, and Soda Vessels from the Boott Mills. In M.C. Beaudry and S.A. Mrozowski (eds), Interdisciplinary Investigations of the Boott Mills Lowell, Ma: Vol III. The Boarding House System as a Way of Life, *121–41*. Cultural Resources Management Study no. 21. Boston: National Park Service, North Atlantic Region.

Bourdieu, P. 1977. *Outline of a Theory of Practice.* (translated by R. Nice), Cambridge: Cambridge University Press.

Browne, Ray B and Browne, P. 1991. Introduction. In R.B. and P. Browne (eds), *Digging into Popular Culture: Theories and Methodologies in Archeology, Anthropology and Other Fields*, 1–9. Bowling Green: Bowling Green State University Press.

Brumfiel, E. 2000. On the Archaeology of Choice: Agency Studies as a Research Stratagem. In M.A. Dobres, and J.E. Robb (eds), *Agency in Archaeology*, 249–56. London: Routledge.

Buchli, V. and Lucas, G. 2001. The Absent Present: Archaeologies of the Contemporary Past. In V. Buchli and G. Lucas (eds), *Archaeologies of the Contemporary Past,* 3–18. London: Routledge.

Burke, P. 1978. *Popular Culture in Early Modern Europe.* London: Temple Smith.

CNN. 2004. FDA: Consider 'alternative' to Celebrex: Pfizer examining data that show higher risk of heart attack. www.cnn.com (17 December 2004).

Dobres, M.A. and Robb, J.E. (eds) 2000. *Agency in Archaeology.* London: Routledge.

Fike, R. 1987. *The Bottle Book.* Salt Lake City: Gibs M.Smith.

Fishbein, M. 1932. *Fads and Quackery in Healing; An Analysis of the Foibles of the Healing Cults, with Essays on Various Other Peculiar Notions in the Health Field.* New York: Friede.

Fisher, G. and Loren, D.D. 2003. Introduction: embodying identity in archaeology. *Cambridge Archaeological Journal* 13 (2), 225–30.

Gould, R. and Schiffer, M. (eds). 1981. *Modern Material Culture: The Archaeology of Us.* New York: Academic Press.

Gramsci, A. 1971. *Selections from the Prison Notebooks.* (edited and translated by Q. Hoare and G. Nowell-Smith), New York: Int. Publishers.

Griswold, W. (ed.) 2003. *Supplementary Excavations at the Kirk Street Agents' House, Lowell National Historical Park, Lowell, Massachusetts.* Occasional Publications in Field Archaeology, no. 2. Lowell: National Park Service, Northeast Region.

Hall, M. 2000. *Archaeology and the Modern World: Colonial Transcripts in South Africa and the Chesapeake.* London: Routledge Press.

Hall, S. 1981. Notes on Deconstructing 'the Popular'. In R. Samuel (ed.), *People's History and Socialist Theory,* 227–40. London: Routledge and Kegan Paul.

Helfand, W. 2002. *Quack, Quack, Quack: The Sellers of Nostrums in Prints, Posters, Ephemera & Books ; an exhibition on the frequently excessive & flamboyant seller of nostrums as shown in prints, posters, caricatures, books, pamphlets, advertisements & other graphic arts over the last five centuries.* New York: The Grolier Club.

Holbrook, S. 1959. *The Golden Age of Quackery.* New York: Macmillan.

Joyce, R. 1998. Performing the body in pre-Hispanic Central America. *Res* 33, 177–65.

Kaplan, S.L. (ed.) 1984. *Understanding Popular Culture: Europe from the Middle Ages to the Nineteenth Century.* Berlin: Mouton.

Kasson, J.F. 1978. *Amusing the Millions: Coney Island at the Turn of the Century.* New York: Hill & Wang.

Leiss, W., Kline, S. and Jhally, S. 1986. *Social Communication in Advertising: Persons, Products and Images of Well-being.* Methuen: Toronto.

Little, B. 1991. Popular Culture, Material Culture: Some Archaeological Thoughts. In R. and P Browne (eds), *Digging into Popular Culture: Theories and Methodologies in Archeology, Anthropology and Other Fields,* 25–35. Bowling Green: Bowling Green State Univ. Press.

Loren, D.D. 2001. Social skins: orthodoxies and practices of dressing in the early Colonial Lower Mississippi Valley. *Journal of Social Archaeology* 1 (2), 172–89.

Majewski, T. and Schiffer, M. 2001. Beyond Consumption: Toward an Archaeology of Consumerism. In V. Buchli and G. Lucas (eds), *Archaeologies of the Contemporary Past,* 26–50. London: Routledge.

Meskell, L. 2000. Writing the Body in Archaeology. In A.E. Rautman (ed.), *Reading the Body: Representations and Remains in the Archaeological Record,* 13–24. Philadelphia: UPenn Press.

Miller, D. 1987. *Material Culture and Mass Consumption.* Oxford: Blackwell.

Mrozowski, S., Ziesing, G. and Beaudry, M. 1996. *Living on the Boott: Historical Archaeology at the Boott Mills Boardinghouses, Lowell, Massachusetts.* Amherst: University of Massachusetts Press.

Orser, C. 1994. Consumption, consumerism, and things from the earth. *Historical Methods* 27 (2), 61–70.

Ortner, S. 1991. Reading America: Preliminary Notes on Class and Culture. In R.G. Fox (ed.), *Recapturing Anthropology: Working in the Present,* 163–189. Santa Fe: School of American Research.

Root, R.L, Jr. 1987. *The Rhetorics of Popular Culture: Advertising, Advocacy and Entertainment.* New York: Greenwood Press.

Ryzewski, K. 2001. Medicine Patterns on the Spencer-Peirce-Little Farm: An analysis of the shift from the usage of home remedies to patent medications. MS on file at Department of Archaeology, Boston University, Boston, Massachusetts.

Shackel, P. 1991. Consumerism and the Structuring of Social Relations: An Historical Archaeological Perspective. In R. and P Browne (eds), *Digging into Popular Culture: Theories and Methodologies in Archeology, Anthropology and Other Fields,* 36–47. Bowling Green: Bowling Green State University Press.

Shanks, M and Tilley, C. 1987. *Re-constructing Archaeology: Theory and Practice.* Cambridge: Cambridge University Press.

Spencer-Wood, S (ed.). 1987. *Consumer Choice in Historical Archaeology.* Plenum: New York.

Spillane, J. 2000. *Cocaine: from Medical Marvel to Modern Menace in the United States, 1884–1920.* Baltimore: Johns Hopkins University Press.

Steward, S.C. 1993. *The Sarsaparilla Kings: A Biography of Dr. James Cook Ayer and Frederick Ayer with a Record of their Family.* Cambridge: Scott C. Steward.

Strinati, D. 2000. *An Introduction to Studying Popular Culture.* London: Routledge.

Thomas, N. 1991. *Entangled Objects: Exchange, Material Culture, and Colonialism in the Pacific.* Cambridge: Harvard Univ. Press.

Toulouse, J.H. 1970. *Bottle Makers and Their Marks.* New York: Thomas Nelson, Inc.

Traube, E.G. 1996. 'The popular' in American culture. *Annual Review of Anthropology* 25, 127–51.

Victorian Trade Cards Collection. 2001. Digital collection, Miami University Library, Oxford, Ohio. www.digital. lib.muohio.edu/tradecards (1 May 2006)

Wilson, R.L. 1981. *Bottles on the Frontier.* (edited by Edward Staski), Tuscon: University of Arizona Press.

Young, J.H. 1960. *The Toadstool Millionaires: A Social History of Patent Medicines in America before Federal Regulation.* Princeton: Princeton Univ. Press.

Young, J.H. 1974. *American Self-dosage Medicines: An Historical Perspective.* Kansas: Coronado.

Other Sources

Here Today, Here Tomorrow: Varieties of Medical Ephemera, online exhibit, National Library of Medicine, www.nlm.nih.gov/exhibition/ephemera/ephemera.html (23 September 2003).

History of Medicine Archives, United States National Library of Medicine. National Institutes of Health, www.nlm.nih.gov/hmd/ (24 March 2006).

SLAVERS, SWASHBUCKLERS, AND SALVORS: THE ETHICS OF PUBLIC PRESENTATION IN NAUTICAL ARCHAEOLOGY

Brian W. Gohacki

Introduction

Nautical archaeology today faces a profound challenge. Despite continued international efforts over the past three decades to enact legislation protecting underwater heritage (Giesecke 2002: 577–80), the number of professional salvors exploiting historic shipwrecks has risen at an alarming rate. Profit-driven salvage, despite its demonstrated negative impacts on archaeological site integrity and analytical rigor (Miller 1987; Kechington *et al* 1989; Johnston 1989; Mather and Watts 2002), has increasingly been viewed by governmental regulators and the public at large as an acceptable balance between academic research and free enterprise. A substantial, well-developed body of literature addressing the ethical problems inherent in the practice of underwater salvage exists (eg, Elia 1995; 1992; Mather and Watts 2002), and I will not rehash arguments that have been made elsewhere. Rather, this chapter will explore the various strategies by which salvors have successfully come to dominate public discourses on nautical archaeology and in turn use them to publicly legitimize a body of practice that is inherently at odds with effective archaeological inquiry. These strategies, often carried out with the help of professionally trained archaeologists and other heritage professionals, result in a public deemphasizing of the importance of controlled archaeological methodology, long-term artifact preservation, and critical interpretation of the past in favor of sensationalism and wild speculation (Johnston 1989; Bass 1990; Goodheart 1999).

While such criticisms apply to salvage operations on many different types of submerged archaeological sites, I will specifically examine how salvors have exploited slave ships, a symbolically potent class of vessels that is little understood in historical and archaeological terms. The origins of this paper lie in observations I made while conducting a seminar project on slave ship archaeology as well as in background research that I conducted with Krysta Ryzewski on the possible 1850s wreck of the reputed slaver *Gem* in Newport, Rhode Island. Considering the current popularity of African diasporic archaeology among historical archaeologists, it is surprising that while the two slave ships excavated by private salvors, and archaeologists working with them, had each received full-length publications, extensive media coverage and accompanying museum exhibitions, only five pieces of archaeological literature concerning slave ships and written by authors not associated with for-profit salvage were in publication at the time. Furthermore, just one, a monograph on the slaver *Fredensborg* written by amateur archaeologist Leif Svalesen (Svalesen 2002), was greater than article length. What is worse, each of these publications exhibited the typical deficiencies of nautical archaeological scholarship, weaknesses that help to explain the ineffectuality of the subdiscipline in countering the challenges posed by treasure hunters.

Unlike most modern archaeologies, nautical archaeology as a discipline has remained generally uninterested in a problem-based, theoretically informed anthropological approach to the past (Gould 1981, McGhee 1998). Rather, nautical archaeologists tend to conduct themselves like architectural historians, in that they seem content to describe the minutiae of ship construction without attempting to contextualize ships, their cargoes, and the people who traveled in terms of wider cultural processes. This obsession with ship construction has led to a narrow focus on 'oddity' vessels: the biggest, oldest, most obscure, or otherwise outstanding examples of maritime technology. As late as 1987, prominent nautical archaeologist Anne Giesecke (1987: 12) estimated that of 12,000 known shipwrecks in US waters, only 5% were 'historic' or 'had a story to tell about their past.' Likewise, investigations into more technologically nondescript vessels are often driven by their associations with famous historical episodes or time periods (Gould 2000: 10–11). These same biases are plainly evident in archaeological articles on slave shipwrecks. Graeme Henderson's 1974 excavation of the former Portuguese slaver *James Matthews* (interim report published in 1976), for instance, is mainly interested in the ship as a rare example of slave ship construction from the mid nineteenth century, a period when the British Royal Navy pursued an official policy of destroying vessels captured engaging in slaving activities. Likewise, Abbass' and Zarzynski's (1998) investigations of what they contend is the *Gem* are almost exclusively descriptive, with almost no attempt to contextualize the ship's use. A small cadre of behavioralist archaeologists conducting programs of comparative research on less glamorous sites (Gould 2000; Muckelroy 1978; McCarthy 2001; Souza 1997) has offered an encouraging alternative to the status quo in nautical archaeology. However, their success has been constrained on one side by a lingering general antipathy toward theory among nautical archaeologists, and by the rejection of behavioral theory among terrestrial historical archaeologists in favor of more ideologically-centered interpretive frameworks.

Dismayingly, the increasing success of salvors in positioning themselves as legitimate scholars (Cockrell 1990: 14) has exposed this lack of theoretically situated analyses as an increasing liability. The first major wave of historic salvage, typified by Mel Fisher's pillaging of the galleon *Atocha* and the Gold Plate fleet, was aimed at an extremely small subset of vessels notable for their material value. While initial bonanzas such as these did prove lucrative to salvors, both through sales of artifacts and through investments by venture capitalists, the ensuing profusion of treasure-hunting enterprises could not support itself on a series of financially disappointing hauls (Throckmorton 1990). In response, salvors used to selling their projects by employing popular fantasies of the past quickly realized that history, not gold, was their most valuable commodity. At first, their attempts to exploit this realization were awkward and heavy-handed. A tactic typical among unscrupulous salvors was to plant unprovenienced artifacts on famous wrecks (Gould pers. comm.), thus increasing their market value through historical association. Fisher himself was accused of pioneering this kind of scheme by selling fake Spanish doubloons allegedly recovered from the *Atocha* (Carrier 1998). However, spurred on by the mass-market success of projects like Ballard's quasi-archaeological explorations of the *Titanic*, the savviest treasure hunters soon concluded that the profits generated by selling countless books, videos, and museum tickets would far outstrip those from the sale of a handful of US $5,000 teapots to unwitting collectors. Thus was born the phenomenon of wreck recovery as popular culture event.

Treasure hunters had put on museum exhibitions before; Mel Fisher himself was forced, as part of his settlement with the state of Florida over the *Atocha* haul, to reserve 20% of his finds for museum display (Elia 1992: 103). But what began as begrudging compliance soon took on a life of its own. Wrecks once deemed worthless by gold-obsessed salvors suddenly became fair game for uncontrolled excavation, their artifacts fodder for the newest private gallery or blockbuster traveling exhibition. Whereas many archaeologists could rationalize a modicum of tolerance for salvage activity before, it was not long before they would have to engage with the problem head-on. The kinds of high-profile wrecks favored by archaeologists, treasure-poor but easy sells to a popular audience, were the first obvious targets.

The discipline was neither intellectually nor legally ready to deal with the salvors' new tactics. As scholars spent years debating the usefulness of different approaches to the problem, from inaction to cooperation to overt political challenge, salvage continued unabated, and its practitioners refined their strategies. With the passage in the US of the 1987 Abandoned Shipwrecks Act, ownership of wrecks in US territorial waters was turned over to individual states, resulting in a hodgepodge of laws governing the preservation and salvage of abandoned vessels. Against this confused legal backdrop salvors began to employ various strategies to gain access to wrecks in different localities (Pelkofer 1987: 114), usually centered on the question of ownership. Despite the transformation of the American maritime salvage industry as whole from an asset-recovery business to a pollution-mitigation industry (Zarzynski *et al* 1996: 43), treasure salvors portrayed archaeological resistance to their activities as standing in the way of a long tradition of American free enterprise (Cockerell 1990; Mather and Watts 2002: 598). Fighting the battle for legal opinion on a state-by-state basis with limited resources, anti-salvage archaeologists have focused their efforts on influencing regulations for the *in situ* preservation of wrecks (Arnold and Mclaughlin-Neyland 1994, Hannahs 2003), often openly welcoming private sector and enthusiast involvement (Halsey 1994: 110–11).

While in many areas, the efforts of archaeologists have been met with appreciable success, savvy salvors quickly realized that their problem was a political one, which could in many cases be solved by publicly positioning their work as superior to that of archaeologists, and that museums were the place to do it. Already eyeing the potential financial value of the huge pool of marketable wrecks ignored by archaeologists, vessels that might be little-known, but which hold strong cultural, emotional, or dramatic appeal to particular segments of society, salvors quickly realized that these sites hold value in other ways. By moving away from unselfconscious treasure hunting towards allegedly academic investigations of neglected vessels, salvors have managed to cloak themselves in a new mantle of legitimacy. By selling the story, rather than the loot, they can truthfully claim that, to quote Barry Clifford, 'no artifacts will be sold' (Webster 1999), at least physically, neutralizing one

of their most common criticisms (Bass 1990). Boding even worse for anti-salvage archaeologists, salvors can honestly say that they are bringing information to the public about kinds of wrecks that academic archaeologists have written off as unimportant.

The practical results of the legitimacy imparted by such activities are depressing. Simplistic salvor-owned museums, offering lots of flash but little in the way of contextualization or critical analysis, have become popular tourist destinations (especially troublesome, given Throckmorton's (1990) estimate that the state of Florida alone could be making over US $0.5 billion each year had it invested from the start in public nautical archaeology museums, supplied objects by research archaeologists, rather than settling on a 25% cut from privately salvaged artifact sales). Traveling exhibits have netted millions of dollars at respected national and international museums willing to turn a blind eye to archaeological critiques. Multinational corporations have thrown their financial muscle and their respected names behind salvage projects (*Henrietta Marie Exhibit Catalog* 1995: 3). Television specials and glossy magazine articles (Steinberg 2002; Webster 1999) tout the salvors' discoveries, often sneering at the concerns of archaeologists. Many academics, including archaeologists, have been swayed by the salvors' case into working with them, believing that the recovery of knowledge ultimately trumps concerns with professional ethics and well-established standards of research-driven archaeological practice.

The ramifications of this trend for archaeologically and historically sound interpretations are also troubling. Giesecke (2002: 583) convincingly argues that driven by profit rather than a theoretically grounded research design, salvage operations, even those conducted under the auspices of trained archaeologists, will always attempt to maximize financial profit while minimizing operating costs at all points in the recovery, conservation, interpretation, and display processes, resulting in an exaggeratedly skewed final product. Even if they could somehow overcome the deficiencies engendered by the salvage process, most professional archaeologists could not use material from salvage operations even if they wanted to. The Council for Underwater Archaeology (Neyland 2002), the Society for Historical Archaeology, the Society for American Archaeology, and several other professional archaeological associations (Noble *et al* 2002) have enacted bans on publications from commercially salvaged sites, rightfully considering them to be hopelessly compromised (Mather and Watts 2002: 594), and archaeologists daring to use such materials risk professional anathema. Meanwhile, in the absence of critical interpretations, salvors have happily busied themselves with producing the kinds of accounts that their audiences have proven to be willing to pay for, that is to say interpretations that merely illustrate popular and politically acceptable views of the past. Given this situation, it is no surprise that alternative or potentially unpopular interpretations are almost nowhere to be found in the accounts produced by salvors, nor has there been any real opportunity for meaningful scholarly review and critique of what interpretations private interests actually have produced.

Since the formalization of archaeology as an academic discipline, archaeologists of different theoretical stripes have argued over the merits of various theoretical paradigms within which to appraise archaeological data (Trigger 1989: 370–29). Despite these differences, however, scholars within the field have arrived at a general consensus (one often shared with the public at large) that the central mission of the archaeological endeavor is the recovery and distribution of knowledge of the past (codified eloquently in the mission statement of the SAA at www.saa.org). Even the curio cabinets of the nineteenth century, despite embodying all of the internalized colonialist ideologies of their producers, shared this intention. With a century's worth of hindsight, today's archaeologists and heritage scholars have come to realize that any depiction of the past, even the most well thought-out, will necessarily be shaped by the ideologically driven decisions of its producers (Russell and Woodall 1998). While no clear consensus regarding the ideal way to address the latent biases in archaeological investigation and presentation has yet emerged, self-reflexive and critical analyses of previous and current work have contributed to a theoretically robust methodology of interpretation that, if not ideal, is increasingly effective at producing accurate and informed pictures of the past (Trigger 1989: 382–84). The following case studies, however, illustrate the ways in which the commercialization of underwater archaeology, by eschewing these methodologies in favor of financial expediency, seriously compromises the factual accuracy and critical integrity of both primary archaeological data and the interpreted accounts made available to the public.

Case Study 1: The *Henrietta Marie*

The types of problems engendered by commercialized archaeological salvage are probably best exemplified by the recovery and subsequent commercialization of the *Henrietta Marie*, a slave ship wrecked off Key West, Florida in 1701. It was first discovered in 1972 by divers employed by Mel Fisher's Treasure Salvors Inc., which, at the time, was engaged in a search for the *Atocha*. Having cleared the site with highly destructive prop-wash deflectors, devices designed to bore indiscriminately into the seafloor by redirecting a boat's propulsive power straight downward, Fisher's men noted the presence of several sets of iron shackles, but no treasure, and quickly moved on, having determined the site was of no value to them (Clifford 1999). It was not until 1983 that the wreck would be investigated again, this time by an archaeologist named David Moore, then studying for his MA at Eastern Carolina University. While Moore's investigations at the site were self-initiated, after the first few years of work the Fisher organization began to recognize the potential marketability of the wreck and began devoting large amounts of capital to remove and conserve the artifacts that would provide the basis for their 1995 traveling exhibit *A Slave Ship Speaks*.

As the excavations continued and concrete plans for the exhibit began to take shape, the Fisher group used the ship's association with the slave trade to attract the support of a broad spectrum of national organizations, including the Association of Black Scuba Divers, historically black universities, and the National Geographic Society (Steinberg 2002). In order to lure corporate sponsors for the exhibit, the Fisher Corporation produced fliers overtly connecting the opportunity for corporate image building with the raw emotions associated with slavery. One such flier, reproduced on the Mel Fisher Web Site (www.melfisher.org) explicitly compares the exhibit with one of the most successful black-themed American pop culture productions of the past century. 'ASTONISHING,' its headline shouts, 'Not since *Roots* has there been an event in African-American history that provides such an excellent sponsorship opportunity.'

The advertisement is replete with emotionally charged imagery, including a drawing of shackles in the upper left and a huge reproduction of the infamous 1789 *Brooks* diagram, illustrating the conditions aboard a Middle Passage slaver. The Fisher organization's use of this drawing is particularly telling, given its well-known use as a propaganda piece by late eighteenth-century British abolitionists. While no one can argue against slavery being one of the most despicable and dehumanizing institutions the world has ever seen, the exhibit promoters' choice of this arguably atypical image, specifically designed to depict the worst abuses of the slave trade (Garland and Klein 1985), starkly reinforces an impression of their willingness to overlook more sophisticated, broader-based analyses in favor of maximized emotional impact, and hence, profit (*cf* Moeller's 1999 discussion of profit and sensationalism in popular visual media).

As the exhibit's debut approached, its (predominantly white) planners took steps to generate advance interest among their target audience, placing multiple ads in popular African-American publications like *Ebony* and *Jet*. Upon its arrival in 1995, the exhibit was widely hailed both in the black media and in the mainstream press. In the succeeding years, the associated media blitz would continue unabated. Exploiting the exhibit's wild popularity, journalist Michael Cottman wrote not one, but two successful books (1995; 1999) recounting his experiences diving on the *Henrietta Marie*, which in turn helped to boost the exhibit's attendance further. The exhibit would receive even more exposure when, in August 2002 (Steinberg 2002), it achieved the holy grail of the commercial culture industry, a full-length feature article in *National Geographic Magazine* - for better or for worse the arbiter of scholarly legitimacy for a large portion of America's populace. *National Geographic* has been criticized elsewhere for its often problematic presentations of cultures past and present (Lutz and Collins 1993; Gero and Root 1996), and its feature on the *Henrietta Marie* is no exception, essentially parroting the Mel Fisher line, while downplaying criticisms by archaeologists of the Fischer Organization's handling of the vessel's investigation, recovery, and exhibition.

The overall result was a resounding success for the once notorious Mel Fisher Organization. The American public, corporate America, and important segments of academia came to embrace Fisher's *Henrietta Marie* project as the ideal example of a successful and socially conscious private salvage operation. In terms of actual contributions to cultural and historical scholarship, however, the project was an unmitigated disaster. Moore's unpublished (and, given his association with salvors, probably unpublishable) thesis (1989), representing the only substantial archaeological document on the wreck, languished on a shelf at Eastern Carolina University. In the meantime, the exhibit and its associated catalog remain the only widely available publications on the ship. Both, however, possess major problems. In the exhibition, the artifacts recovered from the ship function merely as illustrations, fetishized material synecdoches for a familiar script composed of an amalgamation of information from historical documents and simplistic popularized notions regarding the horrors of slavery. Little attempt is made to address the underlying causes of slavery in political, social, or economic terms; and enslaved Africans are portrayed as passive victims, with scant attention paid to active and habitual resistance strategies during the slave experience. The exhibit catalog is somewhat better, with multiple articles by non-archaeologists attempting to contextualize the history of the *Henrietta Marie* in terms of larger cultural processes. Yet even here the cultural significance of material evidence - how the objects were used, and the meanings they held - is ignored. The artifacts are simply presented in schematic line drawings with solely descriptive labels (*Henrietta Marie* Exhibit Catalog 1995).

The complete reluctance on the part of the Fisher group to use the artifacts in any analytical sense is the greatest failure of the *Henrietta Marie* project. Unfortunately, despite their superior recovery methods, the atheoretical framework still clung to by most nautical archaeologists makes it unlikely that they could be expected to do much better a job of interpretation. This situation does, however, suggest a point of weakness in salvors' claims of legitimacy that, in the event of a more theoretical turn in the subdiscipline, could be used by self-reflexive nautical archaeologists and archaeologically aware exhibitors to present persuasive arguments demanding more rigorous investigations.

Case Study 2: The *Whydah*

The salvors of the second wreck to be considered here have used similar methods to those used by the Fisher organization, but with several interesting variations. Like the *Henrietta Marie*, the *Whydah* was the wreck of an early eighteenth-century slaver salvaged by private interests. Few in the general public, however, are familiar with the vessel's role in the slave trade, for it is much more famous for its one-month career as the flagship of the pirate 'Black' Sam Bellamy, lost off Cape Cod in 1717 while carrying a sizable treasure. Barry Clifford, the treasure hunter who discovered the ship in 1982, freely admits that it was 'gold lust' (Webster 1999) that initially drove him to search for the vessel: its discovery made international news, with headlines trumpeting the US $400 million treasure allegedly soon to be recovered (Elia 1995: 23). Initial uncontrolled blasting of the site by Clifford's group, Maritime Explorations Incorporated (MEI) was quickly halted by legal action by the State of Massachusetts, which claimed ownership over the vessel, but the case was eventually settled in Clifford's favor in 1988, although he was obliged to conduct his subsequent recovery operations under the auspices of a revolving cast of archaeologists (Elia 1992).

As the recovery proceeded through the early 1990s, it soon became apparent that the *Whydah* haul would not live up to investor expectations, prompting a shift in tactics on Clifford's part. Following a strategy innovated by Mel Fisher, Clifford began to market his efforts differently. Repositioning himself as the guardian of the *Whydah's* history, he pledged that he would not sell any artifacts from the wreck but instead maintain the collection intact at his new museum on Provincetown's Macmillan Wharf. Like the *Henrietta Marie* exhibition, the *Whydah* museum's popularity has been enhanced by complimentary and uncritical media productions. Clifford himself authored a self-congratulatory book, entitled *Expedition Whydah* (Clifford 1999), featuring a dashing photograph of the author front and center on the cover, with the ship itself pushed to the background, and romanticized tales about his project inside. As with the *Henrietta Marie*, *National Geographic* lent its imprimatur to the *Whydah* project, with a slick article (May 1999), web site (www.nationalgeographic.com/whydah/), and television program (1999) documenting the wreck, again downplaying criticisms from legitimate scholars (Webster 1999).

However, despite his success with *National Geographic*, Clifford's efforts at maintaining a front of archaeological respectability, both methodological and interpretive, have been, compared to Fisher's, clumsy at best. Two years before the conference enacted a ban on papers generated by for-profit salvage operations (Johnston 1989: 148), the Society for Historical Archaeology (SHA) meetings hosted a session devoted to the Whydah in which archaeologists and professional salvors presented their findings (see Underwater Archaeology Proceedings from the SHA

Conference 1987). While at the time, Clifford's presence at the conference lent his operation an air of credibility among archaeologists not enjoyed by most salvors, the papers presented seem less inclined toward establishing a well-formulated research protocol, then as *ex post facto* rationalizations for previously uncontrolled recovery operations. For example, Robert McClung (1989), an EMI employee, in a paper entitled 'Supporting Archaeological Research in the Real World,' chides archaeologists for their resistance to the project. Yet, he describes prop washing as controlled archaeological excavation and makes an artificial semantic distinction between artifacts (objects of academic value) and treasure (objects of financial value).

A visit to the Whydah Museum reveals a continued failure to responsibly deal with the material generated by the excavation. Upon entering the museum, visitors are immediately greeted by unconserved ship's timbers drying and cracking atop 'treasure chests' that the woman working the register informed me had come from 'flea markets and Barry's Grandmother's attic.' Inside the museum itself, other poorly conserved artifacts degrade in the air or are simply displayed in saltwater tanks. Human remains are callously treated throughout the museum, nowhere more so than in a fanciful and fantastically macabre diorama of 'conditions on the bottom,' featuring a simulated 'corpse' the docent informed me was constructed from human bones and modern materials. Before visitors are admitted to the main exhibit gallery, they are led to a side room to sit through a 28-minute video biography of Clifford playing up the importance of his finds and deriding the efforts of archaeologists and heritage regulators.

Regarding the subject of the history of piracy, the museum's admitted focus, the exhibition is sorely lacking in substance. While Clifford vaingloriously plays up the *Whydah's* short stint as a pirate ship, he, like the Fisher group, has made no attempt to use the evidence in critical interpretations of the culture of piracy itself, especially those that might touch upon politically sensitive, but incredibly important and interesting issues like homosexuality or racial resistance (*see* Bly 1998). Much of the museum's focus seems rather to be on Clifford himself. Displays claiming to present accurate reinterpretations of pirate history instead perpetuate romantic popular visions of egalitarian and race-blind swashbuckling adventurers, using language strikingly similar to that which Clifford uses to describe himself, in effect anointing him as their modern day successor.

Clifford's presentation of the ship's (and part of its crew's) previous role in the slave trade can be called no less than shamefully inadequate, consisting of only one-and-a-half pages in the museum catalog (McLean 1996: 10–11), passing references in Clifford's book, and a small display in the museum that compares unfavorably in size and prominence to a nearby one recounting John F. Kennedy Jr's participation in the project in the early 1980s. Even more offensive are displays of Akan gold recovered from the wreck. Accompanying signage fails to explain this treasure for what it is: accumulated profit from the repeated buying and selling of human bodies and other commodities along the West African coast (see Behrendt 2001). Instead, the exhibit presents it merely as gleaming booty from Clifford's latest adventure. Clifford's preoccupation with gold and downplaying of slavery are even worse in his book (eg, 1999: 232) where several pages are devoted to loving descriptions of the gold, while even the most obvious articles of slavery - branding irons, and other restraints - receive less than a paragraph's attention.

Constructing Informed Aternatives

Given the destructiveness of these projects to the physical, contextual, and informational integrity of archaeological resources, and also to scholars' abilities to conduct theoretically meaningful work, it is obvious that nautical archaeologists need to reassess not only their responses to salvage activity, but their entire *modus operandi*. For better or worse, in order to repossess the popular and legal mandates that salvors have managed to acquire, nautical archaeologists must become overtly political in their practice. No longer can we busy ourselves with studies of extraordinary architecture, publishing our results only in academic journals for the consumption of like-minded scholars. We need to ask bigger questions, and we must find it within ourselves to engage the public in meaningful ways. This is not to say, of course, that we should attempt to beat the salvors at their own game by producing our own publicly accessible but factually bowdlerized accounts of the past. Rather, we need to offer alternative visions of the past based upon anthropologically informed studies of a diversity of wrecks, ones that allow popular audiences to acknowledge, understand, and interact with historical complexity without pandering to entrenched racial or political ideologies.

This strategy will necessarily entail a much broader comparative approach to the practice of nautical archaeology. While particularizing investigations and accounts of wrecks will still be necessary in order to gain deeper understandings of the construction and specific use-histories of individual vessels, all analysis must be considered in terms of broader cultural developments, not just typologically. Scholars need to ask themselves not only why particular vessels were built in certain ways and used by certain people for certain purposes, but also how and why the materiality and uses of various vessels are similar to or differ from each other in different systemic contexts. Ships must be treated not as static and systemically isolated objects, but as complex archaeological *sites* - simultaneously loci of human activity and conveyers of people, things, and ideas across much larger cultural, economic, and historical contexts. Pointing to the recovered remains of specific vessels such as those discussed here and using them as stand-ins for large-scale cultural phenomena such as slave trading or piracy is simply unacceptable. To do so is to take a facile reading of the value of archaeological evidence, relegating it to a role of mere illustration of preexisting historical interpretation, rather than treating it as the rich primary informational source that it is.

With regards to our knowledge of slave ships and their place in the development of modern global culture, the potential contributions by archaeology are almost boundless. An electronic search of the *Transatlantic Slave Trade* database (Eltis and Nwokeji 1999) reveals 825 ships known historically to have been wrecked during slaving activities and an additional 55 abandoned. Even ignoring additional ships that engaged in slaving illicitly or went undocumented for other reasons, it seems that enough sites should exist in accessible locations to provide not just one or two good examples of slave ships, but rather a sample large enough for meaningful comparative and diachronic analyses to be made. A program of archaeological investigation of these wrecks, in conjunction with existing documentary evidence and oral traditions, has the potential to contribute deeply to a much more nuanced and sophisticated understanding of the global development and practice of slaving. Such an understanding would recognize the human toll of the trade but move beyond a simple condemnatory position and seek deeper, more complex understandings of the Middle Passage as an ongoing historical phenomenon taking place aboard ships, but situated across vast stretches of geographic and historical distance. Furthermore, such interpretations need not be couched strictly in materialist terms of capitalist economic development (Richardson 2001, Klein *et al* 2001). As the vehicles upon which enslaved Africans of many cultures were first thrown together and removed from their continent, slave ships represent one of the first stages for the creation of a global African cultural diaspora. Considering Harris' (1996) contention that it is the common social condition of slavery that has led to the creation of more unified pan-African identities, evidence of the formation of new social arrangements and resistance strategies aboard slave ships has the potential for shedding light on some of the earliest processes of domination, resistance, and transculturation by which diasporic identities were forged.

Even more importantly, once comparative studies have taken place, it is incumbent upon any archaeologist conducting them to disseminate his or her findings not only through the usual academic channels of journals and monographs, but also through museum exhibitions and popular media presentations. The success of the problem-riddled *Henrietta Marie* exhibit has shown that the public thirsts for untold histories, and that it believes that archaeologists, or facsimiles thereof, have the ability and authority to provide them. Without more compelling alternatives, however, archaeologically based exhibitions will be lost in a crowd, and we will continue to lose not only the ability to deliver our own interpretations effectively, but we may also lose our identity and authority as archaeologists (Smith 2002). With well-developed legal protections - comparable to those for terrestrial archaeological sites - still missing underwater, popular discourse has become the main arena in which the battle for control of underwater heritage is fought. Slick, successful exhibits embraced by the general public go a long way toward securing the approval of well-meaning policy makers for private salvors. Only through a conspicuous, sustained campaign of engagement with the public can nautical archaeologists create a demand for informed, unsensationalized accounts of the slave trade and the past in general, accounts next to which the distortions and shortcomings of those produced by private interests become glaringly obvious (Johnston 1993).

A successful response to the *Henrietta Marie* and *Whydah* exhibits and media campaigns would have to be carefully planned in order not to fall victim to the kinds of simplistic analyses that plague privately produced exhibits, or, worse yet, to validate their approaches and content. A responsible exhibition should both reflect and continue the process of contextualization undertaken during the research phase. The kind of self-referential, vessel-centric approach is inherently awkward and difficult to reconcile with contextualizing narratives, and for this reason, a better strategy would be to shift the subject of the exhibition away from particular slave ships and toward the slave trade *in toto*. Considering the broad geographic, cultural, and historical depth of the subject, the ideal scenario would perhaps be an entire museum focusing on the slave trade. However, the potential benefits of a wider museum audience and concomitant increased media exposure suggest that for practical reasons, a traveling feature exhibit would be more effective in changing public perceptions.

Such an exhibition must be both informed and interactional, reflecting the actual contributions of archaeology to knowledge of the slave trade, and presenting these findings in ways that challenge audiences to participate in the interpretive process. Given the subject's sensitive nature, exhibits should take care to present slavery in a compassionate and humane way but should not compromise factual or analytical integrity for the sake of raw emotive power as the *Henrietta Marie* exhibition does. Rather, the topic should be presented in a dignified and restrained way, one which does not shrink away from the brutality of the trade but which allows audiences to digest its reality and come to their own intellectual and emotional conclusions.

Finally, exhibit managers must take great care to ensure that associated media productions follow the same standards of rigor as the research and exhibition. Doing so will be much more difficult than it would seem at first glance. It is an unfortunate fact that for-profit heritage media giants have a stranglehold on the US popular psyche and are the only outlets capable of producing the kind of large-scale popular awareness that they do. For this reason, it is important that scholars work with mass-media outlets but do so in an extremely cautious manner so as to ensure that any resulting productions neither distort interpretations nor convey any unintended messages. *National Geographic*, in particular, is notorious for allowing its staff writers to rewrite articles written by academics in order to make them more palatable to a mass audience, often simplifying or excising important interpretations (Gero and Root 1996). For this reason, it is of utmost importance that exhibitors act decisively to make themselves heard by the creators of media productions before they are released.

The suggestions made in this paper address the uniquely specific circumstances surrounding the subject of the archaeology of slave ships. However, many of the critiques presented are broadly valid for large swaths of the interpreted and depicted past. Issues of commercialization, homogenization, and ideologically driven soft-pedaling continue to confound museum and other heritage scholarship and practice (Kirby 1988, Roberts 1997). Fortunately, the greater awareness of these problems generated by modern heritage studies has provided us with the tools we need to fight back against this trend. And fight we must, for the results of our disengagement are readily apparent. This struggle will no doubt be protracted and unpleasant, but we can no longer afford to be anything but political.

References

Abbass, D.K. and Zarzynski, J.W. 1998. The Rhode Island ship 'Gem': Slaver or Propaganda. In L.E. Babits *et al* (eds), *Underwater Archaeology*, 74–8. Tucson, Arizona: The Society for Historical Archaeology.

Arnold, J.B. III, and Mclaughlin-Neyland, K. 1994. State Responses to the Abandoned Shipwreck Act of 1987. In D.H. Keith and T.I Carrell (eds), *Underwater Archaeology Proceedings from the SHA Conference 1994*, 114–18. Pleasant Hill CA: The Society for Historical Archaeology.

Bass, G. 1990. After The Diving is Over. In T.L. Carrell (ed.), *Underwater Archaeology Proceedings from the SHA Conference 1990*, 10–13. Pleasant Hill CA: The Society for Historical Archaeology.

Behrendt, S. 2001. Markets, transaction cycles, and profits: Merchant decision making in the British slave trade. *William and Mary Quarterly* 58 (1), 171–204.

Bly, A. 1998. Crossing the Lake of Fire. Slave resistance during the Middle Passage. *The Journal of Negro History* 83 (3) (Summer, 1998), 178–86.

Carrier, J. 1998. Sunken Treasure's Sinking Fortunes. *New York Times*.

Clifford, B. 1999. *Expedition Whydah*. New York, NY: Cliff Street Books.

Cockerell, W.A. 1990. Why Dr. Bass Couldn't Convince Mr. Gumbel: The trouble with treasure revisited, again. In T.L. Carrell (ed.), *Underwater Archaeology Proceedings from the SHA Conference 1990*, 13–18. Pleasant Hill CA: The Society for Historical Archaeology.

Cottman, M. 1995. *Spirit Dive*. New York: Three Rivers Press.

Cottman, M. 1999. *The Wreck of the Henrietta Marie*. New York: Harmony Books.

Elia, R. 1992. The ethics of collaboration: Archaeologists and the *Whydah* project. *Historical Archaeology* 26(4), 105–17.

Elia, R. 1995. Nautical shenanigans. *The INA Quarterly* 22(3), 23.

Eltis, D. and Nwokeji, U. (eds). 1999. *The Transatlantic Slave Trade*. New York: Cambridge University Press.

Garland, C. and Klein, H.S. 1985 .The allotment of space for slaves aboard eighteenth-century British slave ships. *William and Mary Quarterly* 3d Ser., 42, 238–48.

Gero, J. and Root, D. 1996. Public presentations and private concerns: Archaeology in the pages of *National Geographic*. In I. Hodder (ed.), *Contemporary Archaeology in Theory*, 531–47. Cambridge, MA: Blackwell Publishers.

Giesecke, A. 1987. Creative Financing and Project Management. In A.B. Albright (ed.), *Underwater Archaeology Proceedings from the SHA Conference 1987*, 12–13.

Giesecke, A. 2002. Wrecked and Abandoned. In C. Ruppe and J. Barstad (eds), *International Handbook of Underwater Archaeology*, 573–84. New York: Kluwer Academic.

Goodheart, A. 1999. Into the depths of history. *Preservation* 51(1), 36–45.

Gould, R. 1981. Looking Below the Surface: Shipwreck Archaeology as Anthropology. In R.A. Gould (ed.), *Shipwreck Anthropology*, 3–22. Albuquerque: University of New Mexico Press.

Gould, R. 2000. *Archaeology and the Social History of Ships*. Cambridge: Cambridge University Press.

Halsey, J.R. 1994. Shipwreck Law and Underwater Management. In R.P. Woodward and C.D. Moore (eds), *Underwater Archaeology Proceedings from the SHA Conference 1994*, 108–13. Pleasant Hill CA: The Society for Historical Archaeology.

Hannahs, T. 2003. Underwater Parks vs. Preserves: Data or Access. In J.D. Spirek and D. Scott-Ireton (eds), *Submerged Cultural Resource Management*, 5-16. New York: Kluwer Academic.

Harris, J.E. 1996. The Dynamics of the Global African Diaspora. In A. Jalloh and S.E. Maizlish (eds), *African Diaspora*, 7–21. College Station, Texas: Texas A+M Press.

Henderson, G. 1976. James Matthews excavation, summer 1974. Interim report. *The International Journal of Nautical Archaeology and Underwater Exploration* 5(3), 245–51.

Johnston, P.F. 1989. Between The Devil and The Dark Blue Sea: Archaeology and the Council of American Maritime Museums. In J.B. Arnold III (ed.), *Underwater Archaeology Proceedings from the SHA Conference 1989*, 148–49. Pleasant Hill, California: The Society for Historical Archaeology.

Johnston, P. 1993. Treasure salvage, archaeological ethics, and maritime museums. *The International Journal of Nautical Archaeology* 22, 53–60.

Kechington, T., Carter, J.A. and Rice, E.L. 1989. The Indispensability of Non-artifactual Data in Underwater Archaeology. In J.B. Arnold III (ed.), *Underwater Archaeology Proceedings from the SHA Conference 1989*, 111–20. Pleasant Hill CA: The Society for Historical Archaeology.

Kirby, S. 1988. Policy and Politics: Charges, Sponsorhip, and Bias. In R. Lumley (ed.), *The Museum Time Machine: Putting Cultures on Display*, 89–101. New York: Routledge.

Klein, H *et al.* 2001. Transoceanic mortality: The slave trade in comparative perspective. *William and Mary Quarterly* 58 (1), 93–118.

Lutz, C. and Collins, J.L. 1993. *Reading National Geographic.* Chicago: University of Chicago Press.

Mather, I. and Watts, G. 2002. Ethics and Underwater Archaeology. In C. Ruppe and J. Barstad (eds), *International Handbook of Underwater Archaeology,* 593–608. New York: Kluwer Academic.

McCarthy, M. 2001. *Iron and Steamship Archaeology: Success and Failure on the S/S Xantho.* New York: Kluwer Academic.

McGhee, F.L. 1998. Towards a postcolonial nautical archaeology. *Assemblage* 3, www.assemblage.group. shef.ac.uk/3/3mcghee.htm (1 June 2006).

McLean, R. 1996. *Quest For a Pirate.* Catalog. Key West, Florida: Barry Clifford Museum.

McClung, R. 1989. Supporting Archaeological Research in the Real World. In A.B. Albright (ed.), *Underwater Archaeology Proceedings from the SHA Conference 1987*, 46. Pleasant Hill CA: The Society for Historical Archaeology.

Miller, G. 1987. The second destruction of the Geldermalsen. *The American Neptune* XLVII (4), 275–81.

Moeller, S. 1999. *Compassion Fatigue.* New York: Routledge.

Moore, D.D. 1989. Anatomy of a 17th Century Slave Ship: Historical and Archaeological Investigations of the *Henrietta Marie*. MA Thesis. Eastern Carolina University.

Muckelroy, K. 1978. *Maritime Archaeology*. New York: Cambridge University Press.

Neyland, R.S. 2002. Open Letter to US Commission on Ocean Policy. www.oceancommission.gov/publicomment/octcomments/neyland_comment.pdf (1 June 2006).

Noble, V., Kelly, R. and Wilkie, N. 2002. Joint Statement to the US Commission on Ocean Policy, The Society for Historical Archaeology, The Society for American Archaeology, The Archaeological Institute of America. www.oceancommission.gov/publicomment/octcomments/noble_comment.pdf (5 May 2002).

Pelkofer, P. 1987. The Abandoned Shipwreck Act and State Law: A Legal Perspective. In R.P. Woodward and C.D. Moore (eds), *Underwater Archaeology Proceedings from the SHA Conference 1994*, 114–18. Pleasant Hill, California: The Society for Historical Archaeology.

Richardson, D. 2001. Shipboard revolts, African authority, and the Atlantic slave trade. *William and Mary Quarterly* 58 (1), 69–92.

Roberts, L. 1997. *From Knowledge to Narrative: Educators and the Changing Museum*. Washington D.C.: Smithsonian Institution Press.

Russell, A. and Woodall, J.N. 1998. The roles of archaeology and ideology in the reconstruction of an eighteenth-century North Carolina Moravian dwelling. Paper presented at the *31st Conference on Historical and Underwater Archaeology*. www.wfu.edu/anthropology/archeology/library/SHA.htm (1 June, 2006).

1997 *A Slave Ship Speaks, The Wreck of the Henrietta Marie* – Museum exhibition. Mel Fisher Maritime Heritage Society.

Smith, S. 2002. Education: The Power Tool of Underwater Archaeology. In C. Ruppe and J. Barstad (eds), *International Handbook of Underwater Archaeology*, 585–92. New York: Kluwer Academic.

Souza, D. 1997. *The Persistence of Sail in the Age of Steam*. New York: Kluwer Academic.

Steinberg, J. 2002. Last voyage of the slave ship *Henrietta Marie*. *National Geographic Magazine* 202 (2), 42–61.

Svalesen, L. 2000. *The Slave Ship Fredensborg*. Bloomington: Indiana University Press.

Throckmorton, P. 1990. The World's Worst Investment: The Economics of Treasure Hunting with Real Life Comparisons. In T.L. Carrell (ed.), *Underwater Archaeology Proceedings from the SHA Conference 1990*, 61–72, Pleasant Hill CA: The Society for Historical Archaeology.

Trigger, B. 1989. *A History of Archaeological Thought*. New York: Cambridge University Press.

Webster, D. 1999. Pirates of the Whydah. *National Geographic Magazine* May 1999, 64–77.

Zarzynski, J., Abbass, D.K., Benway, B. and Farrell, J. 1996. 'Ring-Around-A-Radeau' or, Fencing in a 1758 Shipwreck for Public Access and Preservation. In S.R. James Jr. and C. Stanley (eds), *Underwater Archaeology 1996*, 41–44. Tucson, Arizona: The Society for Historical Archaeology.

THE PARADOX OF PROGRESS: LAND SURVEY AND THE MAKING OF AGRARIAN SOCIETY IN COLONIAL BRITISH COLUMBIA

Jeff Oliver

Introduction

> They had a little map with them, and asked me to show them where they were, of which they appeared to have a very hazy idea (R.C. Mayne, Four Years in British Columbia 1862: 175).

Progress is the idea that 'civilization' has moved, is moving and will continue to move in a desirable direction (Bury 1955: 2). During the colonization of North America in the nineteenth century, progress was usually linked with material changes in the land where the natural environment was 'improved' for farming and other forms of productive investment (Ekirch 1969: 13). Colonialism, in the context of this chapter, refers to the frontiers or margins of the civilized world and how they were appropriated and moulded by Europeans for their interests. Thus, colonial history and the idea of progress are inextricably linked. Following a narrative pattern in common with other many parts of the continent, the history of environmental change in colonial British Columbia has a tendency to rest on two assumptions. First, it is couched in terms of 'impact' where a singular and self-conscious group of colonists intentionally shape a passive landscape for the betterment of 'civilization'. Second, its narrative form follows a simple 'ascending plotline' (Cronon 1992), or 'world growth story' (Gellner 1964), where change is registered along a progressive chronological time scale (see for example papers in Seimens 1976a and Wynn and Oke 1992). Although this is beginning to change in academic circles (cf, papers in Sandwell 1999a), among broader public opinion the notion that colonization uniformly brought progress and civilization to the west coast is still typically unquestioned.

While colonial history is laudable in that it seeks to represent the 'truth' of environmental change, according to recent developments in post-colonial theory it is only a partial truth. Post-colonial theory, an umbrella term for critical approaches that have sought to shed light on the voices of 'sub-altern' groups displaced by colonialist history, suggests that the problem lies in the premise of a static and monolithic view of cultures and of colonial encounters. This body of critique can be separated into two main themes. First, history and environmental change are often confused as the same phenomenon, the natural result of which is a teleology according to which change is perceived as inevitably moving forward in one direction (Giddens 1984: 242). Second, the categories of 'colonizer' and 'colonized' are unrealistic objectifications that disregard the often fluid social boundaries of inhabitation (Gosden 2001: 242). Rather, colonial cultures and encounters were far more complex than this and were constituted by a blurring of this duality into hybrid and often-ambiguous realities.

It is in this context that I want to take a critical look at the idea of progress through the prism of land survey. During the second half of the nineteenth century 'improvements' to the colony of British Columbia began with the establishment of the international boundary and a program of cadastral survey. Establishing a basic infrastructure of survey lines and monuments acted as an important technology to appropriate and give order to what was essentially perceived as wilderness. However, through investigating the gap between the artefact of survey maps and the material effects of land survey 'on the ground', this paper will argue that the seemingly progressive ideal could be muddled and contradictory. Sliding between the abstract scale of cartography and the local scale of experience in the landscape will allow me to argue that there is a very real tension between these different ways of seeing. The process of land survey may have helped to subdue nature, but it also facilitated the construction of cultured wildernesses that served to fragment colonial interests. The material reality of colonial power and the way it was interpreted was not a coherent one-way process, but something that resolved itself at different scales.

The paper concludes by suggesting that land survey and the decisive architecture that the land system attempted to establish was at times antithetical to a unitary vision of progress, and that historians must balance the premise of a colonial discourse with the different ways that it became enmeshed and refigured in different contexts of inhabitation. Shifting between different forms of evidence and scales of analysis, the approach employed can also be seen as an attempt to dissolve the intellectual boundaries between the more abstract spaces of historical geography and the more place-centred focus of archaeology. To the extent that colonialism is often treated as a unilateral means of representing, subjugating and reforming peoples and places, what I will propose can be seen as part of that growing body of work that seeks to write back from the colonial margins (eg, Bender 1999; Clayton 2000).

The colonisation of British Columbia

British interest in the northwest coast begins in the latter half of the eighteenth century. However, it was not until 1858 that the mainland colony of 'British Columbia' was established. In that year, a contingent of Royal Engineers was sent to the Fraser Valley to partake in the International Boundary Commission, to establish a property cadastre and to build the colony's first roads (Woodward 1974–75). In the words of the colonial secretary the engineers were dispatched to 'conquer nature...so that all nations will... gaze on gardens and cornfields...first carved from the wilderness' (Lytton 1858). Over less than a single lifetime, the valley passed through remarkable transformations, changes which took Europe itself millennia to develop (Harris 1997: 68). By the turn of the twentieth century the landscape was remodelled along class lines and reshaped by agrarian values (see Demerit 1995–96: 42). None the less, attempting to recreate the land-based society of rural Britain was not achieved haphazardly. The practice of land surveying helped to create a single cartographic truth, a form of scaffolding upon which settlement and the aspirations of progress could hinge.

Land survey in the Fraser Valley

Of all possessions west of the Rocky Mountains, the Fraser Valley saw the earliest land surveys of British mainland territory. Between 1858 and 1890, most of the valley was carved up into a cadastre, a geometric property grid that was used to help organize Crown land into parcels for an anticipated market of settlers and investors (North *et al* 1977: 45). For newcomers good land meant improved agricultural land, and creating a framework of survey lines that corresponded with maps of land division was the first step in bringing what was perceived to be unproductive wilderness into the clutches of civilization. Quite simply, land surveys helped to organize, control and record the settlement of 'empty' lands (Kain 2002: 11).

The early years of land survey saw a number of different systems used in the valley. However in 1873, following the example of the United States, a more permanent solution was found in the Township and Range System (Taylor 1975: 43; see also Johnson 1990: 135). This system divided the valley into six-mile square blocks, each subdivided into 36 sections of one-mile square. Blocks were hung on meridians running north to south, with baselines and correction lines running east to west. With minor variations the Township and Range System remains the framework for land holding to the present day.

Surveying land that was commonly dominated by tall trees and thick underbrush required a means of demarcating survey lines so that they would clearly stand out. By cutting a clear line of sight through underbrush and blazing nearby trees with an axe, surveyors were able to rough out the line of their traverse. Additionally, trails were cut along the exterior lines of townships, enabling settlers to get through and satisfy themselves as to the quality of the

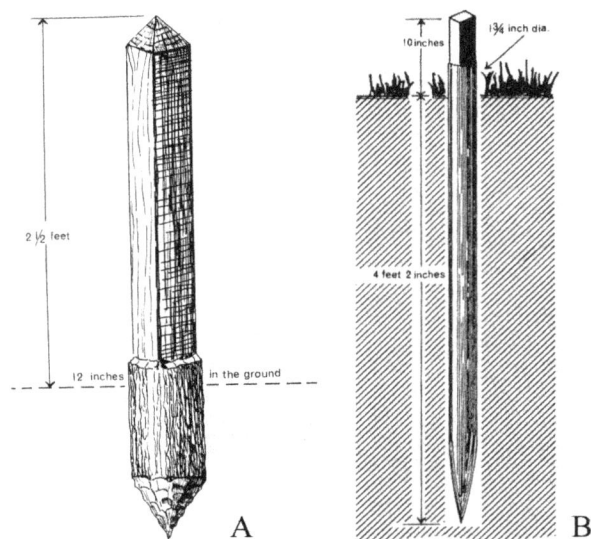

Figure 8. Diagram of survey posts, adapted from Thomson (1967: 52). (A) Wood post, marking section corner 5 inches diameter, 3½ inches square. (B) Iron post marker, township corner.

soil (Fannin in British Columbia Legislative Assembly *Sessional Papers* 1873: 4). In heavily forested areas, such as the valley, the placing of landmarks along survey lines – such as 'corner posts', 'section' and 'half section posts' – planted two feet into the ground, helped settlers to visibly register land divisions. Above ground, posts were squared with three-inch faces (Figure 8). Below ground, they were set on charcoal, crockery or broken glass, a measure to both impede rot and reconfirm their location should they be displaced (Cail 1974: 62; North *et al* 1977; Taylor 1975: 43; Thomson 1967: 51).

Figure 9. Colonial survey party (Chilliwack Archives, P.1484).

The progress of civilization and the 'god trick' of the map

So far I have touched on the more practical role of land survey. However, we must not overlook the fact that it also served an important symbolic purpose. Surveys and cadastral maps (maps that show surveyed property boundaries) were perhaps the ultimate means of legitimizing land divisions through identifying boundaries in the land with specialized signs and symbols, as if they reflected the natural order of things. Moreover, because maps that were produced from land surveys suggested a mathematically precise representation of boundary lines – as they existed

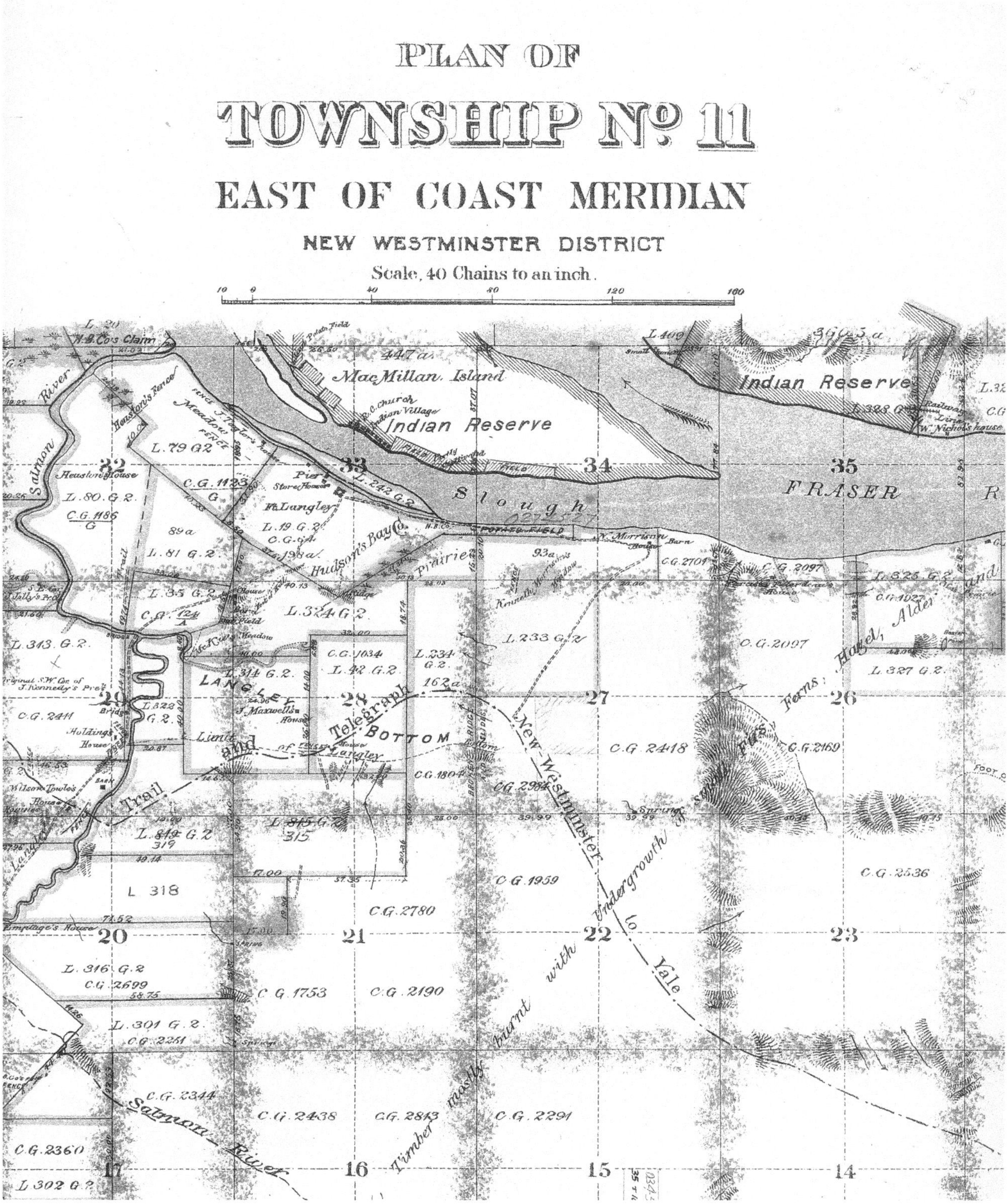

Figure 10. Plan of Township 11 in the central Fraser Valley (detail), Department of the Interior, Technical Branch, Ottawa, 12 July, 1886 (British Columbia Crown Land Registry).

in 'reality' – they bolstered these claims while at the same time framing the landscape through the lens of progress.

By marshalling the authority of the state with the rhetoric of scientific accuracy the surveyor acted on behalf of settler society as an arbiter of power (Figure 9) (Burnett 2000; Edney 1997). Crosscutting older forms of land tenure, they undermined aboriginal claims by 'mapping them out' of the land, effacing their memory with a new geography of boundary lines and an index of place names (Brealey 1995) (Figure 10). Survey landmarks helped to reinforce the power of the state, although they were sometimes contested - for example, Bruce Stadfeld (1999) has showed how in certain contexts local native groups challenged boundary demarcations, particularly along Indian reserves. But land surveying had perhaps a more profound performative quality for those who observed and participated in this reterritorialization. The rehearsed choreography of a disciplined troop of men wielding scientific instruments was a visual display that helped to give their actions a lasting emphasis. Moreover, settlers were not simply passive onlookers to this performance. When land was already occupied they actively joined in by closely scrutinizing this process, legitimizing what they deemed to be an accurate survey by signing their names in the meticulously kept survey register (Ralph 1875).

Drawing on Foucault's arguments about surveillance and control of the body, Cole Harris (1997: 101) has argued that by 1881, the land system acted like a 'disciplinary appendage', with its sprouting fence lines, zones of exclusion, and landowner 'watchmen' backed up by the power of the state. This is not to suggest that other changes like road building, establishing farms or cutting down the forest were less effective in constructing a colonized landscape. Nevertheless, the built environment unfolded far more slowly than the relatively fast paced land survey. In contrast, the 'god trick' of the mapped image, which allowed its users an infinite view of the landscape where everything could be seen from one perspective (Haraway 1991: 189), facilitated vision across the valley, beyond the giant trees 'fringing the river like a gigantic hedge' (Dawson in Cole and Lockner 1989: 10).

Additionally, surveys mobilized the rhetoric of progress by inscribing land with spaces and boundaries equivalent to the ideals of capitalism and 'man over nature'. While most settlers were firmly brought up within the ethos of capitalism, where land was understood as a commodity, maps helped to reinforce the perception of land as an alienable object. Articulated in terms of repetitive symbols, maps suggested that land was equivalent and exchangeable with other such spaces (Harley 1988: 282; Strang 1997: 252). Some maps also included information about local vegetation and soil quality, helping to narrow the definition of land to one of economy. No longer inhibited by the disorientating characteristics of wilderness, the new spatial geometry anticipated the enabling powers of agriculture and its rewards of social improvement.

Crucially, following common practice with other parts of North America, maps of the valley were displayed in public places, such as at Land Offices in Victoria and New Westminster where land grants and land sales were registered (see Home 1997: 37; Kain and Baigent 1992: 307; Spittle 1988). Although in some contexts it was not always this straightforward; in the colony of Vancouver Island, access to survey maps appears to have been through favour by the governor (*British Colonist* 1860). Even if these images were not readily available, most settlers owned a legally binding sketch of the survey of their own land (Harris 2002: 76). It was through consuming these images that newcomers were instilled with a sense of

palpable authority; that the land between the mountains and the gulf was underwritten by the colonial state and the rule of law. To landowners, 'the presence of their property clearly identified on a map…confirmed their stake in the new nation…etching the cadastre into the public mind' (Kain and Baigent, 1992: 307). Moreover, the fact that geographical knowledge was extended year on year, by filling in the blank spaces on the map, created a certain conflation between mapping and the progress of civilization. As one local newspaper suggested, recent government surveys in the Fraser Valley 'wonderfully assisted newcomers in selecting locations for settlement' (*Mainland Guardian* 13 January 1877). This is a notion alluded to not only by historical figures but also by historians of cartography who have equated mapping with the process of civilizing by throwing back the boundaries of *terra incognita* (cf, Farley 1960; Gilmartin 1986).

At this point I want to move from cartography to the 'view from the ground', for I want to show that land survey at this scale was caught up in complex negotiations that problematize its role in evoking a coherent and unified perception of the progress of civilization.

The paradox of progress: a view from the ground

Threading evidence together from an on-the-ground perspective can 'cut reality in different ways' (Gosden 1994: 140) and suggests a far more messy history to the process of land survey. While cartographic victories were proclaimed as methods became more scientific and more accurate, the stability and very materiality of this 'truth' on the ground was contested. Certainly, idiosyncrasies among surveyors and survey systems were one problem. Despite the rigour that many surveyors imposed upon their work, 'it was not always possible to measure what was intended to be measured' (Taylor 1975: 18). The unforgiving terrain and the use of different survey technologies inevitably meant mistakes and fudged results. What is more, however, is that the material effects of survey in many places contradicted the 'natural' order of things portrayed by the map when relationships between colonial interests and the landscape escaped their assumed stable references. In particular I address the reactive qualities of forest ecology and biogeography (Butler 1995; Head *et al* 2002: 176). Assumed to be a simple background for the playing out of colonial desires, the forest was imbued with its own agency (Jones and Cloke 2003) – in this case, a counter agent to progress – when we take into consideration the different ways in which the material effects of surveying (as well as other forms of forest modification) were drawn upon by differently situated social actors.

The living landscape

A major problem with imposing boundaries on the land and ensuring that they stood out was simply that the trees grew back. In contrast to the colonial desire to carve passive wilderness into a new social and economic framework, 'nature' showed the uncanny ability to 'act back' – to reclaim the landscape as successional forest. Paradoxically, areas of re-growth were sometimes described in terms usually reserved for the most primeval wilderness. For example, from 1859 to 1863 Royal Engineers of the British Boundary Commission surveyed a line along the 49th parallel delimiting British from American territory. To demarcate the boundary clearly, a wide avenue of trees was felled on both sides of its axis along the entire length of the border (Figure 11). To reinforce this line cut through the wilderness, the Boundary Commission placed cast iron monuments and wooden posts along its course at regular

Figure 11. Lithograph of boundary line between the colony of British Columbia and Washington Territory, after Whymper (Mayne 1862: frontispiece).

intervals. However, as the line inched eastward over the years, from the Gulf of Georgia into the mountainous interior, older sections of the cut became obscured by new growth. Naval officer R.C. Mayne recorded this phenomenon during routine provisioning of the line:

> These periodical visits to the boundary-line gave us some idea of the rapid growth of the bush in this country, and showed us how completely futile the mere cutting down of trees to mark a boundary in such a county is. We knew the position of the boundary-line, but could not find the stump which had been driven in to mark the spot; and when I tried to penetrate along the line…I found the undergrowth so thick as to be what people unused to that country would consider quite impenetrable (Mayne 1862: 233).

Mayne's observations along the boundary were not isolated. As he was frequently involved in provisioning the Sappers of the Boundary Commission, it became increasingly apparent that land clearance had stimulated fresh growth. During a further trip to a different part of the boundary line a year after the trail had been cut, his party 'hunted for an hour or more' in the bush, later protesting that 'no entrance to the trail could be found' (Mayne 1862: 233–34).

The speedy obliteration of trails was such that Township and Range surveys had to expend considerable effort to bring

nature to a heel. The importance of this is demonstrated by the actual time spent in physically inscribing surveys into the land. In 1874, surveyor Ashdown frequently commented on the many hours and days his party spent, with axe in hand, 'cutting out [the] base line' (1874: 2). Others were required to go to even greater lengths. On the progress of surveying Indian reservations in the valley, one surveyor reported to the government that he made certain to emphasize how 'The lines are well cut and defined, being good trails almost', further describing how corner posts were deeply scored and sunk into the corners of each reserve, and how the attention of Indians was called to blazed trees and other natural features on the boundaries (Launders in British Columbia *Sessional Papers* 1876).

Despite these efforts, contradictory outcomes were apparently felt along even well trodden meridians. In May 1867, when lands north of New Westminster were being surveyed into saleable lots, surveyor Howse – working on the baseline of North Road – reported that 'The roadway… is overgrown with fern and underbrush, leaving only a foot track along the line', which he said was '…badly cut up, the surface being washed away' exposing numerous roots and small boulders (quoted in Harris 1982: 16).

If inscribing the landscape with a property grid was a form of improvement heralding social progress, then what happened when the land was re-colonized and obscured by nature? It would not have been only surveyors that noted the discrepancies between the mapped image and the reality on the ground. Extrapolating from the broader history of environmental alteration in the valley that followed land survey, such as the construction of roads, the felling of timber and the building of railways (Seimens 1976b), combined with the frequent forest fires that accompanied these activities (Perry 1984), forest succession would have been a commonly observed phenomenon. The photographic evidence from the turn of the century certainly bears this out **(Figure 12)**. We need to recognize that people living in and working the land were not ignorant of these changes. Vigorous growth – what forest ecologists call 'secondary succession' (Packam *et al* 1992: 143) – flew in the face of improvements to tame the country. In the lowland forests of the Fraser Valley, the disturbed ground and the invasion of light propagated a quick rejuvenation of buried seeds, roots, rhizomes and invading seedlings, so that in a short succession of years, weeds were quickly supplanted by thickets of shrubs and trees such as alder, and later by the saplings of what would become forest giants, such as Douglas-fir and red cedar.

The lie of the land

Over longer time scales, with the increasing pressure of settlement, we cannot ignore the fact that cadastral surveys helped to shape the physical transformation of the valley whilst simultaneously influencing how newcomers valued land. The sprawling settlement of the city of Vancouver and its suburban tendrils attests to this well enough. Although land surveys underpinned the ability to hold private property, the boundaries they proclaimed were in certain contexts actually seen to be impeding progress.

With the founding of the colony in 1858, most settlers opted to take free land in single 160-acre parcels, improving it materially so as to fulfil the conditions of a government land grant. This was known as 'pre-emption'. Others chose to purchase land outright, and in much larger portions, circumventing the land grant clause that required settlers to improve it. Frequently, these individuals were land speculators who sought to invest in land for reasons that were not always sympathetic to the making of a productive

Figure 12. Successional forest in the Fraser Valley c. 1911 (Surrey Archives, P.180.5.01).

countryside. For these individuals land became viewed as 'real estate' and 'every available piece of land was bought up...not for the purpose of farming, but to hold for a rise in prices' (Gosnell 1897: 270). Land values went up to the extent that they 'never saw an axe or a plough' and remained 'unimproved' (ibid: 270). This strategy failed to pay dividends for many landowners as population and economic opportunities remained relatively low until late in the century, creating little market for land sales (Harris 1997: 86). What it did achieve, however, was to dissuade settlement by unnaturally holding up large blocks of the valley in unimproved conditions.

Whether there is truth to the notion that land speculation slowed the pace of civilization, what is certain is that its material effects were clearly perceived to have adverse impacts on those newcomers who had already settled in the valley. For example, where pre-emptors had homesteaded and cleared land in still isolated parts of the valley, land speculators would swiftly accumulate the surrounding forest, hoping to turn a tidy profit on settlers enticed by the emerging oasis. In the words of a newspaper editor, '...just as soon as you go in and commence improvements, the whole region round about will be *grabbed* by the *Land-sharks* and then you may sigh in vain for society' (emphasis in the original, *British Columbian* 4 April 1861). This emphasis on the 'solitude' of unlucky pre-emptors was not a short-lived occurrence, but persisted in a range of commentaries on settlement in the valley. As late as 1892, it was recognized in an agricultural report 'that much land is held by non-resident owners, which lies in its old primeval state, and is very discouraging to residents, who are thus shut in to a great extent' (British Columbia

Legislative Assembly *Second Report of Agriculture* 1892: 797).

What was good for some was not necessarily good for all. At the scale of lived experience 'on the ground', progress did not adhere to the rules of fair play. A land system that promised to facilitate settlement and capitalist enterprise, for some, began to represent greed. Rather than anticipating visions of agrarian living, survey boundaries reified a cultured wilderness. In places, a wall of living green contradicted the mapped image of control and predictability and it hemmed in and obscured rhetoric about the mastery of land. Forced into exclusion from the rest of society, and deprived of access to markets, progress may have been a word with little resonance for newcomers isolated by the very land system that was thought to promote settlement. Given this rather stark situation, for many, the only option was abandonment (see Sandwell 1999b for the varied causes). And when this happened, land that in the grand narrative would have remained open was instead re-colonized by the forest. It is interesting to see how this parallels a recent argument put forward by John Knight: if non-agricultural people, such as some indigenous societies, were not ecologically passive, can agriculturalists necessarily be as active and unilateral in subduing nature, as they have until now tended to appear (1996: 222)? Based on the evidence, it would appear not.

Conclusion

A close reading of the evidence from colonial British Columbia suggests that the ideal of progress was shot through with ambiguities. Land survey attempted to establish a decisive colonial architecture by ordering the landscape for settler society. It was a form of improvement that established the rudimentary framework for productive investments, while at the same time marginalized aboriginal groups. But colonial history did not always have an ascending plot line; its impact on the land was mediated by its very materiality, which in turn impacted upon human expectations and motivations in unintended ways. Survey lines that helped to hold the country in the grip of the state could be quickly obscured by successional growth and boundaries thought to facilitate settlement were at times antithetical to a unitary vision of progress. What was nature and what was culture depended on what side of the boundary you stood. At this scale people encountered and acted upon very different conditions, often for a very diverse set of reasons. Their stories are a vital part of the historic geography of the area but they are frequently glossed over in our pursuit of the grand narrative. It is not to say that we should ignore the more detached way of seeing embodied in maps. After all, these too had real consequences, such as influencing waves of immigration to the new world. However, given the gap between the efficacy of the map and the view 'from the ground', the growth of the survey system as a disciplinary appendage was not as clear-cut as it has been previously suggested. The inevitability of progress, characterized by literature, science and the history of nations, became questionable in times and places where society's domination of nature came into question. The premise of a colonial discourse did not necessarily trickle down evenly at the scale of individual experience. Intent was blunted and fractured by an agency that lay outside the monolithic colonial goal to remake the world.

Acknowledgements

I am grateful to Mark Edmonds, Ana Jorge and Tim Neal for comments and helpful suggestions on earlier drafts of this paper. I would also like to thank the editors of this volume for their help in clarifying aspects of the text.

References

Ashdown, H. G. 1874. *Diary of a Survey of Saltspring Island, June 8–November 22, 1874*. British Columbia Archives and Records Service.

Bender, B. 1999. Subverting the Western Gaze: Mapping Alternative Worlds. In P.J. Ucko and R. Layton (eds), *The Archaeology and Anthropology of Landscape: Shaping Your Landscape*, 31–45. London: Routledge.

Brealey, K.G. 1995. Mapping them 'Out': Euro-canadian cartography and the appropriation of the Nuxalk and Ts'ilhqot'in First Nations' territories, 1793–1916. *Canadian Geographer* 39, 140–56.

British Colonist. 1860. The Secret Practices of the Land Office. 21 September.

British Columbia Legislative Assembly 1873. *Sessional Papers*. Victoria: Government of British Columbia.

British Columbia Legislative Assembly 1892. *Second Report of Agriculture of the Province of British Columbia*. Victoria: Wolfenden.

British Columbian 1861. Our Land System. 4 April.

Burnett, D.G. 2000. *Masters of All They Surveyed: Exploration, Geography and a British El Dorado*. Chicago: Chicago University Press.

Bury, J.B. 1955 [1932]. *The Idea of Progress*. New York: Dover Publications, Inc.

Butler, S. 1995. Post-Processual Palynology. *Scottish Archaeological Review* 9–10, 15–22.

Cail, R.E. 1974. *Land, Man, and the Law: The Disposal of Crown Lands in British Columbia 1873–1913*. Vancouver: UBC Press.

Clayton, D. 2000. *Islands of Truth: The Imperial Fashioning of Vancouver Island*. Vancouver: UBC Press.

Cole, D., and Lockner, B. (eds). 1989. *The Journals of George M. Dawson: British Columbia, 1875–1878, 2 Vols*. Vancouver: UBC Press.

Colonial survey party c. 1870. Photograph available at Chilliwack Archives, P.1484.

Cronon, W. 1992. A place for stories: nature, history, and narrative. *The Journal of American History* 78, 1347–76.

Demeritt, D. 1995–96. Visions of agriculture in British Columbia. *BC Studies* 108, 29–59.

Edney, M.H. 1997. *Mapping an Empire: The Geographical Construction of British India, 1765–1843*. Chicago: The University of Chicago Press.

Ekirch, A.A.J. 1969 [1944]. *The Idea of Progress in America, 1815–1860*. New York: AMS Press.

Farley, A. 1960. The History of Cartography in British Columbia. Unpublished PhD dissertation, University of Wisconsin.

Gellner, E. 1964. *Thought and Change*. London: Weidenfeld & Nicolson.

Giddens, A. 1984. *The Constitution of Society*. Cambridge: Polity Press.

Gilmartin, P. 1986. Landmark Maps in British Columbia's Past. In C.N. Forward (ed.), *British Columbia: Its Resources and People*. vol. 22, Western Geographical Series, 25–41. Victoria: University of Victoria.

Gosden, C. 1994. *Social Being and Time*. Oxford: Blackwell.

Gosden, C. 2001. Postcolonial Archaeology: Issues of Culture, Identity, and Knowledge. In I. Hodder (ed.), *Archaeological Theory Today*, 241–61. Cambridge: Polity Press.

Gosnell, R.E. 1897. *The Year Book of British Columbia 1897 to 1901*. Victoria: Government of British Columbia.

Haraway, D.J. 1991. *Simians, Cyborgs, and Women: The Reinvention of Nature*. New York: Routledge.

Harley, J.B. 1988. Maps, Knowledge, and Power. In D. Cosgrove and S. Daniels (eds.), *The Iconography of Landscape*, 277–312. Cambridge: Cambridge University Press.

Harris, C. 1997. *The Resettlement of British Columbia*. Vancouver: UBC Press.

Harris, C. 2002. *Making Native Space: Colonialism, Resistance, and Reserves in British Columbia*. Vancouver: UBC Press.

Harris, R. C. 1982. Trails radiating from New Westminster, c. 1865. *British Columbia Historical News* Summer, 14–18.

Head, L., Atchison, J and Fullagar, R. 2002. Country and garden: Ethnobotany, archaeobotany and Aboriginal landscapes near the Keep River, Northwest Australia. *Journal of Social Archaeology* 2, 173–96.

Home, R. 1997. *Of Planting and Planning: The Making of British Colonial Cities*. London: E & FN SPON.

Johnson, H.B. 1990. Toward a National Landscape. In M.P. Conzen (ed.), *The Making of the American Landscape*, 127–45. New York: Routledge.

Jones, O. and Cloke, P. 2003. *Tree Cultures: The Place of Trees and Trees in their Place*. Oxford: Berg.

Kain, R.J.P. 2002. The role of cadastral surveys and maps in land settlement from England. *Landscape Research* 27, 11–24.

Kain, R.J.P. and Baigent, E. 1992. *The Cadastral Map in the Service of the State: A History of Property Mapping*. Chicago: University of Chicago Press.

Knight, J. 1996. When Timber Grows Wild: The desocialisation of Japanese Mountain Forests. In P. Descola and G. Palsson (eds.), *Nature and Society: Anthropological Perspectives,* 221–39. London: Routledge.

Lytton, E.B., Sir. 1858. *Speech by Sir Edward Bulwar Lytton, Colonial Secretary to a Company of Royal Engineers, Leaving London in 1858 for British Columbia.* Manuscript available at UBC Special Collections.

Mainland Guardian 1877. The Fraser Valley. 13 January

Mayne, R.C. 1862. *Four Years in British Columbia and Vancouver Island: An Account of Their Forests, Rivers, Coasts, Gold Fields, and Resources For Conlonisation.* London: John Murray.

North, M., Holdsworth, D. and Teversham, J. 1977. A brief guide to the use of land surveyors' notebooks in the Lower Fraser Valley, B.C., 1859–1890. *BC Studies* 34, 45–60.

Packham, J.R., Harding, D.J.L., Hilton, G.M. and Stuttard, R.A. 1992. *Functional Ecology of Woodlands and Forests.* Dordrecht: Kluwer Academic Publishers.

Perry, T.E. 1984. Land use of Matsqui Prairie region of the lower Fraser Valley in southwestern British Columbia. Unpublished MA thesis, Western Washington University.

Plan of Township 11 in the central Fraser Valley, Department of the Interior, Technical Branch, Ottawa, 12 July, 1886. Map available at British Columbia Crown Land Registry.

Ralph, W. 1875. *Chilliwack and Sumass Preemption Claims.* Unpublished report available at British Columbia Crown Land Registry.

Sandwell, R.W. (ed.). 1999a. *Beyond the City Limits: Rural History in British Columbia.* Vancouver: UBC Press.

Sandwell, R.W. 1999b. Negotiating Rural: Policy and Practice in the Settlement of Saltspring Island, 1859–91.

In R.W. Sandwell (ed.), *Beyond the City Limits: Rural History in British Columbia,* 83–101. Vancouver: UBC Press.

Siemens, A.H. (ed.). 1976a [1968]. *Lower Fraser Valley: Evolution of a Cultural Landscape.* Vancouver: Tantalus Research.

Siemens, A.H. 1976b [1968]. The Process of Settlement in the Lower Fraser Valley. In A. H. Siemens (ed.), *Lower Fraser Valley: Evolution of a Cultural Landscape,* 27–49. Vancouver: Tantalus Research.

Spittle, J. 1988. Early Printed Maps of British Columbia. Maps printed and published in New Westminster, 1861–1866. In B. Farrell and A. Desbarats (eds.), *Explorations in the History of Canadian Mapping: A Collection of Essays,* 193–204. Ottawa: Association of Canadian Map Libraries and Archives.

Stadfeld. 1999. Manifestations of Power: Native Resistance to the Resettlement of British Columbia. In R. W. Sandwell (ed.), *Beyond the City Limits: Rural History in British Columbia,* 33–46. Vancouver: UBC Press.

Strang, V. 1997. *Uncommon Ground: Cultural Landscapes and Environmental Values.* Oxford: Berg.

Successional forest in the Fraser Valley c. 1911. Photograph available at Surrey Archives, P.180.5.01.

Taylor, W.A. 1975. *Crown Lands: A History of Survey Systems.* Victoria: Crown Land Registry Services, Ministry of Environment, Lands and Parks.

Thomson, D.W. 1966, 1967. *Men and Meridians: The History of Surveying and Mapping in Canada, 2 vols.* Ottawa: Department of Energy, Mines and Resources.

Woodward, F.M. 1974–75. The Influence of the Royal Engineers on the Development of British Columbia. *BC Studies* 24, 3–51.

Wynn, G., and Oke, T.R. (eds). 1992. *Vancouver and Its Region.* Vancouver: UBC Press.

Constructing Capitalism: Speculation and Social Relations in the Building Industry, 1700–1850

Martin Locock

Introduction

The origins of this paper lie in an intensive survey of the standing fabric at Castle Bromwich Hall, including the walls of the formal garden, undertaken as part of a programme of archaeological excavation and related research in the early 1990s. Perhaps unusually, these walls can be correlated with documents concerning their construction; this meant that in addition to describing and recording the structures, we were in a position to name the workers who had built them. Documentary research has allowed us to place these people in their social context, and thus to consider whether the forms of business practice and structure they adopted conform to the models of economic development which have been advanced, in particular Marx's account of the early stages of capitalism, with specific reference to the development of the rural economy, and evidence for speculation and risk-taking in the light of Weber's thesis that the 'entrepreneurial spirit' emerged from a distinctively Protestant, non-traditional, context. Comparison between these models and the case study remains problematic because 'early capitalism' has no single signature trait. Rather, it comprises a bundle of behaviours which collectively make up the capitalist mindset (Johnson 1996: 9; Johnson 1999: 146).

Marx's model of the Agricultural Revolution

It is common when discussing Marx to focus on his analysis of urban and industrial activity, but he also analyses rural economic change as a necessary precursor, an 'Agricultural Revolution', that precedes the Industrial Revolution. There has been a good deal of recent debate about the 'Agricultural Revolution', with Brenner arguing that it implies capitalism, and Kerridge that it is marked by increased agricultural output (Allen 1992). Underlying this debate is a variation in which a phenomenon is being described, when it occurs, and what causes it, which has moved some distance from Marx's focus. What Marx meant by *his* Agricultural Revolution was not related to new crops and techniques, or even to new work practices: it was a real, social revolution, which created a rural proletariat that could become the urban proletariat. It is also a process more than an event (Marx 1930: 745).

With the collapse of the feudal system in the late medieval period, the new flexible social structure provided an opportunity for ex-serfs to develop their own status and economy and to establish some control over the means of production (Marx 1930: 844–45), exploiting their rights to common pasture and other resources, and tenure or ownership of smallholdings, as a supplement to paid work for the 'capitalistic' lord, or others. This meant that they enjoyed a degree of freedom of action over their economic fate.

Marx identifies the process of enclosure of common land as effectively a privatisation of the rural landscape by the main landowners (1930: 803), through which, by removing common rights, the less-established lost their independence and were forced to become landless labourers tied to their capitalist employers. Since the new landscape required less labour fewer labourers were needed, so that there was a surplus of population, without rights and property, who were forced to seek alternative employment in rural industry or to move to the towns.

In defining capitalist behaviour, Marx uses the Money-Capital cycle. Pre-capitalists would see holding money as the fixed point, which is then invested (converted to capital) until it yields a profit and can be returned into money, for use as consumption; what he calls the M-C-M cycle. Capitalists, on the other hand, keep capital as capital, and when it generates money, this is re-invested in more capital, the C-M-C cycle, maximising production (Marx 1930: 134).

Castle Bromwich Hall

Castle Bromwich was a small village in Aston parish, southeast of Birmingham, in the West Midlands, on the northern edge of the Forest of Arden, in the historic county of Warwickshire. It appears to have had some open fields in the medieval period, but its economy was largely based on pastoral farming. The wood-pasture economy relied on the use of wastes and woodland for the grazing of animals allowing larger herds of livestock to be maintained. Castle Bromwich Hall was built in 1600 and bought in 1660 by Sir Orlando Bridgeman, a member of the local minor gentry, who extended it. Between 1700 and 1740, an extensive series of walled gardens were laid out by the Bridgemans to the south of the Hall (Figure 13). To the north and east lay the village and common areas occupied by squatters. In the 1740s, the Bridgemans became linked by marriage to the Earls of Bradford, and their main residence became the seat of Weston Park, Staffordshire.

The gardens at Castle Bromwich have been the subject of a long-term restoration project by an independent trust. In 1989–91, extensive archaeological investigations were undertaken, funded by the Leverhulme Trust and published in *Post-Medieval Archaeology*, *Transactions of the Birmingham and Warwickshire Archaeological Society* and elsewhere (Currie 1990; Currie and Locock 1992; 1993; Locock and Currie 1991). The garden walls, although architecturally simple, have some points of interest. The bricks, typical of their time, are simple and hand-made with no frog (indentation in the top). The process of brickmaking was lengthy, starting with the digging out of clay, leaving it to weather, mixing it with sand, water and coarse material (stones or grog), filling a wooden mould, turning out the wet brick and leaving it to harden, stacking in the kiln, and firing. The Castle Bromwich bricks were made from the local clay and probably fired on-site, in a small clamp kiln. Payments for the bricks in the estate records show that 13,000 bricks was the usual kiln-load (Locock 1990b). Some of the bricks were marked while drying prior to firing with tallies, using the same type of

Figure 13. Castle Bromwich Hall by Henry Beighton, published in Dugdale's History of Warwickshire (2nd edition, 1730). The image is of some interest as a blend of accurate depiction and misdirection. The Hall in the centre, L-shaped bakehouse block to the centre right, and the church at the top are shown correctly, but the large coachhouse to the right was still under construction when the drawing was made in 1726, and when completed differed in detail from the design shown here. The avenue of trees in the bottom right had been planted, but did not (as might be expected) march across an enclosed parkland withdrawn from commercial activity: the area formed part of the common pasture of the parish. The garden walls shown separating the various components are shown accurately, but the left edge of the picture does not clip off further formal gardens: at the time, the remainder was still agricultural land, and the rectangular beds shown are fictional. The innocent viewer of the scene would conclude that Castle Bromwich was a quiet rural estate: the fact that the rolling hills in the background concealed the rapidly-developing industrial urban centre of Birmingham would have been unsuspected, and the picture conveniently avoids the cluster of squatter cottages housing paupers which lay just to the right. Reproduced by kind permission of Castle Bromwich Hall Gardens Trust.

numbering, derived from Roman numerals, employed by carpenters: 64 bricks with tally markings have been recorded (Locock 1990a). Tally-marking of bricks in this way is a very rare phenomenon (the author is aware of three examples in the UK), and its use here suggests that the craftsman was more familiar with local carpenters than with other brickmakers. The brickmaking was probably carried out by Abraham Parsons, who is listed in the accounts as 'ye brickman'. He was a local man, born in 1688, the son of one of the paupers who lived 'in Town Houses upon the Common'. From 1703 to 1740, he made 820,000 bricks for the Bridgemans. Although he must have been paid more than £1,000 in total for 'making and burning' the bricks, he does not appear to have saved any money or left any property. It is likely that the actual brickmaking was carried out by a team of three to four people, based on the number of different numbering styles used in the tallying, who were probable drawn from local squatters. The tallies presumably reflect their employment on piecework rates, at so much per thousand.

The bricklayers employed were also local, but from much higher up the social scale. Robert Smith was employed as master bricklayer in the 1700s. He is called a mason in his probate inventory, but he was also a farmer and landowner. As well as his work on the hall, he built a farmhouse for the Bridgemans at nearby Shard End. The other labourers involved were also agricultural tenants on the estate, paying the Poor Rate, and therefore significantly more wealthy than the paupers and squatters.

Rural capitalism

Although there were landless labourers at Castle Bromwich, there were also other tenant farmers enjoying some independence and diversifying into other trades.

One of the features of the wood-pasture economy is that it required less labour than open-field arable farming, especially in the early summer, and it has been suggested that the resulting under-employment (or spare labour capacity) was a factor in encouraging diversification by farmers into other trades (Skipp 1970: 96). In the Forest of Arden, the combination of time, clay and wood fuelled the development of an established brick and tile industry operating seasonally, in response to demand from the nearby towns. In Worcestershire, a parallel development was the growth of the rural scythe-making industry. These industries disappeared in the late seventeenth century, partly because of the exhaustion of wood supplies, but also because of the enclosure of arable land in response to demand for cereals from the developing urban centres (Johnson 1996: 27). In Castle Bromwich, it appears that agricultural diversification changed from manufacture, rather than vanished completely. The farmers had limited scope for business since they could not commit themselves fully to new ventures. In their building work, they were employed on a day rate, probably casually. In some cases they were contracted 'by the measure', implying a degree of trust and freedom, since their work would go unsupervised until completion. It would appear that their profits were re-invested into land, their main interest.

It is hard to say whether the rural proletariat, represented by the squatters on the commons of the parish in the 1680s, were a new feature of the time. The *Poor Laws* from the 1570s were intended to address the social and public order problems caused by paupers (as Marx notes, 1930: 813). The *Settlement Act 1662* dealt specifically with paupers leaving their homes and settling in other parishes, and did so by simply placing the responsibility for their maintenance on the home parish. This mobility was perceived as an attempt by the paupers to exploit the variation in harshness and generosity of different parishes. It may well have been due more to unsuccessful economic migration, with incoming poor unable to find sufficient work. The rural proletariat at Castle Bromwich - the squatters - were not idle, but rather were involved in rural industry, as were those in Worcestershire: nail-making on the commons. The nails used at the Hall were made by Thomas Barebones, who had a forge in the village and was relatively poor, to judge from his contribution to the Poor Rate Levy in 1700 (Locock 1994: 248).

Urban building in the Midlands

Garden building in Castle Bromwich was in many senses peripheral. When towns grow, they need people, and people need houses; it is in the urban centres that the construction industry takes root as an established specialist trade. It is likely that until the middle of the eighteenth century, masons were jobbing craftsmen, employed on a particular task and contributing their labour alone. Contracting 'by the great', for a lump sum for the whole project, was restricted at this period to prestige building projects by architect-builders (Locock 1992). In terms of cash flow, it required resources to finance a project if paid on completion, or even in instalments in arrears. It also required confidence from the client. In the 1720s, the rebuilding of Castle Bromwich Church was overseen by the clerk, who employed the building labourers on a day rate and arranged the buying in of raw materials. It would appear that he was unwilling to rely upon the labourers' abilities to organise this for themselves. Looking at the premiums paid for apprenticeships at this time, the building trades were close to the bottom of the scale, just below clothiers and far below joiners, reflecting the low value placed upon their skills.

In view of the low status and few opportunities for profit that resulted from being paid on piecework, building contractors had to find other ways to develop. Typically, they did so by forming partnerships with other traders who owned or leased urban property. Building density increased in early post-medieval towns as street-frontage properties were replaced by courtyards. This type of work was relatively low-risk in financial terms, since properties awaiting building work could still be rented out. It was not until the early 1800s that there is evidence in the Midlands for what we would recognise as speculative building. John Eglington, in Walsall, leased agricultural land from the Earls of Bradford in order to build houses on this basis (Locock 1992). But the main speculative builders were in fact the landed estates, not the building partnerships; they had the resources, the land and the transport links. By this time, the organising of building work was a much less onerous task, since materials were mass-produced and transported over wide areas. There was scope for a production-line approach to building, transforming it from a trade into an industry. In contrast to the estates, the small building firms had a high failure rate. Although this may partly reflect the personal nature of the partnerships, of which dissolution was a regular part, it probably also reflects the financial strains on them of funding lengthy projects without a certain pay-off at the end, demonstrating that successful capitalists need capital.

Weber, the entrepreneurial spirit and the history of speculation

Max Weber (1930) characterises pre-capitalist society as having values in which the satisfaction of needs is the prime driver of economic activity, and in which the accumulation of great wealth for its own sake was seen as unethical, or uninteresting. This traditional mindset is reflected in the medieval concept of paying the 'just price' for commodities, and the corresponding wariness of charging interest on loans. Weber argues that moving to a capitalist society required a change in ethics, a change that occurred most readily and earliest in the Protestant nations of northern Europe. Pursuit of 'rational' behaviour like the accumulation of wealth was made possible by the break from traditional, Catholic values, and success in business was viewed as a sign of one's membership of the Elect. Weber's account of this change in behaviour and its causation has been the subject of controversy ever since. The history of financial speculation is critical to this debate, and is therefore worthy of examination.

Speculation is profit maximisation in its purest form, since it is essentially an abstract financial activity, in which the commodities involved (if any) are of no lasting interest to the investor. A speculator is serving no need other than making money. The machinery required for active speculation did not emerge until surprisingly late. Any seventeenth-century gentleman or lady, for example, considering what to do with an unexpected legacy had very few options, constrained by risk and liquidity. He or she could retain money as cash as it could be readily used and would preserve its value. He or she could buy property, in buildings or land), to ensure a long-term return in the form of rent, which should preserve its value but would be difficult to sell at a good price if money was urgently required. Or, she or he could explore high-risk investments such as overseas trade, eg, the East India Company, which could make high yields or heavy, if not total, losses, and could not easily be redeemed until the completion of the venture (the Company had developed from earlier, single-voyage, ventures).

The purchase of Government annuities became possible in the later seventeenth century, as Governments sought to borrow money to finance wartime expenditure. Purchase of an annuity would yield an annual return for the life of the purchaser, funded from future Government income. Although bearing a low risk, and having a reasonable rate of return, this was still problematic as an asset because it belonged to a named individual, and was therefore non-liquid.

An important development was the establishment of the Bank of England (1694) as a private enterprise, using money from depositors to lend to the Government, in exchange for future interest payments. Shares in the Bank were much easier to trade than annuities, and were thus more liquid while offering similar returns. Marx notes that by this mechanism 'the funds endow barren money with the power of reproduction' (1930: 836).

These developments added to liquidity and security, but were not exciting, and offered no extravagant profits. Alternatives soon came along, though. In Scotland, the Darien venture, to set up a trading port in Panama, inspired large-scale investment across the population in the expectation of rapid and high returns. So much of the country's capital was invested — one third of that available — that when the venture proved a disastrous failure the economy was faced with collapse and was only secured by the financial settlement that accompanied the Act of Union with England.

In England, the South Sea Company appeared to offer similar opportunities, with similar success. The main purpose of the company was to accumulate Government stocks, in exchange for company shares that could be freely traded. The shares increased in value, in the expectation of future profits, and soon there was a frantic scramble to purchase them. In 1720, the South Sea Bubble burst, since the price of the shares had risen far above their rational valuation. Again, it seemed as if a whole country faced ruin, from Tory grandees through merchants and politicians to the Royal family. Mackay says of the Lords 'A speculating frenzy had seized upon them, as well as the plebeians' (1996: 40). There does not appear to have been any substantial difference in the behaviour of different classes and social groups, contrary to the expectations of Weber's model, which should have seen the more traditional parts of society hanging back from the fray. Again, in the end the speculators were let off the hook, this time by a 'restructuring' of the devalued shares into conventional stocks.

So, within a matter of 40 years, finance had travelled from the tentative invention of the Government annuity as a new secure form of investment, to frenzied speculation in abstract secondary products:

> The English commenced their career of extravagance somewhat later than the French; but as soon as the delirium seized them, they were determined not to be outdone ... But it did not follow that all these people believed in the feasibility of the schemes to which they subscribed; it was enough for their purpose that their shares would ... be raised to a premium (Mackay 1996: 41).

There seems to have been no lack of enthusiasm. On the contrary, their reckless pursuit of possible large returns exposed the investors to so much risk that they could not be forced to bear their losses. This might suggest that there had already existed a pool of would-be speculators who needed only the opportunity, and the encouragement of their peers, to leap in wholeheartedly.

Entrepreneurship and risk management

It may seem surprising that the pool of speculators was drawn so widely, extending into the supposedly cautious and conservative rural landed gentry. But the successful management of a landed estate required some entrepreneurial skill, even if taking a longer-term perspective. If the major assets of an estate were fixed, non-liquid, such as land on long-term leases with fixed rents, great care was needed in managing the revenue. The Bridgeman family wished to create a garden at Castle Bromwich; they took something like 45 years to do so, funded, presumably, from estate revenue. Grand gestures and shorter-term timetables would have cut into capital and threatened the viability of the estate.

Estates work on a generational timescale. In the eighteenth century, there was a widespread expectation that prices and wages were stable in the long term, and that variations were temporary despite the fact that the century actually experienced substantial inflation. In such a context, long-term investments like land for leasing only needed to yield small percentage returns, since the asset itself retained its value.

The main risk that an estate faced was an urgent need for cash, which would mean realising some of its assets, perhaps at a time when land prices were depressed. Surpluses and deficits arising from harvest and prices were hard to predict, and the cash generated by a generally good national harvest may have been much less than a fair crop in a nationally poor year. A fund manager seeking to advise an estate on its financial strategy would find it difficult to recommend a better course of action than to invest in land, with sufficient hedges against having to sell

it at short notice. Bekar and Reed view land ownership as an ideal buffer for agricultural risk management, because it provides a return on investment but retains its capital value for re-sale in all but the most extreme market conditions (2003: 320).

The management of estates, with the idea of buying more land whenever possible, conforms to the C-M-C cycle of Marx (1930: 134), so perhaps even the Bridgemans are capitalists after all. In contrast, the builders they employed on the estate and gardens probably were not. Although they had more freedom and independence than many day-labourers, and some entered into contracts that allowed them to arrange the work themselves, their scope for profit was severely constrained, limited to incremental surpluses that required careful nurturing to grow into usable assets. Abraham Parsons did not manage this; Robert Smith did. It is tempting to explain their divergent paths by pointing to Smith's background in agriculture, his security of tenure, and his diversified activities, as factors that made him well placed to exploit the opportunities that the Bridgemans' building plans presented. Certainly Smith's strategy was similar to that adopted by the small-scale speculators in urban housing later in the eighteenth century, with some success.

Conclusion

The building industry of the later nineteenth century in the English Midlands was recognisably capitalist: speculative, mass produced and profit-maximising. But its development can be traced back to the wood pasture economy of the late seventeenth century, where risk management and social relations were prominent in defining the character of the brickmaking trade and other rural enterprises such as scythe- and nail-making. The Bridgemans were probably more concerned with long-term investment and diversification to spread risk, than with short-term profits.

By the late eighteenth century, as demand for housing in the urban centres of Worcester and Birmingham grew, partnerships between tradesmen with capital and builders exploited the market, but they were careful to minimise outlay on raw materials and work on rebuilding, a long way from the alienation and standardisation that Marx would lead us to expect of true capitalism. The organisation of the industry preserved many of its 'non-capitalist' features into the nineteenth century, notably the many-stranded relationships between those involved, risk sharing and minimisation.

Acknowledgements

Most of the research on which this paper is based was undertaken under the auspices of Leverhulme grant F/656, through Castle Bromwich Hall Gardens Trust, in collaboration with the late Chris Currie. A version of the paper was presented at the CHAT 2004 conference, Leicester.

References

Allen, R.C. 1992. *Enclosure and the Yeoman.* Oxford: Clarendon Press.

Bekar, C.T. and Reed, C.G. 2003. Open fields, risk and land diversity. *Explorations in Economic History* 40, 308–25.

Currie, C.K. 1990. Excavation of an early eighteenth-century garden pond: the West Pond, Castle Bromwich Hall *Post Medieval Archaeology* 24, 93–123.

Currie, C.K. and Locock, M. 1992. Trial excavations in the North Garden, Castle Bromwich Hall, 1991. *Transactions of the Birmingham and Warwickshire Archaeological Society* 97, 77–85.

Currie, C.K. and Locock, M. 1993. Excavations at Castle Bromwich Hall, 1989–91, *Post Medieval Archaeology* 27, 111–99.

Johnson, M.H. 1996. *An Archaeology of Capitalism.* Oxford: Blackwell.

Johnson, M.H. 1999. *Archaeological Theory: An Introduction.* Oxford: Blackwell.

Locock, M. 1990a. The eighteenth-century brickmaking industry in the Forest of Arden. *Warwickshire History* 8, 3–20.

Locock, M. 1990b. Eighteenth-century brickmaker's tally-marks from Castle Bromwich Hall, West Midlands. *Transactions of the Birmingham and Warwickshire Archaeological Society* 95, 95–98.

Locock, M. 1992. The development of the building trades in the west midlands, 1400–1850. *Construction History* 8, 3–19.

Locock, M. 1994. Spatial Analysis of an Eighteenth-century Formal Garden. In M. Locock (ed.), *Meaningful Architecture: Social Interpretations of Buildings*, 231–52. Avebury, Aldershot: Worldwide Archaeological Series 9.

Locock, M. and Currie, C.K. 1991. Castle Bromwich Hall: excavations directed by P Twigg, 1985–1988. *West Midlands Archaeology* 34, 19–26.

Mackay, C. 1996. *Memoirs of Extraordinary Popular Delusions* (reprint of 1932 single-volume edition: 1st edition 1841). New York: Farrar, Strauss and Giroux.

Marx, K. 1930. *Capital: A Critique of Political Economy* (translation from 4th German edition). London: J M Dent & Co.

Skipp, V. 1970. *Medieval Yardley: The Origin and Growth of a West Midland Community.* Gloucester: Phillimore.

Weber, M. 1930. *The Protestant Ethic and the Spirit of Capitalism.* London: Unwin.

SOME GENEALOGIES OF CASTLES IN IRELAND

Andrew Tierney

Introduction

A striking aspect of historical writing on Ireland in recent times is the manner in which it continues to privilege the colonial text while seeking to deconstruct it. There has been much emphasis on how colonial writing sought to shape Irish identity for its own ends but little attempt to engage with how the Gaelic-Irish perceived themselves. Where writers on identity have engaged with Gaelic texts they have more often sought response to the colonial enterprise, thus privileging the themes of colonialism and decline as the defining discourses relating to Gaelic-Ireland. This chapter seeks to broaden the scope of post-colonial investigation into later medieval and early modern Ireland by looking at various discourses surrounding the meaning and ethnicity of buildings. In particular, I attempt to apply the notion of 'genealogy', the central component of the medieval Gaelic-Irish 'archive', to an understanding of buildings. As Jacques Derrida has argued, control of an archive or a people's institutionalised memory is a means to ultimate political and social control. In his explanation of 'archive' Derrida was quick to acknowledge links between architecture and memory. He described the derivation of the word 'archive' from the Greek *arkheion*: 'initially a house, a domicile, an address, the residence of the superior magistrates, the archons, those who commanded' (Derrida 1996: 2). I argue that the histories of the built environment (in this case castles) contained in such archives (be they manuscript collections or books housed and protected by buildings and institutions) were central to how different ethnic groups defined themselves. In particular, such histories established competing 'genealogies' of power during moments of conflict and instability. Like the people who inhabited them, castles were implicated in shifting genealogies, both personal and ideational, their origins subject to distortion and reinvention as the political and cultural climate changed.

Using samples of documents across four centuries this chapter attempts to chart these shifting perspectives on castle origins in an Irish context. I argue that we can only start engaging properly with the meaning of castles when we understand that their status and origins were mutable through time. So, this chapter is an attempt to understand the 'genealogy' of Irish castles in two senses: firstly, the genealogy of ownership that castles can so effectively symbolise, which ties together people with a shared blood lineage and lends legitimacy to their claims of power over both people and land; and secondly, the genealogy of castle form itself, in which notions of architectural development are constructed to coincide with particular ethnic and cultural lineages of power.

The colonial lineage of the Gaelic-Irish and its architecture

Irish genealogical origins were systematised by Irish scholars in the eighth century in the famous *Leabhar Gabhála* or *Book of Invasions*, which charted the origins of the Gaels to Scythia, describing them as the last in a series of eastern tribes to invade and conquer the country (MacAlistair 1938). These early ecclesiastical writers sought to reconcile indigenous legend with the earlier writings of the Spaniard Orosius who had speculated on the geographical origins of the Irish (O'Donovan 1846; Carey 2001). Initially only a few powerful tribes such as the Connachta and Eoghanachta were included in this genealogical system, both claiming descent from a common progenitor, Míl of Spain; but eventually almost all Gaelic-Irish families were incorporated into this system by claiming descent from newly invented sons of Míl (Byrne 2001: 9).

In the fourteenth century, a new tower constructed by the Gaelic chieftain Uilliam Ó Ceallaigh was celebrated by the poet, Godfraidh Fionn Ó Dálaigh, for its similarity to a tower built by Breoghan, the grandfather of Míl, in the north of Spain (Knott 1911: 63 vv.36–37). According to *An Leabhair Gabhála*, it was from this tower that the Gaels first saw Ireland and decided to conquer it. It is perhaps no surprise then to find that the poem was written to celebrate Ó Ceallaigh's reclamation of land which had undergone Anglo-Norman occupation. It is a reassertion of Gaelic identity as fundamentally aristocratic and colonial, bound up with the assertion of power by military force. The poet eulogised his patron by writing 'The grandson of Concobhar of Glandore is not a mere Irishman; William with his curly ringletted, spreading locks, is Grecian and Spanish' (Knott 1911: 65, vs. 41). The poet consciously rejected the characterisation of the Gaelic-Irish as natives (as put forth by colonial writers of the time), rather stressing their aristocratic descent and colonial credentials. The genealogical scheme crafted by Irish writers, which cast the Gaelic-Irish into the role of foreigners on conquered territory was similar to that found in other European countries during the same period.

While highlighting the castle's Milesian predecessor, the poem suppresses the influence of Anglo-Norman culture and blood, which features quietly yet powerfully in the forenames of both poet and patron. Triumphant references to recent military campaigns celebrate Ó Ceallaigh victory over the Anglo-Norman presence in this part of Connacht and might be seen in the context of the Gaelic-Revival of the late fourteenth century. The cooperation and social intercourse between Gael and Anglo-Norman that the names of poet and patron betray also had an architectural dimension and, although William's tower does not survive, one might speculate that the spirit of Breoghan's tower was conjured up as a means of distracting attention from its Anglo-Norman derivation. This was a period in which the Gaelic-Irish were increasingly occupying and building castles of stone for the first time. So there was a process of cultural assimilation on the part of both Anglo-Normans and Gaelic-Irish on one level, and the artificial and learned construction and maintenance of genealogical identity on another. But the Gaelic-Irish discourse surrounding the ethnicity of aristocratic dwelling places was largely confined to poetry, demonstrating that there may have been a knowing and almost self-conscious indulgence in archaic terminology as a means of projecting an image of ancestral continuity and cultural distinction in the face of Anglo-Norman colonisation.

If we look at Gaelic annalistic writing from the twelfth century onwards there is acknowledgment of the foreign context of 'the castle' in the use of its Irish form 'caisleán'. The word first appears in the early to mid twelfth century in relation to the building projects of Toirdhealbhach Ó Conchobhair, King of Connacht and his son, Ruaidhrí, last high king of Ireland. A little known poem to Toirdhealbhach Mór describes his travels to foreign kings in France and England suggesting that he personally imported the castle (either motte and bailey or stone) into Ireland (McKenna 1939: 4–6). The annalists record them as constructing 'caisleán' in places such as Galway, Athlone and Tuam amongst others. The use of the term *'caisleán'* is particularly striking at this date because it simply disappears from a specifically Gaelic-Irish context for the following 150 years. During this time Gaelic-Irish annalists use it exclusively to describe the buildings being erected by Anglo-Norman colonists. The failure of 'caisleán' to develop and spread amongst the Irish during this period may have been due to both the unsettling economic affects of the Anglo-Norman conquest and their symbolic association with colonial oppression. Where Gaelic-Irish kings did engage with 'foreign style' buildings, such as Aodh Ó Conchobhair at Cloonfree before 1309 (Simms 2001; O'Conor and Finan 2002), poets are able to acknowledge such influences while continuing to compare their subjects with ancient Gaelic royal strongholds such as Tara and Cruachain.

The royal sites, which also included Aileach, Dún Ailinn and Eamhain Macha, were the backbone of poetic analogy in poems written to eulogise later medieval Gaelic-Irish strongholds – be they stone castles or some other form of fort. As already stated above, from the second half of the fourteenth century Gaelic-Irish septs began both occupy the castles of vanquished Anglo-Normans colonies and construct their own castles for the first time. In this fact, we find strong parallels between the archaeological record and the annalistic one, as the term 'caisleán' suddenly reappears to describe Gaelic-Irish building activity in the late fourteenth century, the period which immediately precedes the tower house boom of the fifteenth century.

The tendency to suppress the term *'caisleán'* in poetic compositions in favour of antique words such as 'brugh' (fairy palace) or the rather vague 'tigh' (house), continued throughout the later medieval period. There was no value in acknowledging the Anglo-Norman contribution to Irish culture from the Gaelic-Irish perspective. The Irish had invested heavily in the idealisation of ancient royal sites as symbols of political sovereignty and, in ideological terms at least, these were proposed as the genealogical forerunners to later Gaelic-Irish building projects.

The mythopoetic conception of a Gaelic lineage of royal palaces was dependent on the idea of the high kingship and its imminent resurrection from within one of the numerous small polities of later medieval Ireland. The palaces were thus as ethereal and ill-defined as the ambitions of the patrons that paid to hear them described. The Battle of Kinsale of 1601, which saw the Gaelic-Irish defeated under the leadership of Aodh Ó Néill and Aodh Ruadh Ó Domhnaill, was singled out by Irish writers as a turning point in the history of Gaelic-Ireland. The Gaelic-Irish perspective on the battle was presented by Lughaidh Ó Clérigh, historian to Aodh Ruadh, who bemoaned the passing of the Gael in his biographical account of his patron. Aodh Ruadh had died following the Battle of Kinsale when he journeyed to Spain to seek the further assistance of the Spanish king. Ó Clérigh records that on his way he stopped at La Corunna to visit what was regarded as one of the most symbolic antiquities of Gaelic antiquity:

> When Ó Domhnaill landed at Corunna, he goes a-journeying and visiting the town and goes to see Breoghan's tower. It gave him much satisfaction to land there for he thought it a good omen of success that he should have come to the place from which his ancestors had obtained sway and power over Ireland formerly (Walsh 1948: 341).

The tower (Figure 14) was a Roman lighthouse of the third century (Carey 2001: 10), but had become a symbol of the foreign origins of the Gaelic-Irish. Ó Clérigh describes Ó Domhnaill, in his preparation for another Spanish invasion of Ireland, returning to that singular point of origin to reassert his identity as the heir to a conquering tribe. But he wrote this with the hind-sight that Ó Domhnaill would not lead a second Gaelic invasion of Ireland but die in his attempt. Similarly Florence Mac Carthaigh, a captive held on suspicion of pursuing a Gaelic-Spanish alliance, would in the years following the Battle of Kinsale and the flight of the Earls recall the ruins of the Tower of Breoghan from his prison in the Tower of London:

> …some of the ancientest of Spanish writers holde, and ours also…Brigancia to be upon the sea…and make mention of a tower which he built near the city upon the sea, the ruins of which tower that standes within half a mile of Corunna down towards the sea on the west side of the haven or bay is called still Tower of Brighan (O'Donovan 1856: 214).

What is striking about these references to the Tower of Breoghan is that they render it for the first time in the flesh. While these writers may have a propagandistic purpose in mentioning it, they also realise it as a ruin in the present. One gets the sense that the circularity of the Gaelic past has been suddenly made linear. The appearance of the Gaelic ruin, not as metaphor but as a material reality, signals that the past has been consigned to the past without any necessary implication of resurrection or return. So we might argue that the necessary corollary to the ruination of the Gaelic-Irish castle in sixteenth and seventeenth century Ireland (and end of the Gaelic order) was the ruination of its mythopoetic predecessor.

Evidence of this ideological collapse can be found elsewhere. Following the Battle of Kinsale in 1601, and the flight of the northern earls (1607), a dispute arose between Tadhg Mac Bruaidheadha, a poet from the southern half of Ireland patronised by the O'Briens, and the poets from the northern half of Ireland, regarding which region had the stronger genealogical title to the possession of Ireland. Collectively entitled *Iomarbhagh na bFileadh* or 'Contention of the Poets' it constitutes a very heated debate over the respective qualities of north and south throughout history. Joep Leerssen (1994) has written on the contemporary political context of the debate in relation to the shifting position of Thomond (County Clare) during the composition of Connaught in the late sixteenth century. According to Leerssen, genealogical considerations explain the attempts (eventually successful) of the O'Briens of Thomond to maintain County Clare as part of Munster despite repeated attempts by the Crown to join it with Connacht, an idea that made sense

Figure 14. 'Breoghan's Tower' at La Coruňa

geographically due to the territory's location west of the Shannon (Leerssen 1994: 20–21). The genealogical divide between the descendants of the two sons of Míl, Eibhear and Eireamhon was compacted by their division into two geographically separate parts of Ireland, a division that according to legend dated back to the time of the two brothers themselves. While the poems of the contention consist mainly of arguments over literary lore there is also a small but interesting discourse surrounding the royal sites of Ireland. It gives an insight into their perspectives on the material aspects of their own past.

The leader of the northern poets, Lughaidh Ó Clérigh, boasted that most of the ancient royal sites of Ireland such as Teamhair, Eamhain Macha, Cruachain, and Aileach were in the northern half of the island rather than the south (McKenna 1918: 23 vs. 38). The response to this claim by his southern antagonist, Tadhg Mac Bruaideadha, introduced a new discourse to poetic writing. He referred to the contemporary material condition of these royal sites and speculating about their true usage, writing:

> [Weak] as a claim to title are the bare useless forts which differ not from any other spot except that they were built long ago. Short was the time that some of them spent in honour – we both know it now. Your folk had no connection with them except to rule there some time (McKenna 1918: 41 vv. 105–106).

Mac Bruaideadha was arguing that not only were the forts now useless and bare but also difficult to differentiate from other similar settlements in the landscape. He also adds that possession of a fort at one point in time did not necessarily imply ancestral foundation. These were stark and unsettling claims that broke away from the idealisation of ancient royal sites that had been so much a feature of Gaelic-Irish poetry. Mac Bruaideadha emphasised his point by contrasting these 'bare useless forts' with both the old Gaelic forts of the south and thriving contemporary towns such as Luimneach (Limerick), Portlairge (Waterford) and Corcach (Cork). He was aware that the north possessed little urban development and sought to emphasis this front. The response by Ó Clérigh gives some further idea of how the lineage or genealogy of sites might be contested at this time:

> Talk not to us of your forts. They are only graves… all who got Inis Fáil (Ireland) chose to remain here (in the north). The marks of their dwelling here prove it. As Éire's kings chose the fairest places, which of your fair western places did any king inhabit before Brian? You should not boast of those ports of the Muimhnigh, Corcach, Portlairge, Luimneach. They are new places founded by the Gaill [foreigners] and concern not our old division (McKenna 1918: 63 vv. 61–65).

Just as Mac Bruaideadha had done, Ó Clerigh, challenged the interpretation of the southerners' monuments as actual forts. But in his reference to 'the marks of their dwellings' invoked archaeological evidence to champion the authenticity of the northern palaces. Ó Clérigh quickly dismissed Mac Bruaideadha's claims to cities such as Cork and Limerick which he knew were originally foreign (Norse) settlements.

These arguments foreshadow to a remarkable degree the debates of eighteenth- and nineteenth-century antiquaries over the ethnicity and authenticity of Irish antiquities. Yet it is important to see that these arguments were first conducted from within the societal structure of Gaelic-Ireland itself. This discourse signals a rupture in the traditional mythopoetic perspective on the royal palaces of the ancient Irish. Could such palaces any longer be convincingly betrayed as the precursors of Gaelic-Irish castles if their material status and origin was open to question? We might also note, in a wider context, that the poets in the contention began to query the veracity of many of their own textual sources, books which were previously regarded as unquestionable authorities on the Irish past. At this point material culture, like the written text, was about to give birth to its own discourse, in which it becomes a source of explicit contention for the first time. The participants of this contention understood that kingship and royal lineage had an important material dimension that could speak on its own terms.

Excavating power: material genealogies of the English colonial order

Another poet in the contention, Mathghamhain Ó hIfearnáin, observing their arguments about ancient monuments, made a pertinent observation when he advised: 'Listen not to the words of these sages. The foreign soldier is the conquering wolf. He set no store on their pride' (McKenna 1918: 117 vs. 14). If the Gaelic-Irish themselves were willing to challenge the nature and quality of their material heritage in regional quarrels over genealogical supremacy, then it is easy to see how much more challenged it might be by English colonial expansion. One has only to understand

Figure 15. Clonony Castle, Co. Offaly

the rigorous schematisation of Gaelic genealogical knowledge, closely bound up with the lore of place names and historical events, to see how vulnerable it was to outside interference. Genealogy of blood was the means of maintaining dynastic legitimacy, political boundaries and social dominance. It is no surprise then that colonists to Ireland in the sixteenth and seventeenth centuries would assert themselves through narrating opposing genealogies of power, ones that deliberately set out to undermine Gaelic-Irish claims to historic legitimacy as rulers. In early seventeenth-century Ireland new English arrivals were to seek their colonial predecessors in the Anglo-Norman landscape, and justify their reclamation of the country through, amongst other methods, the establishment of their colonial lineage in stone.

This new perspective on the Irish past is best illustrated in the writings of the colonist Mathew De Renzi (MacCuarta 1987 and 1993b). In the early seventeenth century De Renzi was granted Clonony castle (Figure 15), which is situated in the heart of MacCoghlan country (part of present County Offaly) on about a hundred acres. The crown had confiscated the castle from the rebellious *Tanaiste* of the Mac Coghlan sept (Loeber 1980: 124). The MacCoghlans, led by the recently knighted Sir John MacCoghlan, were at the time on relatively good terms with the Crown and could not risk upsetting this harmony by any outward aggression towards De Renzi (MacCuarta 1987: 111). Therefore, they responded to his presence, not through physical violence but through a kind of boycott (Loeber 1980: 124), effectively a slow form of siege warfare on a castle which was completely isolated from Crown assistance.

Not to be intimidated, De Renzi was able to counter-attack with equally non-violent yet effective strategy. Being of a scholarly disposition he consulted Gaelic written sources and studied their local folklore, gathering useful information about the MacCoghlan sept and their origins in the territory. It quickly became apparent to him that centuries earlier an English colony had been forced out of the area by the Gaelic-Irish. De Renzi became determined to find the evidence for this expulsion as a means of furthering the colonial claim. He began to research the building history of the area to discover who had built what and when they had built it (Mac Cuarta 1993b, 8).

He soon launched an audacious counter attack on the sept chieftain, Sir John MacCoghlan, by targeting the very foundations of his enemy's main seat, Garrycastle, situated not far south of Clonony. De Renzi complained to the Lord Deputy that the inhabitants 'deny very steefly that the English made ever any castles or had any hand in their country' (Mac Cuarta 1987: 131) and later reported: '[the MacCoghlans] saey that the castle of Garrecastle is the auntients in all that countrie and causd the barrony to be calld after that, wich is not so but onely done out of delusion, [so that] the Englische should not suspect that their antecessours had bene maisters of that countrie' (Mac Cuarta 1987: 157).

De Renzi argued that during the earlier colonisation of Ireland an English baron named Sir Richard Tuite had built Athlone castle to the north of MacCoghlan territory. It was here, he claimed, that Sir Richard had, in an attempt to assert his authority, imprisoned the leader of the MacCoghlan sept, Amhluibh Og (Mac Cuarta 1987: 157). This 'savage' had subsequently escaped and rampaged against the colony with his followers, resulting in the eventual destruction of the first English settlements and castles in the region. De Renzi argued that the Irish of this period were keenly aware of the monumental significance of English incastellation and sought not only to destroy English settlements but the memory of them too:

They went and threw downe the Benghar, Cuil an Fiamaigh, Lisderg, Esker castle, because it should be no monument hereafter against them by the Englisch... and then perceiving the English conquest to stand and continue, they threw downe all the rest of the castles builded by them wich is to be seene yet at this day (Mac Cuarta 1987: 158)

To show the true significance of these events, he showed Chichester the genealogy of Sir John MacCoghlan, which led directly to Amhluibh Óg, the one time occupant of Athlone Castle's prison. He showed that Garrycastle was built by Felim Maol, the imprisoned rebel's great great grandson (Mac Cuarta 1987: 158); and so, he argued his case that Garrycastle could not provide the MacCoghlan's with a claim over the country, and that it was actually begotten by the descendant of a murdering criminal long after the English had built their castles in the area. In other words, the English had inscribed their claim on the landscape first through their earlier construction of stone castles (Figure 16). That De Renzi should so quickly challenge the dynamics of the MacCoghlans' dynastic relationship with castles is a tribute to his understanding of the symbolism of castles. In addition, De Renzi reported that, following their outrage against the colony, the Gaelic-Irish, had deviously concocted Gaelic genealogies for the surviving English so that they should forget their true origins (Mac Cuarta 1993 b: 8). He also understood that memory could be manipulated if a people's material culture and environment was destroyed.

In order that the plantation of the area succeed it was necessary now, De Renzi argued, to reciprocate such behaviour by creating the conditions for a similar cultural amnesia within the Gaelic-Irish world:

Their bards and croniclers wich keepes their descents, who will ever be plotting to come to that againe wich their antecessours had, and to disturb and subvert the conquest. Therefore fitt it weare that those weare drowned as neare as it weare possible, whereby [the people] might not know in time from whence they came.' (MacCuarta 1987: 120)

While Gaelic-Irish poets were condemned to death in the sixteenth century by the English Crown for rousing rebellion, the English government did not enact similar laws against historians as De Renzi evidently thought necessary. Nevertheless, the general effects of colonisation appear to have made such draconian measures unnecessary.

De Renzi's vision of cultural change soon began to take effect and by the end of the seventeenth century colonial families held most of the King's County (Loeber 1980: 132). The schools of history and poetry were quickly dispersing and their books destroyed, even in De Renzi's time. The situation led one chronicler of the MacCoghlan's, Connell Mageoghegan, to warn (in the newly acquired English tongue): 'the posteritie are like to fall into mere Ignorance of any things happened before theire tyme' (Murphy 1896: 8).

While the English are not known to have destroyed many Gaelic castles deliberately (as De Renzi had claimed the Irish had done to the early English castles), they did distort the histories that surrounded them. No longer was the legendary Tower of Breoghan seen as the worthy precursor to a Gaelic castle, but rather colonial adventurers began to attribute Gaelic-Irish castles to the 'Danes', claiming

Figure 16. Clonmacnoise Castle, Co. Offaly – destroyed by the Irish, according to Matthew De Renzi

they were built, in the words of the English traveller John Dunton in 1699, 'as curbs to the neighbouring Irish' (Harrington 1991: 145). Alternatively, they were attributed to the Anglo-Normans or later to the Elizabethan English themselves. The Irish were portrayed as ethereal figures, existing outside of Ireland's new cultural landscape or, as Henry Wallop put it in the seventeenth century, 'secure only in their forest-forts, and in the wilderness state of their region…naturally jealous of the stone towers which enabled the Englishry to keep the rich lands they had gained' (Hore 1862–3: 56).

The new colonists were creating a genealogy of colonial power in Ireland by describing a relatively seamless transition from 'Dane' to 'Norman', effectively excluding the Gaelic Irish from the history of power within the island. This was expressed through new antiquarian theorising on 'Danish mounts' and round towers, particularly in the work of Thomas Molyneaux who regarded the Danes as having ruled Ireland from the eighth until the twelfth centuries thus omitting the Irish from history altogether (Molyneaux 1755: 191).

The Gaelic-Irish Response

A Gaelic-Irish response to the colonial appropriation of Irish antiquities can be found in the work of the last of the Gaelic historians of the hereditary order, Dubhaltach Mac Firbisigh, who finished his monumental manuscript book of genealogies, *An Leabhar Genealach*, in 1650 (O'Raithbheartaigh 1932: i). His aim, stated in his preface, was to 'illustrate the diligence of the historians and the error of those who say that there were no stone works in Ireland till the coming of the Foreignors or Norsemen therein' (Ó Raithbheartaigh 1932: 15). He drew on Gaelic history as it had been fashioned in the eleventh century *An*

Leabhar Gabhála, or *Book of Invasions*. Mac Fhirbisigh focused his attention on the journey of the Gael, creating a genealogy of great Middle Eastern and European cities and palaces, such as Jerusalem and Rome, whilst also including the royal seats of Ireland such as Tara and Aileach, listing the Gaelic names of their builders as evidence of their ethnicity. Thus, on the morphology of early Irish buildings he wrote: '…we have no doubt that they were made like works in other kingdoms about the time in which they were made, and wherefore should they not, for no invasion came to Ireland but from the eastern part of the world, that is to say, Spain' (O'Raithbheartaigh 1932: 18–19). It is interesting to note that he employs the word 'caisléan' or 'castle' as well as the more ancient term 'rath' to refer to some of these ancient buildings. This is unusual in that the word 'caisléan' was very rarely used in Gaelic writing to refer to ancient royal and mythopoetic sites. I would suggest that Mac Firbhisigh was attempting to forge a link or 'genealogy' between the castles of the Gaelic-Irish in his own time and those of the distant past. He must have been aware that this was anachronistic and that the Anglo-Normans were most closely associated with the term in the annals of the twelfth, thirteenth and early fourteenth centuries. His account of Gaelic building activity in Ireland makes no mention of any Anglo-Norman influence as they were outside the exclusive genealogical parameters of his history. He comments that those castles constructed in the distant past were better built (O'Raithbheartaigh 1932: 19), suggesting a thesis of cultural decline rather than development, the very inverse of new English notions of man's development from barbarity to civilisation.

Ruadhrí Ó Flaithbheartaigh, another seventeenth-century Gaelic-Irish commentator on the early forts of the Irish, didn't use the term 'caisléan' but nevertheless presented early Irish dwellings as a civilising influence on the country:

> The new adventurers (ie, the sons of Míl), after subduing the island, began to erect fortresses, and places of defence, called in Irish Rathe and Duna; and to cultivate and improve the country, by cutting and clearing the wood-land parts. From that period there has been a continued succession of kings of the posterity of the Milesian line, in Ireland and Scotland to the first of May of this present year of our Lord 1684, for the space of 2699 years (O'Flaherty (1685)1793, 33).

This scheme of history, with its 'improvements' and 'clearing of woods', is, of course, a knowing response by Ó Flaithbheartaigh to charges of incivility laid down by recent colonial writers about the Gaelic-Irish themselves. Edmund Spenser, for example, wrote of the Irish man that 'the wood is his house against all weathers' (Hadfield and Maley 1997: 57). Spencer and other colonial writers urged the cutting down of Ireland's woods as a means to quelling rebellion and imposing order. The new English colonist had represented themselves as the 'improvers' but Ó Flaithbheartaigh here writes them out of history by making a direct link with the old Irish kingship and the restored Stuart line (of Gaelic lineage) which offered hope for the return of confiscated lands.

Mac Firbisigh's presentation of the materiality of the Irish past was also an assertion of an essentially dominant, colonial identity – an idea that De Renzi was aware of from his reading of Irish texts and which he employed in arguing the relative legitimacy of English colonialism in Ireland (see MacCuarta 1993 b: 8). For Mac Firbisigh, and other Gaelic chroniclers, the eleventh-century *Leabhar Gabhála* was central to their ethnic identity, charting the history of Ireland as one of conquest by the sword, the Gael being the last and most dominant in a line of colonies that migrated from the east. This was the perspective on the past that allowed those Gaelic poets employed by colonial lords to argue that the Anglo-Norman invasion of Ireland was justified by the terms of Ireland's history as set out in the *Book of Invasions*. They did not seek to present architectural form or style as expressive of ethnicity – as we have seen above they did not promote the idea of an exclusively *Gaelic* style. Castles, represented usually in terms of size, materials, and defensibility, were expressive only of class and therefore might be understood as common to all aristocracies. Seathrún Ó Céitinn, another seventeenth-century defender of the Gaels, argued that regarding the habitations of the Irish, like must be compared to like, pointing out the similarities between aristocratic Gaelic culture and aristocratic English culture; likewise he commented on the equally poor state of both the Gaelic and the English peasantry (Comyn 1902: 55).

However, if there was nothing inherently Gaelic in the form of such structures, then their origins, like the buildings themselves, might be freely re-granted to others. It was not until the arrival of nineteenth-century Romantic nationalism, a movement based on the inversion of colonial stereotyping, that Irish writers and antiquaries would attempt to locate cultural difference in the material record, a task which would create its own problems (Tierney 2004).

As Ireland was anglicised throughout the seventeenth and eighteenth centuries the native Irish, or at least the idea of them, continued to be synonymous with barbarism. The colonial antiquary Edward Ledwich, writing in 1790, put forth his case against them in the following terms:

> The wild and rude manner of life of the Irish made them look on castles and the confinement within them with abhorrence…The reader has already anticipated me in remarking, that all our castles till the time of James I were built by English masons and on English plans…(Ledwich 1790: 290–91).

By the early nineteenth century local traditions regarding the origins of some Irish castles had inevitably come to reflect the ideas forwarded by their new occupants. The castle occupied by the de Renzi, for example, came into the hands of multiple colonial families and by the early nineteenth century, when John O'Donovan was conducting the Ordnance Survey of Antiquities, its ethnic origin had been changed in local tradition: 'Tradition says that this castle was built by the English family of Bullen, which is much to be questioned as Mageoghegan [native translator of the Annals of Clonmacnois, see above] makes it the seat of the Sliocht Ross Mac Coghlan' (O'Donovan in O'Flannagan 1926: 89).

Garrycastle, Sir John MacCoghlan's castle, once the source of so much Gaelic-Irish ancestral pride, was by the early nineteenth century only noted for its 'Danish rath'. (Lewis 1837, vol. ii: 512). After the amateur defence of Gaelic castle-building by the Limerick antiquary Sylvester O'Halloran, in the 1770s (Tierney 2004) it was not until George Petrie's Royal Irish Academy paper in the 1830s that any methodical survey was attempted that was inclined to the Gaelic interest (Tierney 2005).

A new genealogy without castles

Due to the force of the eighteenth-century penal laws, by the twentieth century the average Irish Catholic could trace their genealogy back only to the start of the nineteenth century and, if lucky, to the remains of a thatched cottage. So it is perhaps not surprising to find that Gaelic castles, unlike round towers and high crosses, failed to function as symbols of Irish identity within the Catholic nationalist agenda as their existence tended to annihilate a long cultivated ethnic polarity. In formal terms, castles, and in particular those known as tower houses, represent a point of cultural commonality rather than difference, as they had been inhabited by old English, Gaelic Irish and Elizabethan colonist. But in the twentieth century they have thus been understood as part of the visual history of colonialism in Ireland.

However, due to the fact that Gaelic culture by the early nineteenth century had become almost exclusively the preserve of the peasantry (Leerssen 1996: 1) the process of equating that social strata with an aristocratic past led to the occasional unsuccessful proclamation of castles as 'heirlooms' of the proletariat. But this was a heritage thrust upon them from without. Alice Stopford Green, the nineteenth-century Anglo-Irish nationalist historian, celebrated at length the plebeian, Catholic appropriation of Castle Jordan at Ardglass, Co. Down, in 1911 (Stopford Green 1912). Tellingly, the castle was a gift to 'the people' from the antiquarian Francis Joseph Bigger, a member of the Belfast protestant gentry who nevertheless was of strongly nationalist outlook. Having a great interest in the history of Gaelic-Irish families, Bigger decided to rename the castle 'Sean's Castle' after the sixteenth century Gaelic aristocrat Sean O'Neill. The castle (Figure 17) was hung with banners of Gaelic chieftains and songs were sung to recall their memory, while local people dressed up in

Figure 17. Jordan's Castle, Ardglass, Co. Down

period costume and re-enacted life in the castle. All were allowed to enter freely and food and drink was shared as an exercise in communal identification, led and blessed by the parish priest. Bigger arranged for limelight images of the people (shown going about their work in the village) to be projected onto the wall of the castle so that they could literally see themselves in its fabric (Stopford-Green 1912: 152).

Joep Leerssen has observed similar transpositions of elite culture onto the peasantry during this period, describing how Lady Gregory reconstructed the language of the *Táin Bo Cuailgne* (a written narrative taken from medieval manuscripts) so as to locate it as part of the oral tradition of the storytelling peasantry. As Leerssen put it, 'the elite culture of two thousand years ago [was] to be ploughed back into the soil, into the contemporary demotic culture of the peasantry' (Leerssen 1996: 206). It is perhaps telling that despite the efforts of Bigger to recall the days of 'the noble Gael' at Sean's Castle, the people, when left in the building to entertain themselves, recalled their past not through a celebration of Sean O'Neill but rather through 'the sorrowful decadent songs of modern Ireland – songs of famine, emigration, lamentation, and woe' (Stopford-Green 1912: 154). There was after all a huge cultural and class difference between the modern peasantry of the early twentieth century and the supposed Gaelic owners of the medieval past. The priest reminded them 'to act with courtesy and good breeding when they entered it' and young men 'took off their hats' when looking at the image of Sean O'Neill (Stopford-Green 1912: 151–2).

Interestingly, despite these nationalist theatricals, all the historical evidence points to this castle having been English in origin (a fact of which Bigger must have been aware) and had been called 'Jordan's Castle' in memory of Simon Jordan, the Englishman who had defended it against

the O'Neills during the Tyrone Wars (Lewis 1837: 51). In 1911 an old house in Ardglass (next to Jordan's Castle), associated with the nationalist hero Edward Fitzgerald - 'the intrepid martyr to the freedom of Catholic Ireland' (Stopford-Green 1912: 148) - had been purchased by a golf club 'reputed to be faithful above all to English interest', and proudly displayed 'the imperial flag'. This probably prompted Bigger to come up with a nationalist response, which he did by appropriating Jordan's castle, previously a symbol of British loyalism (Stopford-Green 1912: 149). In this context Bigger's purchase of the castle, his renaming and invention of its past, and presentation of it as gift to the Irish people must have been deliberately provocative towards the Loyalist community of Ardglass. Although not directly associated with the castle, Sean O'Neill was known to have at some time in the past 'cast out the English' and 'forcibly patronised himself on Lecale [the larger area in which Ardglass is situated]' (Stopford-Green 1912: 141). Following the partition of Ireland in the 1920s the castle came into the hands of the British government and the name was changed back to Castle Jordan by which name it is known today.

However Irish nationalism and indeed republicanism had little use for heritage that invoked an aristocratic past and castles seemed to recall only images of violence and oppression. The Irish priest, Eoin Ua Mordha, expressed this Catholic Republican attitude to castle architecture when writing about Queen's County [later County Leix, now County Laois] in 1920, just at the start of a war that would see the burning of so many colonial 'Big Houses'. He played off what he saw as a protestant ascendancy tradition of the picturesque by celebrating not the monuments themselves but the empty and anonymous spaces that surround them. Speaking of one of the county's most conspicuous symbols of colonial power he wrote: 'Not to Lea Castle, then, would I go on pilgrimage; but I would go to the fields around – to repeople those blank spaces with the frieze-coated men who are the bravest figures of our past. To the silent, deserted marshes of Inchicooly would I go' (Ua Mordha 1920: 30).

His pointed invocation of native pilgrimage in opposition to the ascendancy pursuit of tourism is perhaps a reaction against the use of 'pilgrimage' itself as a sentimental element in the content of a particularly Irish form of the picturesque (most famously in the watercolours of George Petrie). But it was not just the colonial symbolism of castles that he dismissed. While wrongly attributing another Queen's County castle, Dunamase, to the Ó Mordha sept (it was actually Anglo-Norman), he nevertheless rejected it as something which 'had existed only as 'a focal point of battle between feuding aristocracies' (Ua Mordha 1920: 22). Too much blood, he argued, had been spilled at Dunamase Castle 'to accommodate itself willingly to…modern life' (ibid). Arguing that sentiment was misplaced 'on those grim and desolate skeletons of the past' (ibid: 29), he saw the landscape through the lens of the crowded schools of industrial Manchester where he taught the children of Irish immigrants destined to lives of urban drudgery. In a period of mass emigration it was the Irish land itself that people wished to return to. He wrote:

> The real romance of Leix [now County
> Laois] lies not in those castles, those
> awesome spectres of past murders. The
> real romance of Leix lies in the memory
> of the longings and strivings of all the
> hearts that beat through all the centuries
> in this wide territory. The real romance
> is in the visions plain to the eye of
> historical memory, of all the men whose
> spirits still keep an interest in it. For this

territory does not wholly belong to the
men whose day now is; but all the men
who ever turned a spade full of its soil,
or who ever fertilised it with a drop of
their sweat…(ibid).

When the descendents of Irish emigrants returned they may
have enjoyed viewing Irish castles but their real sentiment
was reserved for the humble cottages of their grand
parents and great grand parents. This is well illustrated
by the reactions of tourists to one of Ireland's earliest
tourist attractions at fifteenth-century Bunratty Castle,
Co. Clare. The castle was built by the Gaelic-Irish family
of Macnamara and its restoration in the 1950s was soon
after accompanied by the restoration of a small nineteenth-
century cottage of the same family that had been rescued
from the runway of nearby Shannon airport. One local
man involved in the project said of the tourists who came
to Bunratty that

> they were a lot more interested in the
> thatched house than they were in the
> castle because they could all understand
> the workings of a thatched house. There
> was a lot of people who were coming
> from America around that time, and
> they'd come into the castle and say
> they'd give anything to see the thatched
> house…it related to their own home they
> had gone out of fifty or sixty years. You
> used to see them going to their handbag
> taking out their handkerchief and wiping
> their eyes – it was really bringing them
> back (Share 1995: 150).

Although Bunratty Castle had been built by the Gaelic-Irish
it no longer reflected the Irish experience of emigration
and oppression. Irishness had become about oppression
and woe, experiences epitomised in the memory of the
famine. The Gaelic-Irish origins of the castle had for a long
time been forgotten. It had been attributed to the Anglo-
Normans for most of the post medieval period (Tierney
2005: 330).

Conclusion

When thinking about the role and meaning of castles in
medieval and post medieval Ireland we have to realise
that there were wider narratives into which they had to
be understood and presented. In a sense what we see in
the mythopoetic compositions of the Gaelic poets is an
attempt to conserve the idealogy of the Milesian history
of the seventh and eighth centuries in a world which has
become culturally diverse. This narrative is tied up with
an exclusively aristocratic ideology, where the relationship
with the landscape is one of dominance. There is an irony
here when we consider the attempts by the colonial English
to insist on the native origins of the Irish people. The
colonised were largely presented as natural, if corrupting,
elements of the landscape. Yet the claims the Gaelic-Irish
made to the landscape of Ireland were similar to those of
the colonial English: brute force and the colonisation of
a native population. However, little reference is made in
contemporary scholarly writings on Gaelic-Ireland to this
self-conception – largely due to the fact that the Milesian
origin story was long ago discredited as being a fabrication.
While the term 'Milesian' was once common in writings
about Irish history in the nineteenth century it is now
rarely mentioned as historians wish to distance themselves
from anything legendary or non-factual. I would suggest
that we must start to re-engage with it as the central 'fact'
of the medieval Irish discourse on identity. Castles and

forts are presented as key participants and agents of these
settlements and oppressions by both ethnicities, whether it
be De Renzi's reassertion of the materiality of the Anglo-
Norman conquest in his rediscovery of the ruins of the first
colony, or Ó Flaithbheartaigh's account of the building of
forts by the Milesians as a means to control the country in
the early stages of conquest.

In the later period the tendency of Irish people to distance
themselves from castles as a symbol of a nationalist past
is a phenomenon closely bound up with genealogy, as the
connection between people and castles was largely ruptured
by the collapse of Gaelic record keeping in the seventeenth
century. The rise of the thatched cottage as a nationalist
icon in modern Ireland, on the other hand, is a corollary
to the recommencement of the Catholic genealogical
record in the early nineteenth century when Irish language
and culture had become associated exclusively with the
peasantry. This ambiguity in Ireland's relationship with its
native past is best captured at Bunratty Castle where the
unresolved meaning of the Irish castle has been countered
by the ever expanding 'folk park' with its array of thatched
cottages, the first stop on the itinerary of the returning
American diaspora.

Acknowledgements

I would like to gratefully acknowledge the funding of
the Irish Research Council for the Humanities and Social
Sciences, the advice of my supervisor Tadhg O'Keeffe and
fellow student Hanneke Ronnes. Also my thanks to the
editors for their help in preparing this paper.

References

Byrne, F. 2001. *Irish Kings and High Kings*. Dublin: Four
Courts Press.
Carey, J. 2001. Did the Irish come from Spain? The legend
of the Milesians. *History Ireland* 9 (3), 8–11.
Comyn, D. 1902. Foras feasa ar Éireann. Part 1 :
Introduction and the First Book of the History. London:
Irish Texts Society.
Derrida, J. 1996. *Archive Fever: a Freudian Impression*.
Chicago: University of Chicago Press.
Gleeson, D.F. and Gwynn, Rev.A. 1962. *A History of the
Diocese of Killaloe*. Dublin: M.H.Gill and Son.
Hadfield, A. and Maley, W. (eds). 1997. *Edmund Spenser,
A View of the State of Ireland*. Oxford: Blackwell.
Harrington, J.P. (ed.). 1991. *The English Traveller in
Ireland*. Dublin: Wolfhound Press.
Hogan, W.J. 1977. Introduction. In J. Hardiman (ed.).
1846. A Chorographical Description of West or H-Iar
Connaught written in 1684 A.D. by Roderic O'Flaherty,
unpaginated. Dublin: *Irish Archaeological Society*.
Hore, H.F. 1862. An account of the barony of Forth,
in the county of Wexford, written at the close of the
seventeenth century. *Journal of the Royal Society of
Antiquaries of Ireland* 7, 53–84.
Kiberd, D. 1996. *Inventing Ireland. The Literature of the
Modern Nation*. London: Vintage.
Knott, E. 1911. Filidh Éireann go haointeach. *Eriú* 5,
50–69.
Lacey, B. 2001. The Grianán of Aileach – A note on
its identification. *Journal of the Royal Society of
Antiquaries of Ireland* 131, 145–49.
Ledwich, E. 1790. *The Antiquities of Ireland*. Dublin: A.
Grueber.
Leerssen, J. 1994. *The Contention of the Bards (Iomarbhágh
na bhFidleadh) and its place in Irish Political and
Literary History*. London: Irish Texts Society.

Leerssen, J. 1996. *Remembrance and Imagination*. Cork: Cork University Press.

Lewis, S. 1837. *A Topographical Dictionary of Ireland*. London: S. Lewis & Co.

Loeber, R. 1980. Civilization Through Plantation: The Projects of Matthew De Renzi. In H. Murtagh (ed.). *Irish Midland Studies*, 121–35. Athlone.

Macalister, R.A.S. 1938. *Lebor gabála Érenn: The Book of the Taking of Ireland. Part iv*. Dublin: Educational Co. of Ireland.

MacCuarta, B. 1987. The letters of Matthew De Renzi. *Analecta Hibernica* 34. Irish Manuscripts Commission. Dublin: Stationary Office.

MacCuarta, B. 1993a. Conbhubhar Mac Bruaideadha and Sir Matthew De Renzi (1577–1634). *Éigse* 27, 122–26.

MacCuarta, B. 1993b. A planter's interaction with Gaelic culture: Sir Matthew De Renzi (1577–1634). *Irish Economic and Social History* 20, 1–17.

McKenna, L. (ed.) 1918 *Iomarbhágh na bhFidleadh The Contention of the Bards* Vol. I. London: Irish Texts Society.

McKenna, L. 1939. *Aithdioghluim Dána: A Miscellany of Irish Bardic Poetry*. Vols. 1 & 2. Dublin: Irish Text Society; Vols. xxxvii & xl. Dublin: Educational Company of Ireland Ltd for the Irish Texts Society.

Molyneux, T. 1755. A Discourse concerning the Danish Mounts, Forts, and Towers in Ireland. In G. Boate *A Natural History of Ireland in Three Parts,* Dublin: Printed for Geo. and Alex. Ewing.

Murphy, D. 1896. *The Annals of Clonmacnoise being annals of Ireland from the earliest period to A.D. 1408*. Translated into English A.D. 1627 by Conell Mageoghagan. Dublin: University Press for the Royal Society of Antiquaries of Ireland.

O'Conor, K. and Finan, T. 2002. The moated site at Cloonfree Co. Roscommon. *Journal of the Galway Archaeological and Historical Society* 54, 72–87.

O'Donovan, J. 1843. *The Tribes and Customs of Hy-Many, commonly called O'Kelly's Country*. Dublin: Archaeological Society.

O'Donovan, J. 1856. Letter of Florence Mac Carthy to the Earl of Thomond, on the ancient history of Ireland. *Journal of the Royal Society of Antiquaries of Ireland* 4, 203–29.

O'Flanagan, Rev. M.1926. Letters containing information relative to the antiquities of the King's County collected during the progress of the Ordnance Survey in 1839. Typescript in 2 vols. Dublin.

O Flaherty, R. 1793 [1685]. *Ogygia or, A chronological account of Irish events: collected from very ancient documents, faithfully compared with each other and supported by the genealogical and chronological aid of the sacred and prophane writings of the first nations of the globe /* Written orginally in Latin by Roderic O'Flaherty, Esq. Tr. by the Reverend James Hely. Dublin: W. M'Kenzie.

O'Malley, D.J.S. (ed.). 1972. Aspects of George Petrie V: An Essay on Military Architecture in Ireland previous to the English Invasion [by George Petrie] *Proc. R.I.A.* 72, Sect C, 219 – 65.

Ó Raithbheartaigh, T. 1932. *Genealogical Tracts 1*, Irish Manuscripts Commission. Dublin: Stationary Office.

Parker, J.H. 1859. S*ome Account of Domestic Architecture in England from Richard II to Henry VIII, Part I*. Oxford and London: John Henry and James Parker.

Share, B. 1995. *Bunratty: Rebirth of a Castle*. Dingle: Brandon.

Simms, K. 2001. Native Sources for Gaelic Settlement: The House Poems. In Duffy *et al* (eds), *Gaelic Ireland c.1250–1650*, 246–67. Four Courts Press: Dublin.

Stopford-Green, A. 1912. *The Old Irish World*. Dublin/London: M.G.H Gill and Son.

Tierney, A. 2003. A note on the identity of Aileach. *Journal of the Royal Society of Antiquaries of Ireland* 133, 183–86.

Tierney, A. 2004. The Gothic and the Gaelic: exploring the place of castles in Ireland's Celtic revival. *International Journal of Historical Archaeology* 8 (3), 185–98.

Tierney, A. 2005. Pedigrees in stone? Castles, Colonialism and Gaelic-Irish Identity from the Middle Ages to the Celtic Revival, Unpublished PhD Thesis, University College Dublin.

Ua Mórdha, E. 1920. *Three Hills: Ossary, Leix, Lancashire*. Dublin: CTS.

Walsh, P. (ed.) 1948. *The Life of Aodh Ruadh O Domhnaill transcribed from the Book of Lughaidh Ó Clérigh*, London: Irish Texts Society.

Wakeman, W.F. 1861. The Mediaeval Houses or Castles of Ireland. *Duffy's Hibernian Magazine 3 (16)*, 155–59.

CULTURES OF ANTIQUITY AND THE PRACTICE OF ARCHAEOLOGY IN BRITAIN AND IRELAND (C.1700-1850): A POST-COLONIAL PERSPECTIVE

David Harvey

Introduction

Recent years have witnessed a growing concern with issues involving the popular presentation and interpretation of ancient sites and monuments (Bender 1998; Cooney 1994; Gingell 1999; Pearce 1999). Notions of social construction, cultural formation, domination and resistance have been key themes of much of this work, which has sought to re-invigorate the wider arena of archaeology and heritage studies, showing them to be politicised and somewhat problematical practices. This focus on how ancient heritage resources are produced and consumed today, however, prompts us to explore how the interpretation of such sites became entangled within the politics of identity construction, inclusion and exclusion in the past. This chapter explores aspects of the production and consumption of ancient heritage in Britain and Ireland during the eighteenth and early nineteenth centuries, with a particular focus on how they were related to discourses of race, imperialism and colonialism.

Following Catherine Hall's work on 'cultures of empire', this paper centres upon the place of contemporary descriptions and interpretations of ancient sites within discourses of domination and resistance (Hall 2000a; Hall et al 2000). Invoking an idea of 'cultures of antiquity', such archaeological descriptions are seen as forms of cultural power through which races, peoples, societies and places were 'imaginatively managed'. Reviewing contemporary descriptions of Avebury (Co. Wiltshire, England) and Newgrange (Co. Meath, Republic of Ireland), the paper explores how ancient sites reflected wider notions of emerging national identity and imperial ambition, together with apparent senses of colonial domination and resistance (see Figure 18).

The practice of seeking to uncover the symbolic and cultural meanings of seemingly normative objects and practices, such as ancient monuments and archaeological endeavours more generally, is now commonplace (see Chippendale et al 1990; Tilley 1994; Cresswell 1996; Bender 1998 for instance). Indeed, referring to how one should approach the subject of landscape studies, Bender (1993: 3) argues that 'the landscape is never inert, people engage with it, re-work it, appropriate it and contest it. It is part of the way in which identities are created and disputed, whether as individual, group or nation state'. This chapter follows a similar intellectual pathway when examining ancient monuments, seeing Avebury and Newgrange as dynamic and complex sites that people have engaged with, re-worked, appropriated and contested for centuries.

Ancient monuments such as Newgrange and Avebury have always been rendered intelligible, described and otherwise represented in manners that reflect particular views and ideas. For the most part, this production of knowledge has been controlled by antiquarians, natural scientists, archaeologists etc, who have sought to legitimate their claims through academic respectability. Despite such claims to objective enquiry, however, these interpretations

and representations of ancient monuments need to be viewed within their societal and temporal context in order to be fully understood. Thus, we need to interpret these representations from a theoretically informed and critical perspective in order to understand the complex social matrix that produced them.

Ancient sites are supremely malleable. No one can really know their *true*, original meaning, and so they have become valuable resources to be marshalled in the service of contemporary agendas in every era (Harvey 2001; 2003; Holtorf 2001). They were used to justify and support the existence and supremacy of the Catholic Church over a thousand years ago, and have been used to support an emerging sense of nationhood in more recent times. Even today they are used to justify, and often to add a certain 'spiritual gravity' to a range of practices and ideas, from neo-paganism and spiritual freedom to discourses of exclusion and control of 'unruly elements' in the population (Boholm 1997; Kohl and Fawcett 1995; Atkinson et al 1996; Diaz-Andreu and Champion 1996). Rather than taking such concepts as 'ancient monumentality' for granted, therefore, we should seek to interpret the context of their social production, thereby answering Ogborn's (1996: 223) call for work that seeks to understand the situatedness of knowledge production.

Driver and Gilbert's (1998) work opens up an avenue of investigation into how colonial power works through the language of everyday lives both in the colony and in the colonial metropole. This is no less prevalent in areas of academic and antiquarian enquiry. This chapter explores how aspects of colonial power and domination can be read through the antiquarian discourses associated with Avebury and Newgrange. At Avebury, the label of civilisation was consciously associated with quasi-religious ideas, so as to draw legitimating moral sustenance in support of a British Protestant world view. Avebury, therefore, became an important element of cultural capital, defined, described and used by those who were culturally empowered in society. Having established that ancient monuments can be seen as tools of cultural domination, both reflecting, and also (re)-interpreted according to wider cultural and political requirements, the paper will then explore how these processes were enacted within the context of eighteenth-century Irish cultural politics. In this respect, contemporary descriptions of the important site of Newgrange will act as a basis for examining aspects of how a notion of civilisation was negotiated within a complex arena of cultural domination.

In order to contextualise this study, we need first to consider how the language of ancient monuments may become entangled with the politics of domination, inclusion and exclusion within the context of eighteenth- and nineteenth-century discourses of race and colonialism. In other words, we need to account for how 'cultures of antiquity' may be placed within discourses of civilisation and 'cultures of empire', both within and beyond the colonial metropole.

Figure 18. Location map

Ancient monuments, colonialism and domination

Throughout the nineteenth century, the world was made popularly intelligible through a racialised sense of Self and Other (Hall 2000a). As Ploszasjska (1999; 2000) has noted, academic credence was thereby supplied to both racist attitudes and a global-scale colonial system of resource exploitation. In order to make sense of how such scientific and antiquarian endeavour was connected to histories of imperialism, we need to perceive the building and maintenance of empires as being much more than mere territorial expansion, and to follow Hall's (2000b: 2) prompt to reconnect ideas of race, nation and empire. In this context, the descriptions of ancient monuments that are the subject of this paper were tied to specific imaginings of nationhood and imperial destiny through racialised senses of civilisation. Practices of domination and subordination in the colonial world were made palatable through recourse to ideas of civilisation, with colonisers producing 'knowledge' about what is (or is not) civilised, and categorising others accordingly. However, in the same way processes of colonisation should not be seen in such a two-dimensional manner. Categorisations of civilisation itself should be problematised. Drawing from post-colonial theory therefore, such socially contingent categories of civilisation should be recognised as negotiated terms.

Descriptions of ancient monuments should be seen as discourses of domination and resistance. Such descriptions both reflected and helped to instil certain attitudes towards race and ideas of civilisation, and their investigation should be seen as an important part of the wider project of exploring the 'cultures of empire'. In the same way as Ryan (1997) saw the photographic archive as representing a form of collective colonial memory for instance, descriptions of ancient sites comprise a body of work that reinforced a pervasive and persistent set of cultural attitudes towards the rest of the world. Imperial attitudes found sustenance in such archaeological and antiquarian descriptions that reflected a deep-seated faith in, and enduring loyalty to, a sense of the 'civilising mission'. In this respect, such archaeological and antiquarian description, were forms of cultural power through which other people, societies and places were 'imaginatively managed' (Hall 2000b:

14). As Hall *et al* note, such 'forms of cultural power, organised through academic descriptions such as history, anthropology and philology were as significant in the maintenance of colonial rule as the political, economic and military policies which had been more frequently attended to' (2000: 52).

Recent years have witnessed an increasing amount of work that has sought to place the archaeological endeavour within a socio-political context, with a particular interest in examining the practice of archaeology within the context of the fabrication and support of nationhood (Shanks and Tilley 1987; Diaz-Andreu 1993; Tierney 1996; Dietler 1998). While much of this body of work could be said to have taken a cue from Trigger's (1984) seminal paper that categorised archaeological practice into nationalist, colonialist and imperialist styles, further examination of his latter two categorisations does not seem to have extended very far. For Trigger (1984: 363–65), *imperialist* archaeology was that practised in globally dominant states, such as Britain during the nineteenth century, where European 'progress' towards a greater civilisation was seen as both inevitable and highly beneficial. The study of prehistory was seen to 'prove' the supremacy of European peoples, thereby providing intellectual respectability for colonial practices. This in turn reinforced what Trigger (ibid: 360–63) sees as colonial archaeology, whereby archaeological investigation sought to demonstrate 'primitiveness' and a distinct lack of civilisation within the ancient remains of a 'native' population. These categories require further investigation, both in terms of detailed case studies and in the light of more recent theoretical developments. In particular, we need to move beyond the notion of there being a simple, dichotomous construction of Self/Other or coloniser/colonised, with its instrumentalist overtones, and instead view archaeological and antiquarian endeavours in the eighteenth and nineteenth centuries as socially constructed and meaningful practice. In this respect, both archaeological knowledge, and a sense of civilisation were contingent and negotiated; products of the state of the discipline in specific places, at particular times and 'channelled through the idiosyncratic understanding and personalities of individual archaeologists' (Trigger

1995: 266). Rather than placing over these social practices a simple colonial template founded upon the constructed knowledge of hindsight therefore, we need to attempt to explore what these monuments meant within their own context.

Avebury: Protestant Druids and ideas of providence

Perhaps foremost in the context of the construction of popular cultural identity in eighteenth- and early nineteenth-century Britain and Ireland is that of religion (Colley 1986; 1992; Connolly 1992; Samuel 1998). Colley (1992: 10–58) argues that it was a common investment in Protestantism that was crucial to the construction of British identity over the long eighteenth century. This Protestant comradeship may be seen both in the formation of a sense of self – as a fortunate, selected race, and also through a wider world view that portrays (Catholic) others as uncivilised, untrustworthy and brutal. Avebury was recognised, perhaps even over Stonehenge, as the most important ancient monument in Britain, a position that generated extensive literature and antiquarian discussion relating to its supposed origins and meaning (Malone 1989; Burl 2002). A key theme in the process of knowledge construction revolved around a discourse of civilisation; a Protestant providence, with the constructed heritage of Avebury being founded upon a siege-mentality form of anti-Catholicism, together with a sense of destiny to recapture and re-interpret the ancient sites of areas that had been 'polluted by Popery' (Harvey 2003: 478–80).

For Stukeley (1724; 1743), Avebury was a totem: a reminder of past glory and a crutch for present fears, dilemmas and, most importantly, actions. As William Cooke, a fellow believer in the propriety of British druids over others exclaims:

> Here, while an inundation of infidelity is breaking in upon us, the mind of men, well ordered, will be able to resist the torrent, secure in its ancient barrier; in that defence which reasonable souls can judge alone sufficient for their safety and salvation. (Cooke 1754: 69)

This quotation demonstrates very well how ancient monuments, as artefacts from the past, may become entangled within present-day concerns and ideals. Avebury had been preserved by God's providence, and this providence demanded action in order to fulfil one's duty. The fabricated heritage of Avebury lent Protestant Britain support, by legitimising the claim that Britain was a New Jerusalem, under siege from a Catholic Other.

The idea of Protestant providence was common in early modern England. In popular circles, the Fire of London was often blamed on Catholics, with London's preservation and rebirth as a global centre of power and commerce linked strongly to a sense of paying for the city's serendipity as a moral duty for God's providence (Cressy 1994). At Avebury, the popular descriptions by Henry Browne (1823), which were published in several editions over the first half of the nineteenth century, demonstrates the importance of this link between the representation of ancient heritage and the implied superiority of Protestant Britain. This link was communicated to a broader audience in Henry Browne's tourist guide to the ancient remains, in which he clearly states the connection between Avebury (*Abury*), God's providence and national purpose:

> And we have, indeed, in this our little island, so mighty a testimony to the

unerring word of God (Browne 1823: 40).

> Oh, unthinking Englishman! direct your eyes throughout the habitable globe, and what part of it is there in which the name of England is not known? [...] In Abury we find nothing whatever but that which bespeaks the glory of God (ibid: 42).

Browne develops this by arguing that it is Britain (and Avebury in particular), which is God's chosen spot on earth, and that He (*sic*.) has chosen us for a reason:

> Will the Geologist deny its separation from the continent by the Flood? Can we as Christians, venture to assert that there is no appeal to man in this Almighty act of Omniscience? (ibid: viii)

> [The preservation of Avebury and Stonehenge gives] an ascendancy in importance to this our country over all others – an ascendancy which we see paralleled at the present moment in its being alone selected to make known the revealed will of God throughout the earth. And is this little spot, an island, ...destined before all others to this great, this mighty, this most glorious of ends! (ibid: vii)

Crucially, the evidence for this line of thought is found in physical form in the structures of Avebury and Stonehenge. It seems that it is not just Britain's moral duty but also its destiny to bring its version of civilisation to all corners of the world. Developing this theme of colonial domination being both mirrored and enacted through cultural domination, Henry Browne recognises the importance of such groups as Bible Societies and British School Societies in fulfilling what he sees as Britain's duty:

> Look at the amazing effects arising out of the Bible Societies, of the Missionaries, and of the British and Foreign School Society, and where is the nation of the earth that is now to be compared to England – to England, I say, as a Christian – for in no other respect, though she has been till of late permitted to hold the absolute dominion of the greater half of the terraqueous globe, does she stand in so exalted a station, and on so permanent a basis (ibid: 41).

Developing from the ideas of Trigger (1984), therefore, we see here a strong sense of what he categorises as imperialist archaeology, whereby a dominant global power is justifying its expansionist policies by referring to supposed archaeological truths. This demonstrates that such 'imperialist' archaeological *knowledge* is found to be located away from the time and space of the supposed 'heart of Empire', in metropolitan centres, and within the cultural politics of more everyday subject material. Moving away from seeing processes of imperial practice simply as economic expansion elsewhere, we instead see imperial experience as shaping identities at home through the construction of a particular cultural landscape of ancient heritage. For Henry Browne, Avebury is a physical incarnation of God's will for the British to dominate the world, and its preservation is correspondingly linked, not to pious views of conserving the heritage of ancestors, but to more present-centred identity politics:

Do not then, my countrymen, let these testimonies to your unparalleled eminence, even from the beginning of time, [i.e. Avebury and Stonehenge] stand unprotected. Oh! Let not the rude and ignorant demolish what is left of these venerable piles, these truly precious relics of antiquity; – acceptable, I cannot but believe, even in the sight of God himself (Browne 1823: 41).

The heritage process, whereby particular sites are first identified, then categorised, then interpreted and lastly protected and preserved, is inexorably bound up with wider cultural experiences and agendas of self-identification and imperial discourse. Britain's ancient heritage is seen here to act as a legitimating totem for acts of cultural domination and subjugation. Conversely, it is important to see such narratives as representing a product of imperial experience. Echoing Fanon's (1967) conception of the European metropole being a creation of the Third World, the reification of ancient heritage in Britain should be seen as being filtered through established relationships with other peoples in other parts of the world.

Having seen how ancient monuments in Britain were reified through notions of providence and the self, let us now turn to Ireland, where a similar antiquarian culture in the eighteenth century understood and portrayed ancient monuments within the context of contemporary identity politics of exclusion and inclusion. The value of invasion as a harbinger of civilisation is strong in these accounts, which reflect contemporary notions that denigrated 'native Irish' culture.

The domination of Newgrange

The discourse surrounding the ancient site of Newgrange, indicates how the construction of knowledge about ancient monuments may collide with wider cultural agendas, practices and experiences. Unlike Avebury, Newgrange was seen by almost all eighteenth-century commentators as definitely *not* built by local inhabitants. Rather, the civilisation that was represented at such sites as Newgrange needed to be 'imported' through successive tribes of invaders and colonisers, who were beacons of civilisation in an otherwise uncivilised country, and by implication, totems for the veracity of invasionist thinking (see for instance Pownall 1773; Vallancey 1781; Ledwich 1781; Beauford 1786). Very often, these descriptions simply ignore any native Irish origin theories at all, but by invoking Phoenicians, Danes or Ancient Egyptians as the builders of Irish monuments, they automatically imply that it is with diffusion, often through colonial expansion, that civilisation springs and blossoms.

The place of diffusionist assumptions in processes of cultural domination and subjugation has been shown by Driver (2001: 7), among others, with invasion being seen as the inevitable mechanism of progress. Invasionist hypotheses in archaeology, therefore, would seem to spring from these same cultural assumptions, and would also act to justify the 'naturalness' of contemporary arrangements in Ireland, where plantation and resettlement were seen as completely necessary for 'improvement'. In an account of the Newgrange site in 1726 for instance, Thomas Molyneux utilises the 'seven yard perch' for the basis of all his measurements and interpretations. Since the seven yard perch existed as the basic unit of Irish plantation measurement and landscape division during the seventeenth and eighteenth centuries, we can situate this description as an attempt to make sense of the monument

within existing structures of landscape domination and control (Herity 1967: 133). In essence, therefore, knowledge of Newgrange was constructed as evidence of a previous attempt to improve the island of Ireland, to be understood alongside such landscape 'improvements' that were contemporary to Thomas Molyneux's own time.

Over the rest of the eighteenth century, such Anglo-Irish antiquarian and archaeological luminaries as Colonel Charles Vallancey, Edward Ledwich, William Beuford and Governor Thomas Pownall (among others) continued this trend of representing and interpreting Newgrange as a product of a previous attempt to encourage civilisation in Ireland. Thomas Pownall, in particular, gives an exceedingly full account of his ideas in his paper in the journal *Archaeologia* (1773). Thomas Pownall was a career colonial administrator, successively the Governor of New Jersey, Massachusetts and lastly South Carolina before retiring to become a traveller and antiquarian. He was unapologetic about the so-called 'improvements' of his own age and was very keen to link the building of Newgrange with former periods of invasion:

The same zeal which now animates the missionaries of Christian faith did always animate the Magi [...] to propagate their Patriarchal faith and religion amongst the uncivilised inhabitants of the world. [...W]e find them settled in the British Isles, [...] called by a Celtic name *Druids*[.] To the establishment of these holy fathers the Celtic inhabitants of these isles owe their civilisation, the art of husbandry and agriculture (Pownall 1773: 243–44).

In fact, by invoking ancient Magi, Phoenicians *and* Danes as all having an input into the bringing of such civilisation to Ireland, Pownall appears at pains to be supporting anyone but the Irish themselves as harbingers of 'polite society'. In common with other commentators of his time, a message of innovation through diffusion is strong, with invasion and subjugation being entirely natural and necessary in order to replace existing (uncivilised and outmoded) patterns with the new system of order and control.

In common with Pownall, and reminiscent of Giraldus Cambrensis's oft-quoted comment about the incivility of non-Norman peoples in the twelfth century, Edward Ledwich's (1786) description of Irish antiquities launches into a completely unsubstantiated monologue, which reflects his own socio-cultural position and attitude more so than it represents his subject matter of ancient monuments.[1]

The Irish had quitted the hunter and advanced to the shepherd state, the second stage in the civilisation of mankind; but their manners were little altered; their food, their domestication and every other circumstance showed, that the liberty, the ferocity and untamed nature of tenants of the forest, were far from being reclaimed (Ledwich 1786: 120–21).

Following Lilley's (2002: 24) analysis of Giraldus Cambrensis's commentaries within the context of the much earlier Anglo-Norman colonisation of Wales and Ireland, Ledwich's description here is an example of how the imagined geographies of the Irish were used to re-enforce the marginality of colonised peoples during the eighteenth century. Just as in medieval Wales, ideas of exclusion and inclusion were bound up with notions of civility; and just as in medieval Wales, it was those in power that monopolised the means to define and describe the landscape through their notions of what it was to be civilised. In this sense, the political, economic and cultural domination of Ireland was mirrored by the domination of the presentation and definition of ancient monuments in Ireland.

Sites such as Newgrange, were interpreted according to a wider agenda, that, with hindsight, appears to be promoting the idea of British imperial rule as the civiliser. It is the idea that such practices of 'improvement' being brought by the British colonisers was *not* something that is novel, which is perhaps the most important idea. The work of the British is not new, but is founded upon the heritage of previous sea-faring nations. In this respect, a historical precedent is found and identified to act as a guide for the future, with a sense of destiny on the part of the British 'mission' to civilise the world being paramount.

Conclusions

So far, the examples of Avebury and Newgrange seem to indicate a fairly straightforward situation of how 'cultures of antiquity' may be seen to support a contemporary systematic programme of colonisation and imperial expansion. However, the instrumentalist nature of this framework of 'colonial domination', must also be recognised and problematised. Although it may seem easy to make a link to the idea that British imperial attitudes found sustenance in such archaeological descriptions that reflected a deep-seated faith in a sense of 'civilising mission', one should be careful not to construct purely on the benefit of hindsight a simple dichotomous understanding of Self/Other or coloniser/colonised, ascribing a certain 'colonial attitude' onto these eighteenth- and early nineteenth-century descriptions. These archaeological and antiquarian endeavours were socially constructed and meaningful practices, which need to be explored within their own context.

At Avebury, we need to explore the sort of memory that Henry Browne is invoking through his descriptions. In this respect, Browne's (1823) work reflects the retrospective memory of writers such as William Stukeley (1743), writing almost a century earlier. Consequently, although Henry Browne's archaeological descriptions reflected certain racial assumptions and a sense of Protestant civilising mission, we should be careful not to confuse Browne's prospective memories of Avebury with the retrospective construction of barefaced imperial ambition and justification of later years. Taking a similar broadly post-colonial perspective, it is very difficult to ascribe Thomas Pownall's (1773) views on Newgrange as being either pro- or anti-Irish in any simple, dichotomous sense, and many of the later eighteenth-century writers such as Edward Ledwich or Colonel Vallancey, were undoubtedly very proud of their Irish connections. Rather than relying upon a one-dimensional 'colonial template' of Irish-British relations, therefore, one should explore the nature of how these archaeologists constructed their identities – the very *sorts* of Irishness that they ascribed to.

With both Avebury and Newgrange, Colley's (1992) work on the formation of Britishness during the long eighteenth century is instructive here, advocating the notion that it was a sense of Protestant self-identification that was the most important factor in the construction of British national identity at this time. Importantly, Colley is not arguing that British identity was effacing other identities – one could still be proud to be Irish – but that it was through the self-identification of Protestantism that a loyalty towards Britain, its monarchy, state and growing

empire, was articulated (Kumar 2003: 140–47). At Avebury, Henry Browne's (1823) work is not premised on the later expansion of the British Empire in the nineteenth century. Rather, it harks back to an earlier construction of Britishness as a non-Catholic bulwark, waving a supposed flag of freedom towards continental despots. Similarly, rather than necessarily and consciously 'undermining' Ireland through their descriptions of Newgrange, the eighteenth-century antiquarian scholars discussed herein were imaginatively managing a sense of Irishness that made space for their own identification as 'loyal' Irishmen, bringing civilisation and improvement to the island of Ireland.

Although ostensibly about 'the past', heritage only has meaning in the present (Graham *et al* 2000; Harvey 2001). One key and often overlooked element of the heritage process, however, is the way it seeks to promote a particular vision of the future through recourse to an imagined past (*cf* Gruffudd 1994; Gruffudd *et al* 1999, for instance). Interpretations of ancient monuments, therefore, must be understood within the context of how knowledge about them was produced; in this case, contingent upon the agendas, views and constructed identities of eighteenth- and early nineteenth-century 'cultures of antiquity', which were, in turn, situated within broader discourses of knowledge. In addition to understanding this 'present context', however, we must also recognise the importance of a prescribed future, or fabricated destiny being invoked through this process of knowledge construction. The production of ancient heritage at both Avebury and Newgrange is unavoidably bound up with ideas of self-identity and the definition of people around the world. In this sense, civilisation is performed through the interpretation of certain ancient sites. In particular, a context of religious bigotry seems to have infused itself upon the fabricated landscapes of the ancient world, with ancient Britain populated by proto-Protestant crusaders, struggling against idolatry, while the population of Ireland, as the following quotations from Deane's (1830) treatise on serpent worship attest, became tainted by, what was seen as, continental persuasions:

> The prevalence of the Celtic superstition in Ireland is marked, even now, by stupendous monuments: but the Druids of this island assimilated themselves rather to those of Gaul than of Britain (Deane 1830: 252–53).

> The ancient religion of Gaul, though established by Druids, was not so pure as that of Britain; neither did it retain so strong a hold upon the affections of the people. There was in it more of idolatry, and less of priestcraft. (ibid: 254)

Avebury was portrayed as a marvellous result of God's providence for His chosen people. It acted as a totem around which all (Protestant) British subjects could gather, and it extolled the virtue of their 'civilising mission' across the entire globe. Newgrange on the other hand, was interpreted during the eighteenth century as evidence of how civilisation was diffused through invasion; as a justification for the status quo of an Irish identity politics that sought to exclude a large section of the (Catholic) population from power, portraying such division and domination in Irish society as natural and even beneficial for the 'civilising process'.

Heritage must be seen as a present-centred cultural practice and as an instrument of cultural power. The control over the representation of ancient sites in Britain and Ireland, therefore, was an important resource in the identity politics within these islands. Scholarly endeavour lent such constructed knowledge an air of legitimacy, while the monopolisation of this process of knowledge construction allowed notions of exclusion and domination to become accepted as not merely sanctioned, but inevitable and positively desirable.

Acknowledgements

I would like to thank a number of people for comments on earlier drafts of this paper, including Brian Graham, Peter Finlay, Kazuhiro Uesugi, and, in particular, Nicola Thomas. I would also like to thank both the organisers and audiences at conferences where spoken versions of this paper were presented – the Annual Conference of the Royal Geographical Society – with the Institute of British Geographers (Belfast, January 2002), and the conference of Contemporary and Historical Archaeology in Theory (Bristol, November 2003). The research from which this paper has been drawn, was funded by the British Academy (SG-31126). Any errors or misinterpretations are entirely the responsibility of the author.

Endnote

Giraldus Cambrensis wrote how 'the Welsh, who for so long ruled over the whole kingdom, want only to find refuge together in the least attractive corner of it, the woods, the mountains and the marshes'. He noted, too, that 'they do not live in towns, villages or castles, but lead a solitary existence, deep in the woods' (See Lilley 2002: 24).

References

Atkinson, J.A., Banks, I. and O'Sullivan, J. (eds) 1996. *Nationalism and Archaeology*. Glasgow: Cruithne Press.

Beauford, W. 1786. Of the origin and language of the Irish and the learning of the Druids. *Collectanea de Rebus Hibernicis* 2, 218–49.

Bender, B. 1993. Introduction: Landscape – Meaning and Action. In B. Bender (ed.), *Landscape: Politics and Perspectives*, 1–18. Oxford: Berg.

Bender, B. 1998. *Stonehenge: Making Space*. Oxford: Berg.

Boholm, A. 1997. Reinvented histories: medieval Rome as memorial landscape. *Ecumene* 4, 247–72.

Browne, H. 1823. *An Illustration of Stonehenge and Abury, in the County of Wiltshire, Pointing out their Origin and Character, Through Considerations Hitherto Unnoticed*. Salisbury: Brodie and Dowding.

Burl, A. 2002. *Prehistoric Avebury*. New Haven: Yale University Press, 2nd Edition.

Chippindale, C., Devereux, P., Fowler, P., Jones, R. and Sebastian, T. 1990. *Who Owns Stonehenge?* London: Batsford.

Colley, L. 1986. Whose nation? Class and national consciousness in Britain 1750–1830, *Past and Present* 113, 97–117.

Colley, L. 1992. *Britons. Forging the Nation 1707–1837*. London: Yale University Press.

Connolly, S.J. 1992. *Religion, Law and Power: the Making of Protestant Ireland 1660–1760*. Oxford: Clarendon Press.

Cooke, W. 1754. *An Enquiry into the Patriarchal and Druidical Religion, Temples Etc.. Being the Substance of some Letters to Sir H. Jacob Baronet*. London: Lockyer Davis.

Cooney, G. 1994. Sacred and Secular Neolithic Landscapes in Ireland. In D.L. Carmichael, J. Hubert, B. Reeves and A. Schanch, (eds), *Sacred Stones, Sacred Places*, 32–43. London: Routledge.

Cresswell, T. 1996. *In Place/Out of Place: Geography, Ideology and Transgression*. Minneapolis: University of Minneapolis Press.

Cressy, D. 1994. National Memory in Early Modern England. In J.R. Gillis (ed.), *Commemorations: The Politics of National Identity*, 61–73. Princetown: PUP.

Deane, J.B. 1830. *The Worship of the Serpent Traced Throughout the World, and its Traditions Referred to the Events in Paradise: Proving the Temptation and Fall of Man by the Instrumentality of a Serpent Tempter*. London: J. Hatchard and Son.

Diaz-Andreu, M. 1993. Theory and ideology: Spanish archaeology under the Franco regime. *Antiquity* 67, 74–82.

Diaz-Andreu, M. and Champion, T. (eds). 1996. *Nationalism and Archaeology in Europe*. London: UCL Press.

Dietler, M. 1998. A tale of three sites: The monumentalisation of Celtic oppida and the politics of collective memory and identity. *World Archaeology* 30, 72–89.

Driver, F. 2001. *Geography Militant: Cultures of Exploration and Empire*. Oxford: Blackwell.

Driver, F. and Gilbert, D. 1998. Heart of Empire? Landscape, space and performance in imperial London. *Environment and Planning D: Society and Space* 16 (1), 11–28.

Fanon, F. 1967. *The Wretched of the Earth*. Harmondsworth: Penguin.

Gingell, C. 1999. Visiting Avebury. In G. Chitty and D. Baker (eds), *Managing Historic Sites and Buildings*, 23–34. London: Routledge/English Heritage.

Graham, B.J., Ashworth, G.J. and Tunbridge, J.E. 2000. *A Geography of Heritage: Power, Culture and Economy*. London: Arnold.

Gruffudd, P. 1994. Back to the land: historiography, rurality and the nation in interwar Wales. *Transactions of the Institute of British Geographers* 19 (1), 61–77.

Gruffudd, P., Herbert, D.T. and Piccini, A. 1999 'Good to think': social constructions of Celtic heritage in Wales. *Environment and Planning D: Society and Space* 17 (6), 705–21.

Hall, C. (ed.). 2000a. *Cultures of Empire: A Reader: Colonisers in Britain and the Empire in the Nineteenth and Twentieth Centuries*. Manchester: Manchester University Press.

Hall, C. 2000b. Introduction: Thinking the Postcolonial, Thinking the Empire. In C. Hall (ed.), *Cultures of Empire: A Reader: Colonisers in Britain and the Empire in the Nineteenth and Twentieth Centuries*, 1–33. Manchester: Manchester University Press.

Hall, C., McClelland, K. and Rendall, J. 2000. Introduction. In C. Hall, K. McClelland and J. Rendall (eds), *Defining the Victorian Nation: Class, Race, Gender and the Reform Act of 1867*, 1–70. Cambridge: Cambridge University Press.

Harvey, D.C. 2001. Heritage pasts and heritage presents: Temporality, meaning and the scope of heritage studies. *International Journal of Heritage Studies* 7(4), 319–38.

Harvey, D.C. 2003. 'National' identities and the politics of ancient heritage: continuity and change at ancient monuments in Britain and Ireland, c. 1675–1850. *Transactions of the Institute of British Geographers* 28(4), 473–87.

Herity, M. 1967. From Lhuyd to Coffey. *Studia Hibernica* 7, 127–45.

Holtorf, C. 2001. *Monumental Past. The Life Histories of Megalithic Monuments in Mecklenburg-Vorpommern (Germany)*, hypermedia publication on CD-ROM. Toronto: CITD Press/University of Toronto.

Kohl, P.L. and Fawcett C. (eds), 1995. *Nationalism, Politics and the Practice of Archaeology*. Cambridge: Cambridge University Press.

Kumar, K. 2003. *The Making of English National Identity*. Cambridge: Cambridge University Press.

Ledwich, E. 1781. An essay on the study of Irish antiquities. *Collectanea de Rebus Hibernicis* 2, 81–116.

Ledwich, E. 1786. A dissertation on the round towers of Ireland. *Collectanea de Rebus Hibernicis* 2, 117–43.

Lilley, K.D. 2002 Imagined Geographies of the 'Celtic fringe' and the Cultural Construction of the 'Other' in Medieval Wales and Ireland. In D.C.Harvey, R. Jones, N. McInroy and C. Milligan (eds), *Celtic Geographies: Old Culture, New Times*, 21–36. London: Routledge.

Malone, C. 1989. *Avebury*. London: Batsford.

Molyneux, T. 1726. Manuscripts for *Natural History of Ireland* (dated 1726: TCD MS 883/2).

Ogborn, M. 1996. History, memory and the politics of landscape and space: work in historical geography from autumn 1994 to autumn 1995. *Progress in Human Geography* 20, 222–29.

Pearce, S.M. 1999. Presenting Archaeology. In N. Merriman (ed.), *Making Early Histories in Museums*, 12–27. London: Leicester University Press.

Ploszajska, T. 1999. *Geographical Education, Empire and Citizenship: Geographical Teaching and Learning in English Schools, 1870–1944*. Historical Geography Research Series, number 35.

Ploszajska, T. 2000. Historiographies of Geography and Empire. In B.J. Graham and C. Nash (eds), *Modern Historical Geographies*, 121–45. Harlow: Prentice Hall.

Pownall, T. 1773. A description of the sepulchral monument at New Grange, near Drogheda, in the County of Meath, in Ireland. *Archaeologia* 2, 236–71.

Ryan, J. 1997. *Picturing Empire: Photography and the Visualisation of the British Empire*. London: Reaktion Books.

Samuel, R. 1998. *Island Stories: Unravelling Britain. Theatres of Memory, Volume II*. London: Verso.

Shanks, M. and Tilley, C. 1987. *Social Theory and Archaeology*. Oxford: Polity Press.

Stukeley, W. 1724. *Itinarium Curiosum. Or an Account of the Antiquitys and Remarkable Curiositys in Nature of Art, Observ'd in Travels Thro' Great Brittan*. London: printed for the author.

Stukeley, W. 1743. *Abury, a Temple of the British Druids with some others Described*. London: Innys, Manby, Dod and Brindley, in 2 volumes.

Tierney, M. 1996. The Nation, Nationalism and National Identity. In I.A. Atkinson, I. Banks and J. O'Sullivan (eds), *Nationalism and Archaeology*, 12–21. Glasgow: Cruithne Press.

Tilley, C. 1994. *A Phenomenology of Landscape: Places, Paths and Monuments*. Oxford: Berg.

Trigger, B.G. 1984. Alternative archaeologies: nationalist, colonialist, imperialist. *Man* 19, 355–70.

Trigger, B.G. 1995. Romanticism, Nationalism and Archaeology. In P.L. Kohl and C. Fawcett (eds), *Nationalism, Politics and the Practice of Archaeology*, 263–79. Cambridge: Cambridge University Press.

Vallancey, C. 1781. An inquiry into the first inhabitants of Ireland. *Collectanea de Rebus Hibernicis* 2, 56–73.

Encounters Between Actors, Audience and Archaeologists at the Rose Theatre, 1587–1989

Julian M.C. Bowsher

The archaeological excavation of an ancient, or historical, theatre examines a venue wherein a popular culture was expressed and experienced. The excavation of the Rose playhouse in London provides a stage on which to discuss many aspects of archaeology and popular culture in the past and the present. A theatre specifically – physically and dramatically – informs a number of debates: not only archaeology *of* the theatre, but archaeology *and* (the) theatre, archaeology *as* theatre (cf Pearson and Shanks 2001) and even *archaeologists* as (the) *dramatis personae*.

I thought it prophetic that as I was leaving for the CHAT 2003 conference in Bristol I saw a poster at MoLAS entitled 'Archaeo Rock at the Rose'. In fact this turned out to be a flyer for a gig by archaeologist musicians at the Red Rose Club (Finsbury Park, London, 19 December 2003). Clearly, then, the Rose (excavation) is still being used as a metaphor for popular culture within the archaeological community.

In 1989, the excavation of the Rose theatre became a tourist attraction, particularly after the extensive media coverage. There were even road signs erected in Southwark giving directions to the site. There was an intrinsic interest in the site as the archaeological theatre became a modern theatre venue too. The excavation provided a direct encounter for the twentieth-century audience keen on the 'live entertainment' of archaeology. Archaeologists, as members of a profession hitherto unconnected with 'Shakespearean theatres', were now playing bit parts in the drama. The ensuing political debate questioned our encounters with popular culture, past and present (Eccles 1990). Subsequent excavation of small parts of the Globe, the Hope and possibly the Theatre, are accompanied by full academic reference and less hyperbole.

A distinctive manifestation of popular culture in Tudor London was the theatres and playhouses wherein the flowering of English drama was contained. Theatres were indoor establishments generally tolerated within the City; playhouses were open-air arenas within the less puritanical suburbs. There were four playhouses on Bankside in Southwark: the Rose (1587), Swan (1595), the Globe (1599) and the Hope (1614).

The notion of the 'Shakespearean theatre' of the sixteenth and seventeenth centuries is a result of the bardolatry that has dominated theatre history and it has, until recently, tended to produce the idea that all of these playhouses were similar. There may have been basic similarities but even without the benefits of archaeological excavation, documentary records suggest diversity. Moreover, as far as the Rose is concerned, we might more accurately define it as a 'Marlovian theatre' (Bowsher 2000). Short descriptions occur in passing references and in contemporary legal records of building disputes. Little detail is seen on contemporary maps and panoramas but a drawing of the Swan dated to 1596, and only discovered in the 1880s, revealed for the first time an interior view of one of the playhouses (Foakes 1985: 52–55). Analysis of surviving stage directions has also provided some clues.

Only in the case of the Fortune (built in Cripplegate in 1600) and the Hope where the building contracts survive do we have some detailed documentation.

No such detail survived for the Rose but it was nevertheless famous enough before the excavations of 1989. This was largely due to the unique survival of papers concerning its management, accounts and repertoire, once belonging to its owner Philip Henslowe (Foakes 2002). Thus we knew that it was built in 1587, underwent further building work in 1592 and was demolished by 1606.

Since the discovery of the Rose in 1989 there has been an archaeological debate (eg, Biddle 1989; Wilson 1995), but it was not until 1998 that a preliminary report on the excavation appeared (Bowsher 1998). For the last couple of years, the entire excavation data (including, for the first time, the finds) have been subject to a thorough reanalysis in preparation for full publication. This work was occasioned by a grant from English Heritage leading to a MoLAS monograph (Bowsher and Miller forthcoming). It is, therefore, an opportune moment to examine the broader issues of the multifaceted relationships between 'theatre and archaeology' today.

The excavation revealed for the first time in nearly 400 years, the ground plan of a sixteenth-century London playhouse. Generally, therefore, it was this spatial, rather than purely archaeological, aspect that generated most theatrical excitement and debate, primarily conducted by theatre historians (eg, Cerasano 1989; Gurr and Orrell 1989; Foakes 1991). Peggy Phelan's 'psychoanalysis of the excavation' widened the interpretation of popular culture. Indeed, the 'anal core of analogies and analysis' led her to make a comparison between 'an anatomical diagram of the male rectum and an aerial photograph of the Rose remains' (Phelan 1997: 74, 84; 1998: 66, 67, 76). The Freudian concept of anal retention took on a new meaning that has hopefully reduced the hubris that surrounded the excavation.

For the theatrical community, the discovery of the Rose's size and layout, particularly of its stage, are important for the understanding of past performances, allowing today's actors to encounter their predecessors. Reconstruction has thus largely resulted in 'a number of Globe reconstructions, pseudo Globes and Globe inspired buildings around the world' (Frank Hildy, pers. comm.). Sam Wanamaker's project to build a (new) Globe playhouse on the south bank of the Thames heralded an era of serious debate on playhouse appearance. The Rose excavations clearly influenced the film set for *Shakespeare in Love* (Director John Madden, 1998), and, in a modern setting, the new theatre in Kingston, Surrey. Today's audiences are therefore receptive to the contrived heritage of a 'Shakespearean' or 'Marlovian' theatre / playhouse (cf Hildy 1990; 2004).

It is fortuitous that our re-examination of the Rose remains was taking place at the same time as a reconstruction of the playhouse was being planned by Shakespeare and Company of Lenox, Massachusetts, USA. The company

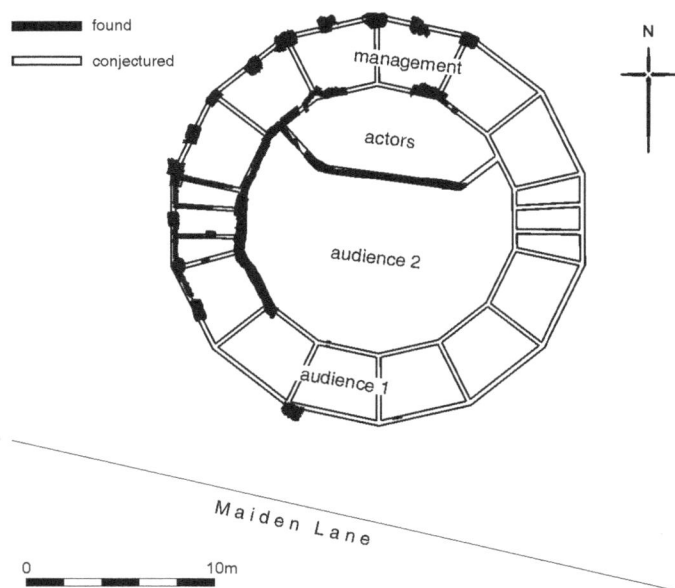

Figure 19. Rose playhouse, phase 1 1587-1592

is therefore working with MoLAS in order to benefit from the archaeological details accrued in the excavations. Moreover, the project has retained the same architects employed at Wanamaker's Globe whose experience has also been of use to the archaeological debate. As in the new Globe, the reconstruction would use traditional materials, such as oak, lime plaster and thatch, and techniques of carpentry construction. There would be constraints imposed by modern building regulations, but the primary intention of the reconstruction is to house a working theatre rather than a museum.

The theatrical use of a reconstruction would provide a serious stage for architects, archaeologists, historians and actors to reencounter and reappraise the original building. We will be able to look at the dynamics of how the building worked: the relationships between the audience and the whole building; between differing areas / classes of audience; between the actors and the stage; and between the actors and the audience.

I will return to the archaeology of theatres – as opposed to the archaeology of theatre. The plan of the Rose revealed fairly simple components: two polygonal rings of walls around a central yard into which a stage projected. The stage was in the northern part of the building and there was some evidence for a main external entrance from the street (Maiden Lane) at the southern end. Within the building there were access points from the yard into the galleries, exactly as the *ingressi* depicted in de Witt's drawing of the Swan. The 'floor surface' of the yard was of hard plaster and raked down towards the stage. This immediately identified differing spatial functions with an audience standing in the central yard and seated in the surrounding galleries, watching actors on the stage. Nevertheless, it also made clear that any 'tiring house' – changing room, store room and theatre offices – must have utilised that part of the galleries immediately behind the stage.

The other major result from the excavation was the discovery that the Rose had been altered at some time, creating a more irregular plan but encompassing a slightly larger stage area. This Phase Two was therefore associated with the unspecified building works documented in 1592 (Foakes 2002: 9). An unexpected outcome of the new research, however, shows some evidence for a relationship

between actors and audiences that is more than merely architectural. An analysis of the spatial distribution of the finds shows a link within those parameters between various users and occupants of the building.

There is, to be sure, little archaeological information on the construction of Phase One (Figure 19). The excavation stopped at the surfaces associated with its first phase, and the only examination of earlier strata was in clearing out later, mostly modern, intrusions within that stratification. Archaeological evidence from the remodelling of Phase Two and its eventual destruction / demolition in 1606 was plentiful. Thus, most of the excavated strata encountered the 'life' of the building as a theatre (Figure 20).

I have always been sceptical about the nature of an 'occupation layer'. Public spaces, including theatres, are cleaned up at the end of the day and little or nothing would be left on the floor. At the Rose what we can see is the *condition* of the yard floor, and infer usage of it. There were certainly traces of wear and tear all over it but the area against the stage front was distinctly churned up. I suggest that this disturbance provides archaeological evidence for 'rocking at the Rose', or, to put it into context, Tudor 'moshing'. This appeared to confirm the 'intimate' encounter with the audience that impressed twentieth-century actors who visited the excavation site.

There were two other areas where there does appear to be archaeological evidence of occupation and use: in precisely those areas utilised by actors and by audience. Much of the material recovered has only recently emerged from sieving soil samples collected during the excavation. It must be admitted that at the time the sampling strategy was biased towards gathering information on biological factors rather than artefact retrieval. Nevertheless, there are now some very useful material indicators and the study of their spatial distribution around the site is proving to be of great interest.

The stage surface itself is assumed to have been wooden boards, raised well above the yard surface. Within the footprint of the stage was a plaster surface that would suggest that there was an under stage area or void, which might have provided storage room and access on to the stage proper through a trapdoor. Over this plaster floor

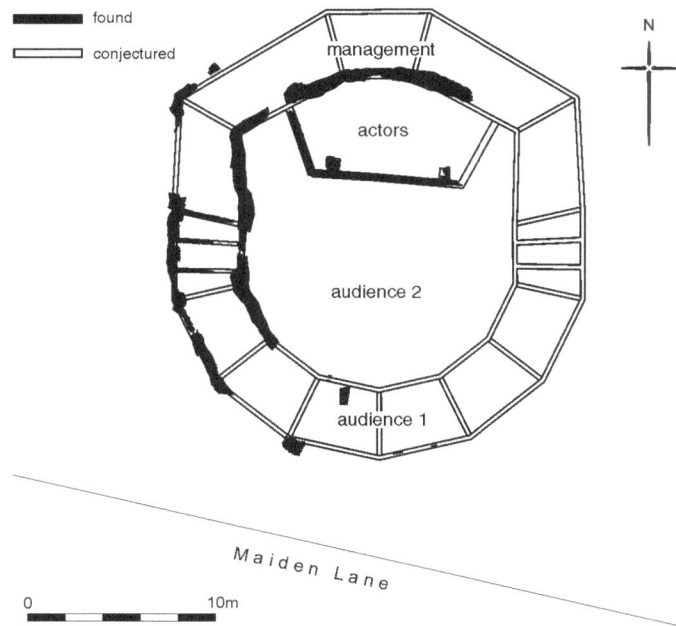

Figure 20. Rose playhouse, phase 2 1592-1606

was a thin humic spread that seems to have been a natural accumulation within what would have probably been a dank, confined space. Material here included a few small dress accessories such as pins, lace chapes and tiny glass beads but also a fragment possibly of a shield that might have been a stage prop. Nearby dumps included a fragmentary buskin; often described as the archetypal theatrical boot.

Secondly, there is occupation debris from below the galleries. The floorboards of the lowest galleries would have been some 18 inches above the ground surface, of redeposited clay. Above this clay was another humic accumulation that included material lying on the clay that we assume fell down through the floorboards. The interpretation of this layer as occupation debris is influenced not just by its content but also by its complete sealing with what were clearly demolition deposits. The assemblage itself included rodent bones, fruit stones and loose hazelnuts. The artefacts were the same sort of dress accessories, but in far greater quantities, as well as some tiny coins. The quality of the material here suggested a middle class component with virtually nothing of aristocratic or high-class association. Material within this layer, therefore, stayed there until found, not by the theatre management, but by later archaeologists. Archaeologists 'clean' (or, encounter) floors in a different manner to innkeepers and theatre keepers.

The alterations that we had defined as Phase Two are best associated with the documentary accounts of 1592. The northern half of the building was enlarged and a new stage that was built some two metres farther back (north) from the old stage. It had a different shape with more 'thrust' into the yard. The reason for this was associated with the outward extension of the galleries and roofing over this stage. Nevertheless, the ground raising deposits now placed either side of the new stage foundations were mostly small homogenous dumps that produced a great amount of material. Much of this, to be sure, was associated with the demolition of the old stage building and included ephemeral fragments of wood and plaster that could not be reused. It is assumed that much of the superstructure was taken down and re-erected where possible on its new alignment.

The artefactual material from these dumps included a slightly wider range of dress accessories as well as shoes. There were also fragments of swords, daggers and scabbards, some of which may have been associated with stage props, and a significant number of drinking and serving vessels. 'Coins' found here were mostly Nuremberg jettons, or counting tokens, rather than state coinage like that found in the area of the galleries. This is in itself an important contribution to the discussion of monetary usage and circulation. It might also be noted here that a large number of broken ceramic 'money boxes' that may have been associated with the management's revenue collecting process were found throughout the site.

The greatest deposition of ground raising material was within the new, larger, yard area. The first idea of perceived audience participation came with its initial excavation when it was found to contain thousands of hazelnut fragments. The 1989 press became very excited: here was direct evidence to support the contemporary sources for 'those nut-cracking Elizabethan theatre goers'. In actual fact the nut fragments were not contemporary litter but only a minor structural element of the material that, bound together, formed a homogenous floor surface. It was very solid and took hefty whacks of a mattock to excavate this surface. The probable explanation is that in the symbiotic encounters of the Tudor building world, one person was putting to good use the waste of another. Hazelnut shells turn out to be the waste product of soap manufacture, an industry attested to in the locality (Orrell 1992).

Thus, the artefactual content of this layer may have been present within the imported material itself. There was actually a very wide range of material, much of it waste associated with the manufacture of goods made from leather, metals and glass. Other items, of a more personal nature, were not only intrinsically interesting but also important because of the *terminus ante quem* of 1592. Many of these pieces may indeed have been associated with public (theatrical) activity and it is uncertain whether the hundreds of dress pins were from the surface, trodden in or buried within this layer. One of the most important items recovered from the excavation was a gold finger ring, which certainly was from well within this floor layer. It would have been tempting to associate it with similar items that formed the repertoire of Philip Henslowe's pawn business, for analysis shows that, despite the precious metal, it was of relatively cheap manufacture. Stylistically, however, it is likely to be somewhat earlier than the Rose.

Conclusions

The excavation of the Rose provided a unique encounter with popular culture: ancient and modern, theatrical and archaeological. Spatial encounters at the site in the sixteenth century revealed working relationships between actors, audience, management and everyday Londoners. The dimensions of the Rose's stage are small by modern standards, and the 'intimacy' with the audience was more pronounced. Modern actors who visited the excavations were generally impressed however, since plays performed at the Rose in the late sixteenth century are still being encountered throughout the world today within a greater variety of settings. Nevertheless, even the modern notion of 'acting in the round' has not necessarily recreated the intimacy of an audience recorded to have been far less sedate than today's. Beyond this encounter between (sixteenth-century) theatre and (twentieth-century) archaeology, a further one was then created between the archaeologists and an 'archaeological audience'. The audience of 1989 was, of course, denied an intimacy by health and safety concerns though they did display vigorous opinions on attitudes towards popular culture in the 1980s.

To compensate for the lack of buried chests containing lost folios, whose encounter was eagerly wished by the 'audience' of 1989, there were plenty of artefacts that informed us about actors, audience and anyone else in the vicinity of Bankside's 'theatre land' in the sixteenth and seventeenth centuries. It is only recently that material culture from London riverside sites has clarified the transition from defined medieval objects to those of the seventeenth century (cf Egan 2005). The Rose excavation placed much of this material into a spatial and functional context. Foremost amongst the artefacts was evidence for dress, though it cannot always be determined who, within the building, left such items for archaeologists to find later. Elizabethan actors are thought to have been clothed in splendour but the numerous fragments of, for example, copper lace (the purchase of which figures heavily in Henslowe's Diary) suggests a more gaudy but false splendour. Amongst the large number of shoes, dress accessories, textile fragments and even pieces of jewellery there was little indication of ostentatious wealth. The findings concur with analysis of documentary accounts of the sixteenth and seventeenth centuries that suggests a largely middle-class audience (Gurr 2004). The material also indicated the presence of men, women and children at the site in the sixteenth century. The twentieth-century 'audience' was almost entirely adult.

The many artefacts discovered at the site could be categorised as everyday items of 'popular culture'. Their presence within the site may even have been accidental but the theatrical context is significant. There was, as we have noted, an importance attached to costume and the presence of weapons in the stage area may suggest props. Items such as tobacco pipes, drinking vessels and even food remains were all at home within a theatre environment. The association of these finds with references to costume in contemporary play texts and particularly in Henslowe's Diary (eg, Orlin 2002) provides a more material encounter with popular (theatre) culture. There were few modern artefacts introduced on to the site: protest banners or television cameras were not deposited as lasting additions to the archaeology of twentieth-century Bankside. The popular culture expressed at the site was given a wider deposition over the airwaves by the media.

Acknowledgements

I am grateful to Dan Hicks and Angela Piccini for encouraging me to present a talk at CHAT 2003. I am also grateful to Mary Guzzy (formerly of Shakespeare & Co.) and Frank Hildy (University of Maryland), and to Geoff Egan and Dick Malt (MoLAS) for advice and encouragement on this written paper. Shortly after finishing the first draft of this paper, I read with sadness of the death of Bristol's father of drama Glynne Wickham. Glynne visited the Rose excavations in 1989 and I benefited from his erudite observations at the time.

References

Biddle, M. 1989. The Rose reviewed: A comedy of errors. *Antiquity* 63 (241), 753–60.

Bowsher, J.M.C. 1998. *The Rose Theatre: An Archaeological Discovery*. London: Museum of London.

Bowsher, J.M.C. 2000. Marlowe and the Rose. In J.A. Downie and J.T. Parnell (eds), *Constructing Christopher Marlowe*, 30–40. Cambridge: Cambridge University Press.

Bowsher, J.M.C. and Miller, P. forthcoming. *The Rose and the Globe – Playhouses of Tudor Bankside, Southwark: Excavations 1988–1991*. London: MoLAS / English Heritage.

Cerasano, S.P. 1989. Raising a playhouse from the dust. *Shakespeare Quarterly* 40 (4), 483–90.

Eccles, C. 1990. *The Rose Theatre*. London: Nick Hern Books.

Egan, G. 2005. *Material Culture in London in an Age of Transition. Tudor and Stuart Period Finds c 1450–c 1700 From Excavations at Riverside Sites in Southwark*. London: MoLAS Monograph series no. 19.

Foakes, R.A. 1985. Illustrations of the English Stage 1580 – 1642. London: Scolar Press.

Foakes, R.A. 1991. The discovery of the Rose: some implications. *Shakespeare Survey* 43, 141–48.

Foakes, R.A. 2002 (2nd edn). *Henslowe's Diary*. Cambridge: Cambridge University Press.

Gurr, A. 2004 (3rd edn). *Playgoing in Shakespeare's London*. Cambridge: Cambridge University Press.

Gurr, A. and Orrell, J. 1989. What the Rose can tell us. *Antiquity* 63, 421–29.

Hildy, F.J. 1990. Reconstructing Shakespeare's Theatre. In F.J. Hildy (ed.), *New Issues in the Reconstruction of Shakespeare's Theatre*, 1–37. New York: Peter Lang.

Hildy, F.J. 2004. Why Elizabethan spaces? *Theatre Symposium* 12, 98–120.

Orlin, L.C. 2002. Things With Little Social Life (Henslowe's Theatrical Properties and Elizabethan Household Fittings). In J.G. Harris and N. Korda, N (eds), *Staged Properties in Early Modern English Drama*, 99–128. Cambridge: Cambridge University Press.

Orrell, J. 1992. Nutshells at the Rose. *Theatre Research International* 17 (1), 8–14.

Pearson, M. and Shanks, M. 2001. *Theatre / Archaeology*. London: Routledge.

Phelan, P. 1997. Uncovered Rectums: Disinterring the Rose Theatre. In P. Phelan, *Mourning Sex: Performing Public Memories*, 73–94. London: Routledge.

Phelan, P. 1998. Playing Dead in Stone, or, When is a Rose not a Rose?. In E. Diamond (ed.), *Performance and Cultural Politics*, 65–88. Routledge: London.

Wilson, J. 1995. *The Archaeology of Shakespeare*. Stroud: Sutton

NOT SURFING BUT DROWNING.
HISTORIC ENVIRONMENT DATA ON THE INTERNET: ADDRESSING INTELLECTUAL BARRIERS TO ACCESS

Martin Newman

Introduction

What better example is there of popular culture than the internet? And at a time when archaeology has never been more popular it would seem to be the ideal way to make large amounts of data on the historic environment available to those who ultimately pay for it. However, there is the potential problem of social inclusiveness as archaeological and architectural data tends to be written by specialists for specialists, therefore making it unintelligible to the majority. In *Psychology of the Internet* Patricia Wallace makes the observation: 'Once an arcane communication medium for academics and researchers, it now sustains almost any human activity you can imagine from shopping to sex, from research to rebellion' (1999: 1).

This chapter is concerned with how the data produced by these academics, researchers and curators working in heritage can be made relevant to a wider audience. Can the same data and web site interface serve public, professional and academic audiences, satisfying all? And if so, how? This examination will look first at the theoretical issues concerned with intellectual barriers. It will then go on to examine the ways in which various projects around the country are addressing them in practice. As a Google search demonstrates, the internet is awash with archaeological information (20,100,000 web sites retrieved on 6 September 2005, an increase of more than 16 million on the figure of 3,470,000 web sites when this chapter was originally researched on 4 May 2003). As would be expected, this information has varying degrees of utility and originates from a wide range of sources: amateurs, professionals, universities, treasure hunters and new-age mystics, to name just a few. The *Publication User Needs Survey* (PUNS) recommended that archaeological archives be made available over the internet (Jones *et al* 2001), something that is acknowledged by English Heritage (Miles 2004). It would seem that for the heritage profession the internet represents the ideal way to publish information about archaeological and architectural sites to make data available to a wider audience. This, however, poses a problem of social exclusivity. Archaeological and architectural data is written largely by specialists for specialists, potentially making it unintelligible to the majority of users – those who ultimately pay for so much heritage research, either directly through taxation or indirectly due to costs of development control passed on to the consumer. These intellectual barriers need to be addressed.

Considerable work has been carried out on the publication of archaeological sites on the internet. For example Caroline Wickham-Jones, writing in *Internet Archaeology*, observes that 'the reader is led deeper and deeper into a maze of information. The writer provides the information and has a duty to make it as easy to understand as possible' (1999). There has also been progress on the dissemination of raw data from archaeological sites through the creation of internet databases such as that for Silchester (Clarke,

Fulford and Rains 2003), which is closely related to the material that this chapter is considering. Both relate to information held in databases that users can subsequently manipulate and interpret.

This chapter concentrates on databases that are wider in scope than an individual site: monument inventories, in particular those of the National Monuments Record (NMR) at English Heritage and the network of nearly one hundred locally based and predominantly local authority curated Historic Environment Records (HERs) in England (formerly known as Sites and Monuments Records). Other inventories exist specific to types of monument and period: The Gatehouse, which confines its information to Medieval Castles (http://homepage.mac.com/philipdavis/home. html), for example, or those resulting from specific projects such as the Survey of the Jewish Built Heritage. Arguably the biggest advances in addressing accessibility issues have been made by public bodies due to the requirements of funding institutions such as the Heritage Lottery Fund, which has aided the majority of HER outreach projects. HERs in England contain records of one-and-a-half million monuments (EH 2003b: 8). The range of material they contain is very broad, both regarding typology and historical contexts: the 2002 content survey showed nearly half of all HERs covering paleoenvironmental sites and 74% recording monuments up to the present day (Newman 2002).

HERs were created primarily for the purpose of planning and development control by local authorities, the first being Oxfordshire in the late 1960s (EH 2003a). Increasingly, they have also become a public record providing services for researchers from the local amateur to the postgraduate student. HERs have had web presences for years: web-based advice was provided in the first edition of the HER *Manual Informing the Future of the Past: Guidelines for SMRs* (Fernie and Gilman 2000: E7). This information will be expanded in the 2nd edition currently in preparation (Gilman and Newman forthcoming), which will itself be an internet publication.

Utilising funds from the National Lottery, the Heritage Lottery Fund (HLF) was set up in 1994 to provide grants to heritage-related projects in the United Kingdom. In 1999, a decision was made to support applications from HERs for improved access through outreach programmes, details of which were published in *Unlocking Britain's Past* (HLF 1999). Since then the number of HERs going online, and the depth of content included, has increased dramatically. However, Paul Gilman recently and quite astutely observed:

> Only a tiny fraction of SMRs have been able to apply for HLF funding…this does not, on the whole indicate a lack of interest in making SMR information more widely available. Rather it is a testament to the lack of resources available to SMRs to support them in the long process of preparing and submitting applications. (Gilman 2004)

This could soon change through the HLF's introduction of Project Planning Grants, which enable HERs to apply for funding to carry out specialist studies such as audience research and to prepare their main bids under the Heritage Grants Scheme (HLF 2002).

HERs are supported by the National Monuments Record (NMR) at English Heritage under the lead role that it was assigned by Government in 1989 whilst part of the former Royal Commission on the Historic Monuments of England (RCHME). As part of this lead role the NMR runs a programme of HER audits and manages the HER Forum, which consists of an email discussion list, twice-yearly meetings and a six-monthly publication *Historic Environment Record News*. The NMR also advises HERs on a range of areas, including data standards and database design and funding applications. The HLF requires that HERs preparing bids for improved access consult the NMR prior to submission (Fraser and Newman forthcoming; EH and ALGAO 2005). Indeed, the NMR advised on the projects used as examples in this chapter.

As well as advising projects in HERs, the NMR is addressing online access via a 'virtual reality' front-end. The NMR's Scottish equivalent has already been made available on the internet by its parent body, the Royal Commission on the Ancient and Historical Monuments of Scotland (RCAHMS). Whereas, the National Monuments Record of Scotland (NMRS) dataset contains details of archaeological sites, monuments, buildings and maritime sites in Scotland, together with an index to the drawings, manuscripts and photographs in its collections. Since going live in 1998 (www.rcahms.gov.uk), CANMORE searches have reached 50,000 (Murray 2004).

So what's the problem?

As part of its funding the HLF expects HERs to address barriers to access. These can come in a variety of forms: barriers created by disabilities are apparent and areas such as accessibility of offices and websites are covered by strict guidelines. Considerable emphasis is also placed on cultural barriers within the context of social inclusion. Often overlooked are intellectual barriers to access. Cultural barriers such as ethnicity and social grouping can create barriers to an interest in aspects of heritage, but the language used can also be a comprehension barrier to some once interest has been established. This is particularly relevant in the context of the supply of data on the historic environment via the internet. Data in HERs and other systems, such as those maintained by English Heritage, have been written by specialists for specialists and designed for use in planning and development control and academic research with little consideration of the general public or non-specialist user. Take the following section from the description of a listed church in Northamptonshire:

> Trefoil-head south door to right of centre. 3-stage buttress between windows, one has circular stone dial. Shallow gabled roof with castellated ashlar

Figure 21. Keys to the Past record for Bamburgh Castle with glossary definition for keep. Courtesy of Durham and Northumberland County Councils.

parapets, corner pinnacle and 2 gargoyles. East elevation has twin gables of chancel and lady chapel. Two 5-light ogee-head windows with reticulated tracery and niches above. Chancel window has cluster shafts. 3-stage buttresses between window. Castellated ashlar parapet with pinnacles. North elevation of Lady chapel of 2-window range with 5-light window with intersecting tracery and cusping to left and 3-light ogee-head window with reticulated tracery to right, both have carved label stops (DoE 1971: 26).

This illustrates two of the most common problems: readability and the use of specialist terminology. Descriptions such as these make difficult reading for adults and are completely unsuitable for schoolchildren. This is a problem that does not concern only monument inventories. Based on user experiences of Çatalhoyuk's website, Ian Hodder observes:

> some people are excluded from the website because of the style or rhetoric used. For example the website is very much aimed at adults…there are dangers that the internet will simply translate old forms of elite knowledge into new forms, increasingly excluding the un-networked (1999).

The example from the RCAHMS mentioned earlier has also experienced problems relating to content:

> Putting the NMRS database online through CANMORE has exposed and highlighted the inconsistencies which, although of little handicap

to experienced and trained users that can follow up their research, lack the mediation required for the majority of users (Murray 2004).

Another common problem is effective searching. Retrieval on specialist systems is often complicated and even free-text retrieval requires knowledge of complex terminology: you have to know what something is called in order to find it.

The HLF can require HERs making bids to improve access by undertaking an HER Audit to ensure the quality of the record they are being asked to support. Quality is, however, a difficult concept to define. For HER Audits this is taken to be the 'fitness for purpose'. However fitness for purpose to support planning and development control differs from fitness to provide a public service (Newman 2003). Yet widespread interest in both historic environment information and access via the internet has been demonstrated through HER audience research.

Solutions

Another example of the problem of intellectual access is apparent in the Somerset HER's record for the Gate House to the Bishops Palace in Wells. It includes very detailed textual description with phrases such as '2 light mullioned window openings with cusped lights under dripmoulds, moulded stone door frame with 4 centred head' (www. somerset.gov.uk/heritage). This may not mean much to the lay reader. Part of Somerset HER's solution is to produce an online glossary describing technical terms,

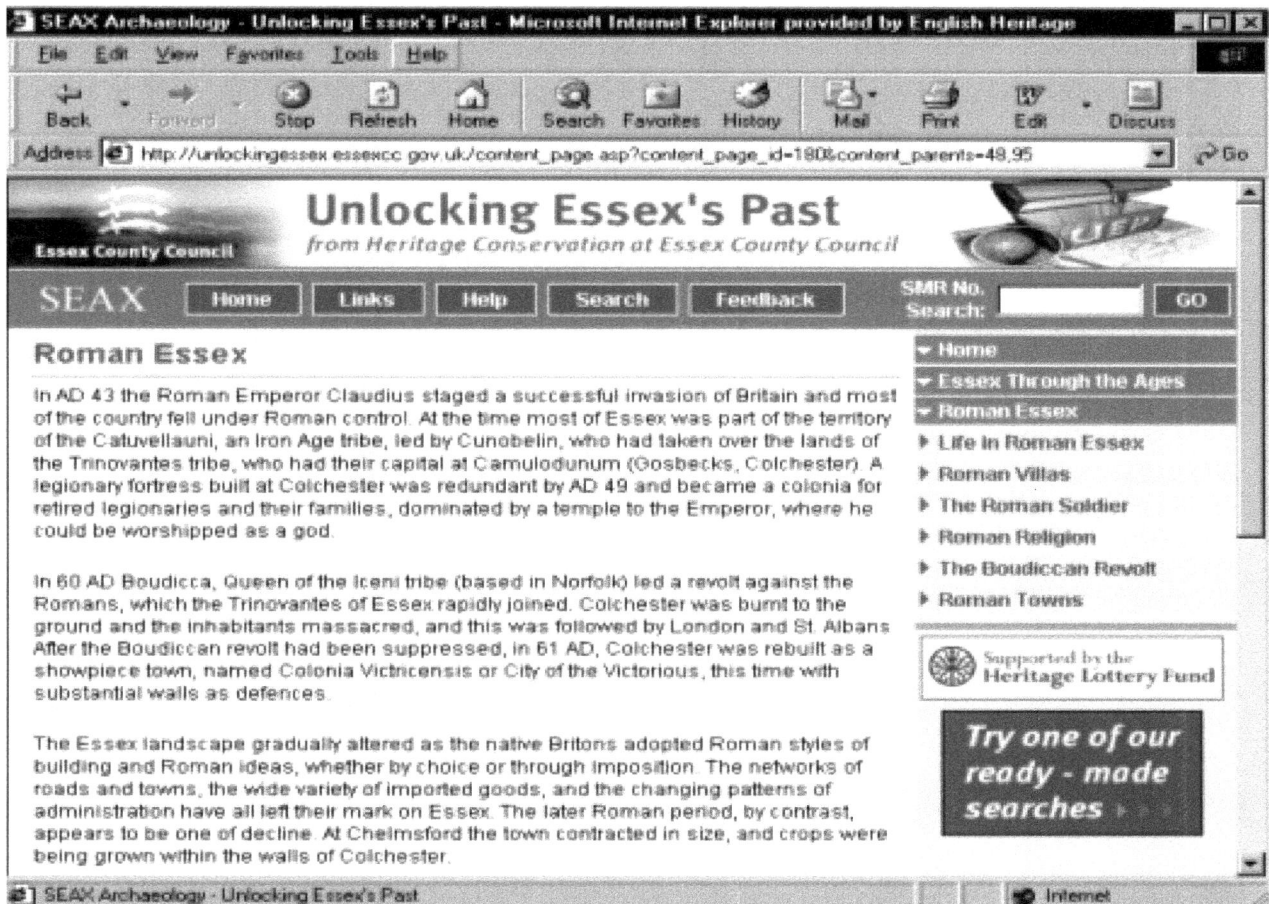

Figure 22. One of the themed essays on the SEAX system. Courtesy of Essex County Council

such as 'dendrochronology', in use in the record. A more time-consuming method is to re-cast descriptions, writing them in 'plain' English. This has been adopted by Durham and Northumberland in their *Keys to the Past* site (www. keystothepast.info), combining it with embedded links to terms in a glossary (see Figure 21).

Audience research indicates wide interest in themed essays on places or topics using sites from the HER as examples. Essex's SEAX system has taken on this approach with essays such as the one below (Figure 22) on *Roman Essex* with links to more detailed essays such as *Life in Roman Essex* and *Roman Villas* (http://unlockingessex.essexcc. gov.uk). This is an approach that has proved particularly popular with school teachers.

Retrieval

As mentioned above, retrieval on specialist systems is often complicated and requires specialist training or knowledge of complex terminology. The NMR and the majority of HERs rely on complicated reference-data structures, such as thesauri, for retrieval. Thesauri are used in many places in HER databases to index records under classifications such as monument types, building materials, maritime craft types and artefact types. The most commonly used is the English Heritage *Thesaurus of Monument Types* (English Heritage 1995), shown in Figure 23.

Thesauri are very powerful indexing and retrieval tools, but are also very complex. They enable a recorder to index at a very precise level, such as 'base cruck house', and retrieve at a very broad level, such as 'house' or 'dwelling'. To use thesauri for retrieval requires a level of understanding of both the structure and the terms they contain. Those unfamiliar with either of these will find their use problematic.

Where this is not such a problem is in locational searching. Audience research consistently shows that the 'what's in my village/town?' question is one of the most common enquiries made. As part of its HLF project, for example, Somerset has adopted a very simple, fast and effective map-based point-click-and-zoom approach for searching its HER via the internet (www.somerset.gov.uk/heritage). Geographic Information Systems (GIS) are currently in use in 88% of English HERs (Newman 2002). GIS provides a powerful tool for the display and retrieval of HER information. As Diana Murray (writing about the Scottish NMR) states: 'GIS frees data from the tyranny of the database' (Murray 2004).

Returning to text-based retrieval, key words can be used either to search all fields or, as in the Archaeology Data Service's (ADS) Archsearch (http://ads.ahds.ac.uk), a particular field, but this can lack the subtlety of structured indexing. Synonyms are common in English: if someone searches for 'cow byre' when the approved indexing term is 'cow house' s/he will not be able to retrieve the

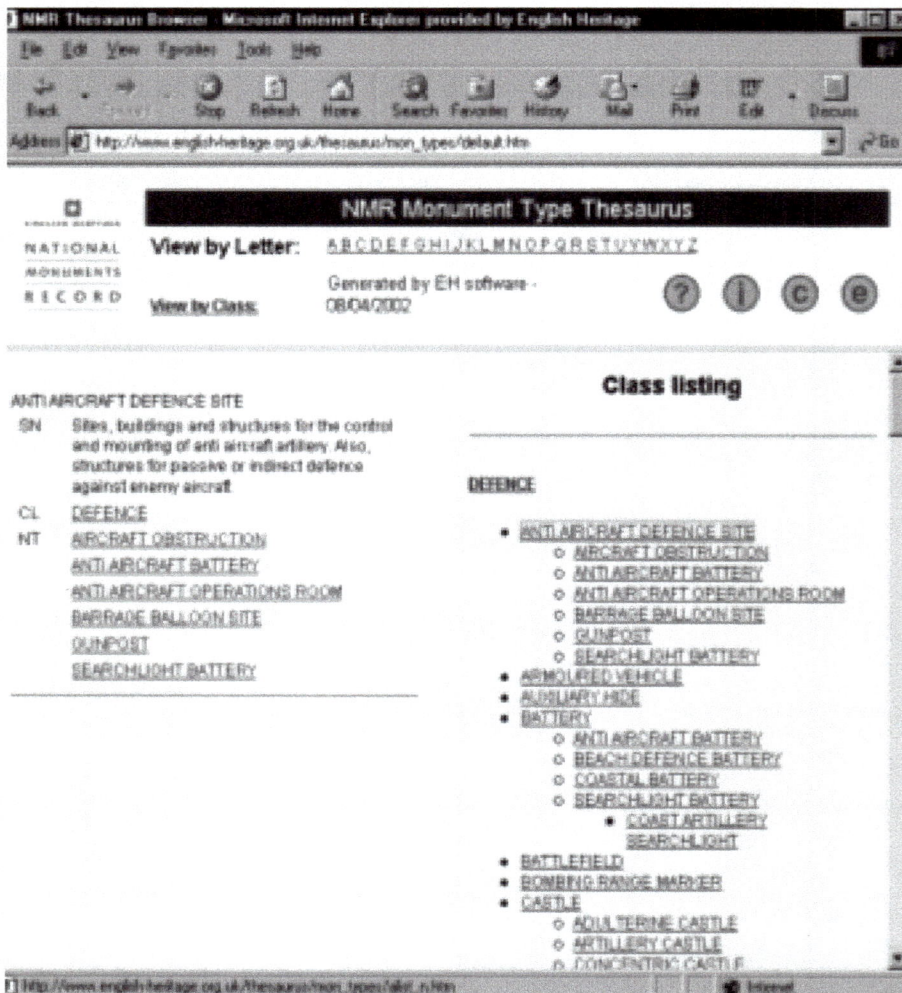

Figure 23. The Thesaurus of Monument Types.

Figure 24. PastScape searching options.

required records. This conceptual problem in the design of relational databases can be addressed by the use of thesauri. Similarly, regarding homographs a common example would be searching for 'banks' and retrieving earthworks when the user is instead interested in the architecture of financial buildings. Some knowledge is, therefore, still required. The ADS hosts data for a number of HERs and as its remit is to serve the academic community retrieval is not as problematic as it can be for those sites aiming at a wider audience. Indexing using structured reference data may be the norm for inventories but requires a level of understanding for retrieval that lay readers do not possess. Two recent projects from EH's NMR are seeking to address this.

PastScape (www.pastscape.org.uk) is an interface utilising graphics with virtual reality animation for searching heritage data sets based around a simple 'what,' 'where' and 'when' approach. A virtual reality entrance takes the user into the National Monuments Record Centre in Swindon to a desk where the searching mechanism is displayed on a PC monitor. This displays the 'where', 'what' and 'when' questions (see Figure 24). The 'what' uses only the top terms from the *Thesaurus of Monument Types* with narrow terms automatically included in the query. A time line and a map of England provide the selection for 'when' and 'where' (Pringle 2000). PastScape now searches the NMR's complete monument inventory although some of the virtual reality aspects have now been removed from the site in order to ensure effective site response for all users, irrespective of the speed of their internet connection.

The Heritage Illustrated Thesaurus (HITITE) is a proof-of-concept system developed with funding from the European Commission's Information Society Technologies fifth framework programme (www.heritage-thesauri.org.uk). It adds images to terms from the *Thesaurus of Monument Types*. As well as allowing users to view monument examples it allows them to enter attributes of a site they

have seen, for example shape, material and size (Figure 25).

HITITE then displays a series of pictures illustrating attributes characteristic of the concepts represented by the terms in the thesaurus. This allows users to identify the type of monument they have seen (Figure 26).

As this is still at the proof-of-concept stage it uses just 500 terms out of the 6,500 in the *Monuments Type Thesaurus*. It has been tested very successfully on a wide range of potential users with particularly high approval rating from school-age children (Carlisle 2002; Byrne and Pringle 2003: 3).

The use of 'virtual reality' in heritage presentation is a fast-growing area, with considerable scope for improving the presentation of information from heritage databases over the internet. An interesting project using the data from the Rijksmuseum in Amsterdam has experimented with using techniques from the electronic gaming sector. This approach is interesting as the project evidences the assertion that 'In a time when human attention span seems to grow ever shorter, computer games are able to keep people focussed for hours' (Nack and Hardman 2004). The benefits of harnessing this approach to keep attention focussed on heritage content are obvious, particularly for the themed essays based on HER data described earlier. There is also the potential use of virtual reality to enhance records for individual monuments in inventories. This has been demonstrated by the virtual reconstructions of sites such as Tintern Abbey and Anne Hathaway's Cottage created for Cadw: Welsh Historic Monuments and the Shakespeare Birthplace Trust respectively (Haig 2003).

Conclusion

The quantity of data on the historic environment being made available online is on the increase. Through the audience research incorporated in their bids for HLF funding and

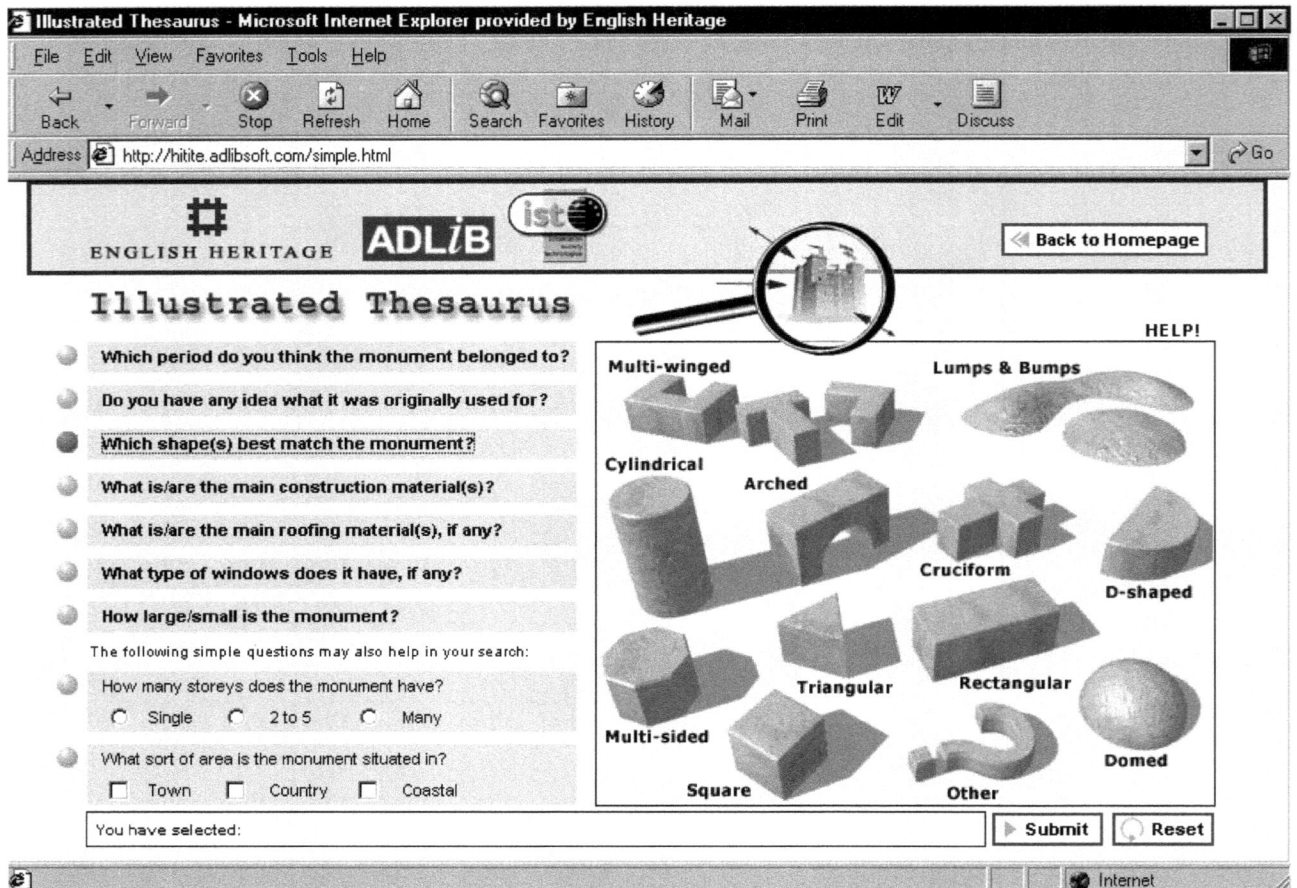

Figure 25. HITITE, options for searching by shape.

the subsequent use figures required to show the success of projects, HERS have demonstrated that a wide-ranging audience exists for heritage data. There remain issues of the intellectual barriers to access created by the nature of the data itself and the fact it is being made available to audiences for which the date was not originally intended. Additionally, the systems used are not sufficiently user-friendly to be made generally available.

However, those HERs that have gone online with financial support from the HLF demonstrate that these problems are not insurmountable. Recasting of data, glossaries and themed essays have all contributed to improving accessibility of these records. Further developments in information technology, including the creation of simplified interfaces that interact with the user through virtual reality, are likely to enhance content for individual monument records and themed narratives. These have the potential to help users remain engaged, whilst delivering information. Virtual reality also has the potential to assist with searching, something that has been demonstrated by parts of the recent HITITE and PastScape initiatives from the NMR. These have also suggested a possible way forward to simplify the retrieval of heritage information for non-specialist users.

The HLF's support for improved access to HERs, including placing them online, has been a success with 11 HERs now making data available online. In an overview published in the Institute of Field Archaeologist Yearbook, this was highlighted as one of the HLF's achievements by its Director of Operations (Johnson 2004).

As for the future, in its response to the recent Government consultation on the future of HERs, English Heritage suggested there was a need for an historic environment portal. This will contain mechanisms for searching and retrieving data from a variety of heritage databases, including the HERs and the NMR (EH 2003c). English Heritage's Chief Executive Simon Thurley reiterated a commitment to this in The Institute of Field Archaeologist Yearbook:

> we consider there is a need to provide seamless access to national and local records on a local, regional and national level and that the best way to achieve this is though a Historic Environment Portal with appropriate mediation and interpretive material for both specialists and more popular access (2004).

Intelligible heritage data that is suitable for all and provided via online inventories is achievable and becoming a reality. The introduction to this chapter referred to Patricia Wallace's *Psychology of the Internet* and in conclusion this chapter ends with another quotation: 'new technologies have incredible power to shape human behaviour and social structures' (1999: 13). Making heritage data available via the internet will play an important role in education, understanding and the enjoyment of heritage. It has the potential to change people's attitudes to heritage and the historic sites in their environment, and thus contribute to preservation through increased awareness within local communities. The greater use of these records will also help them to justify their running costs at a time when local government is continually looking to cut expenditure.

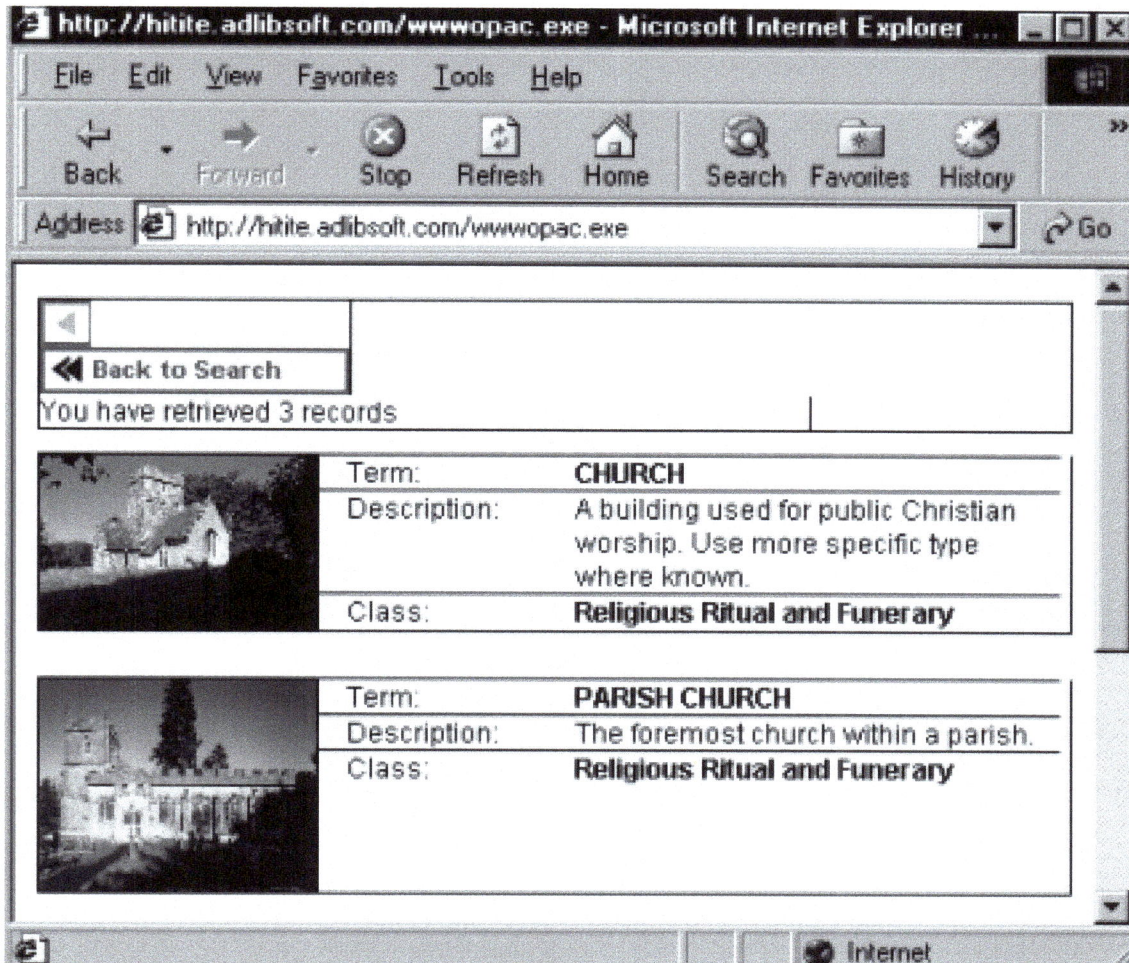

Figure 26. HITITE, results.

Through such expanded recording and use these inventories have the potential to become true Historic Environment Records.

Acknowledgments

I would like to thank Durham, Essex, Northumberland and Somerset County Councils for allowing me to use their HLF projects as examples and include images from their websites. I would also like to thank Edmund Lee and Matthew Stiff for their comments on both the original conference presentation and this paper. I am grateful to my colleagues at English Heritage involved in the PastScape and HITITE projects for allowing me to talk and write about their work, in particular Kieran Byrne, Philip Carlisle and Mike Pringle.

References

Archaeology Data Service. http://ads.ahds.ac.uk. (1 September 2006).

Byrne, K. and Pringle, M. 2003. A User Friendly Future for Online Information. In M. Newman (ed.), *Historic Environment Record News, Issue1*, 3–4. Swindon: English Heritage.

Carlisle, P. 2002. The Heritage Illustrated Thesaurus. An Online Resource, for Monument Identification (HITITE). In J. Hemsley, V. Cappellini and G. Stanke (eds), *Electronic Imaging, the Visual Arts and Beyond 2002 Conference Proceedings*, 167–73. Vasari Ltd.

Clarke, A., Fulford, M. and Rains, M. 2003. Nothing to Hide – Online Database Publication and the Silchester Town Life Project. In M. Doerr and A. Sarris (eds), CAA 2002, *The Digital Heritage of Archaeology*, 401–04. Hellenic Ministry of Culture, Athens.

Department of Environment. 1971. *30th List of Buildings of Special Architectural or Historic Interest, District of East Northamptonshire*. London: DoE.

Durham County Council and Northumberland County Council, www.keystothepast.info (1 September 2005).

English Heritage. 1995. *Thesaurus of Monument Types*. Swindon: English Heritage.

English Heritage. 2003a. *Historic Environment Records, A Guide for Users*. Swindon: English Heritage.

English Heritage. 2003b. *Heritage Counts 2003. The State of England's Historic Environment*. London: English Heritage.

English Heritage. 2003c. *English Heritage response to the DCMS's consultation on the Future of Historic Environment Records*. London: English Heritage.

English Heritage and ALGAO. 2005. *Unlocking Our Past*. Swindon: English Heritage.

English Heritage. www.heritage-thesauri.org.uk. (1 September 2005, no longer available).

English Heritage. www.pastscape.org.uk. (1 September 2005).

Essex County Council. http://unlockingessex.essexcc.gov. uk. (1 September 2005).

Fernie, K. and Gilman, P. (eds). 2000. *Informing the Future of the Past: Guidelines for SMRs*. Swindon: English Heritage.

Fraser, D. and Newman, M. forthcoming. The British Archaeological Database. In J. Hunter and I. Ralston (eds), *Archaeological Resource Management in the UK: an Introduction, 2nd edition*. Stroud: Sutton Publishing Ltd/Institute of Field Archaeologists.

Gilman, P. 2004. Sites and Monuments Records and Historic Environment Records in England: is Cinderella finally going to the Ball? *Internet Archaeology* 15, http://intarch.ac.uk/journal/issue15/gilman_index.html (1 September 2005).

Gilman, P. and Newman, M. (eds). Forthcoming. *Informing the Future of the Past: Guidelines for HERs*. London: English Heritage.

Haig, R. 2003. Virtual Heritage – Making Virtual Reality Work. In M. Newman (ed.). *Historic Environment Record News, Issue 2*, 5–6. London: English Heritage.

Heritage Lottery Fund. 1999. *Unlocking Britain's Past, a Strategic Framework for Support from the Heritage Lottery Fund for Sites and Monuments Records*. London: Heritage Lottery Fund.

Heritage Lottery Fund. 2002. *Heritage Grants, Grants of £50,000 or More* (application pack). London: Heritage Lottery Fund.

Hodder, I. 1999. Archaeology and Global Information Systems. *Internet Archaeology* 6, http://intarch.ac.uk/journal/issue6/hodder/index.html (1 September 2005).

Johnson, S. 2004. How the Heritage Lottery Fund Can Help. In *Institute of Field Archaeologists Yearbook and Directory*. Institute of Field Archaeologists, 23–25.

Jones, S., MacSween, A., Jeffrey, S., Morris, R. and Heyworth, M. 2001. *From the Ground Up. The Publication of Archaeological Projects, a User Needs Survey*. York: Council for British Archaeology.

Miles, D. 2004. Preface: digital dissemination and archiving. *Internet Archaeology* 15, http://intarch.ac.uk/journal/issue15/preface.html (1 September 2005).

Murray, D. 2004, National inventories: from catalogues to computers. *Internet Archaeology* 15, http://intarch.ac.uk/journal/issue15/murray_index.html (1 September 2005).

Nack, F. and Hardman, L. 2004. Generating Multimedia Presentation: It's All in the Game. In Kunz, P. (ed.), *European Research Consortium for Informatics and Mathematics News*, 24–25. ERCIM EEIG, www.ercim.org/publication/Ercim_News/enw57/EN57.pdf (1 September 2005).

Newman, M. 2002. *SMR Content and Computing Survey 2002*. Swindon: English Heritage.

Newman, M. 2003. Auditing Heritage Data –Ensuring Quality. In M. Doerr and A. Sarris (eds), CAA *2002, The Digital Heritage of Archaeology*, 385–89. Athens: Hellenic Ministry of Culture.

Pringle, M. 2000. Using Virtual Reality to Improve Public Access to Heritage Databases over the Internet. In S. Zoran and T. Veljanovski (eds), *Computing Archaeology for Understanding the Past, CAA 2000*, British Archaeological Reports International Series, 329–37Oxford: BAR Publishing.

Somerset County Council. www.somerset.gov.uk/heritage, (1 September 2005).

Royal Commission on the Ancient and Historical Monuments of Scotland, www.rcahms.gov.uk. (1 September 2005).

Thurley, S. 2004. The Heritage Protection Review. In *Institute of Field Archaeologists Yearbook and Directory*, 19–21. Institute of Field Archaeologists.

Wallace, P. 1999. *The Psychology of the Internet*. Cambridge: Cambridge University Press.

Wickham-Jones, C. 1999. Excavation publication and the internet. *Internet Archaeology* 7, http://intarch.ac.uk/journal/issue7/wickham/index.html (1 September 2005).

Concrete Islands

Paul Graves-Brown

All fixed, fast frozen relations, with their train of ancient and venerable prejudices and opinions, are swept away, all new-formed ones become antiquated before they can ossify. All that is solid melts into air, all that is holy is profaned, and man is at last compelled to face with sober senses his real condition of life and his relations with his kind.

(Marx and Engels 1848)

My aims in this essay are twofold. The first is to analyse a modern shopping centre on the basis of a landscape/ observational study treating the site as if it were an historic or prehistoric landscape. In other words, my aim is to concentrate on what one can see of how the site has been laid out, and how it is used and transgressed by its customers. I am not particularly concerned with what people actually do *in* the shops, a topic which has been covered elsewhere (Miller 1998; Miller *et al* 1998), but rather how they access and use the site as a whole, and how this is affected by the design and landscaping. Secondly, and in some senses of related concern, I want to stress the ephemeral nature of such places.

The main focus of this study is the Trostre Park retail centre on the outskirts of Llanelli, Carmarthenshire, Wales. I have been observing and studying this site since 1997, both as an archaeologist and as a frequent customer. In the past few years, Trostre has undergone significant changes, even though it has existed for only some 15 years. To construct a site context I used a fairly standard methodology for desk-top assessment (Institute of Field Archaeologists 2001), yet it proved difficult to document its history and development, or, indeed, to keep pace with the ongoing erasure of that history. That which, at first sight, appeared to be enduring, monumental, has proved to be highly ephemeral. The all-too concrete island can melt into air before our eyes.

Trostre: the background

Trostre Park is situated on the eastern edge of Llanelli, adjacent to the main road to Swansea, and to the bypass that links Llanelli to the M4 motorway. Although an 'out of town' development, the site is surrounded on two sides by the town itself and by the satellite villages of Dafen and Llwynhendy. Historically, the site began as marshland, a *pill* or minor estuary at the mouth of the Dafen river as it flows into the larger Lougher estuary. Although there is limited documentation, it is probable that at least some of the site was affected by early nineteenth-century industrial activity along the north-east side of the Lougher estuary. This area has been heavily exploited for coal and was the location of one of the earliest canals in Britain. The remains of Newcomen and Watt engine houses, and of the Glynea coal pit can still be seen in the vicinity (Dyfed Sites and Monuments Record). The site was developed before UK planning law required archaeological evaluation, and an enquiry with the local planning authority also drew a blank. Since the development took place prior to the 1996 reorganisation of local government in Wales, documentation of the planning process, carried out under the old Llanelli District Council had, I was told, gone into a 'deep archive'. I took this to mean that the documentation probably no longer existed. Hence, there is no available documentation on the construction of the park to indicate the initial developers and architects. Enquiries directed to Tesco (the main retailer on the site) also drew a blank.

The retail park is dominated by the large Tesco supermarket, which has undergone significant extension and alteration. There are a number of other large stores including a 'DIY' hardware store (which has undergone several changes of ownership); several electrical stores (Currys, Comet); carpet stores, shoe shops and a large Halfords motor-parts outlet, also now re-developed. There is also a kind of sub-development on the east side of the access road to the main site, consisting of a McDonald's drive thru, a Blockbuster video store and a Texaco petrol station. At the time of writing, a new area, styled 'Trostre Park South' has opened, including a massive new B&Q DIY hardware store. These developments highlight what I see as one of the fundamental methodological problems of doing contemporary archaeology (see Graves-Brown forthcoming a). Since delivering my paper on this site at the CHAT 2003 conference, the site has undergone, and is undergoing, continual change. The contemporary archaeologist is in the condition of Benjamin's 'angel of history' (1970; see also McLuhan 1967; Winston 1986): we advance blindly into the future, continually trying to understand and interpret an ever-changing present.

Entire unto itself…

In *The Concrete Island* (1974) J.G. Ballard tells the tale of Maitland, a driver who crashes his car onto a large motorway traffic island and is subsequently marooned there. The novel can be seen as part of a trilogy, formed with *Crash* (1973) and *High-Rise* (1975) in which Ballard explores the alienated spaces of modern urban landscapes. I believe it is not too far fetched to regard Trostre as such an island, albeit one that is more frequently visited than those of Maitland or Crusoe. Such islands are formed not by expanses of ocean but by the tacit spatial exclusions that surround and compose them. A shopping centre is, functionally, just a set of buildings, roads and car parks. These create non-spaces that are analogous to Gould and Lewontin's (1979) 'Spandrels of San Marco' – epi-phenomena of functional elements that then take on a life of their own. Thus in the case described by Gould and Lewontin, the spaces between the arches in St Mark's Venice are a by-product of the arch form, but then become the locus for decorative expression.

Trostre, for example, is surrounded by busy roads, farmland and industry. Although on the very edge of Llanelli it has no historic connection with the town. It represents a focus of consumer activity surrounded by a kind of no-

Figure 27. Approach to Trostre Park on foot (video still).

Figure 28. The 'Market Cross' Trostre Park (video still).

mans-land. Virtually all users, staff and goods arrive and depart by road, emphasising the physical dislocation of the site – it does not matter whether it is 100m or 10 km from the nearest habitation. Contrast this with the typical urban shopping area, which will be central and merge imperceptibly into the surrounding residential area.

The physical isolation of the Trostre site is emphasised if one attempts to approach on foot (see Figure 27). From my home it is necessary to cross a busy dual carriageway and two other busy roads on the large roundabout at the entrance to the site. There are no pedestrian crossings and in many places no footpaths. The pedestrian must swim against the tide of traffic to reach the safety of the Tesco car park. The exclusion of pedestrians is typical of shopping 'malls' (see Morris 1988). Indeed, in one case a mall in Buffalo was sued by the parents of a teenager who died trying to cross a busy highway to reach the mall: the owners of the site had refused access to buses (Underhill 2004).

Of course, the attraction of such places is convenience. One can rapidly access the site, park, shop and leave – in contrast to the more complex spatial negotiations needed to use a town centre. Yet this apparent simplification of the negotiation of social space generates some strange effects.

Liminal spaces

Obviously the aim of the retailers is to get customers into their shops as smoothly as possible. Yet they need to manage the periphery of the site and create an overall impression that welcomes. The Tesco at Trostre was originally loosely designed in the 'Essex Barn' style originated in 1978 at the ASDA store, South Woodham Ferrers, Essex (Morrison 2003: 279–80). This now familiar style features sloping terracotta tiled roofs around the periphery of the building and usually a faux clock tower on the top, although these features are purely decorations applied to what is essentially a large steel warehouse. What is perhaps unusual about Trostre is that the stylistic theme extends around two sides of the entire courtyard created in conjunction with the other stores on the site (see Figure 29). Moreover, until recently the theme of a traditional marketplace was echoed in a kind of market cross structure which stood on the edge of the car park (see Figure 28). A true folly, this structure had no practical function, which may explain why it has now been demolished (of which more below).

The purpose of this styling is twofold. Firstly, as Morrison (2003: 279–80) suggests, such designs were intended to

appease planning authorities and local residents who might object to plain undecorated steel warehouses. Moreover, the design evokes a familiar, almost bucolic image of the traditional marketplace, a comfortable trope that serves to offset the stark alienated nature of the space (see Miller *et al* 1988). Here it is interesting to note that Morrison's supermarkets apply the same principle to the interior of their stores – invoking a kind of covered market atmosphere.

Nevertheless, I suggest the car parks and surroundings of these stores remain liminal if not interstitial (see Goss 1993), and as Douglas states: 'danger lies in transitional states simply because transition is neither one state nor the other' (1966: 97). The parking areas and particularly their surroundings are a non-place where normal social rules and practices are in doubt. Like Crusoe's island they appear to belong to no one. Nor are they analogous to any familiar social milieu, a situation underlined by the fact that until recently such areas were not covered by successive Road Traffic Acts, and that there remains some legal ambiguity as to whether a private car park is to be treated as a road.

In order to offset this, Trostre, like other such developments, provides a series of covered ways that lead from the car parks to the shops (see Figure 29). These represent safe passage from the stores and it is no accident that disabled and parent and child parking is placed adjacent to these covered ways. Functionally, these loosely echo the Corridoio Vasario built for the Medici to move between their Florentine palaces unmolested (Boddy 1992).

On the periphery of the site, liminality shades into exclusion, but this is not accomplished by hard boundaries such as fences or walls, but rather by the use of physical landscaping, trees and other planting.

The history of the roundabout

In order to understand these peripheral areas, we need to look at the history of road development. One key element in roads history (at least in the UK) is the roundabout, which can stand as a particular case of all non-spaces (see Figure 30). The first roundabout or gyratory system was Columbus Circle in New York (*c* 1905), closely followed by Eugene Hennard's plan for the Place D'Etoile in Paris (the junction formed around the Arch de Triomphe). In the UK the first roundabout was created as part of the development of Letchworth Garden City in 1910. For our purposes this is significant. The principle architects of Letchworth and Hampstead Garden Suburb were Barry

Figure 29. Covered way at Trostre Park Tesco also showing 'Essex Barn' styling.

Parker and Raymond Unwin. Both had been influenced by John Ruskin and William Morris and were adherents of the Arts and Crafts movement of the late nineteenth century. Hence it is no surprise that their approach to urban planning was essentially that of a landscape garden. Interestingly, the Letchworth roundabout was not intended to exclude pedestrians, but to facilitate the crossing of the junction. Whilst this aspect of roundabout design is now lost, the landscaping approach to such non-spaces continues to this day.

The key point lies in how traditional informal landscape gardens of the eighteenth and nineteenth centuries were intended to be used. Landscaped areas were treated as vistas to be observed from designated paths (or roads/car parks) but were not to be entered. The message was 'keep

Figure 30. Typical landscaped roundabout. Yspyty, Bynea.

Figure 31. Shoppers crossing the main Trostre Park access road between Tesco and the drive thru McDonalds.

off the grass'. This relates to the binary opposition between nature and culture (Miller *et al* 1998). Landscaped areas can operate as socially ambiguous and hence dangerous, wild places. They are islands (within islands), and/or a littoral of wilderness, which either encompass or are interspersed within the cultivated, controlled areas which people are invited to enter.

Islands turned inside out

The conception of the concrete island, has, however, taken a further twist, beginning in the US. This comes about with the development of the enclosed mall or shopping centre. Whilst, as Underhill (2004) points out, the enclosed market has a history dating back to the famous markets of Cairo and Damascus, the modern mall originates in the post-World War Two suburbs of the US. The first true mall was constructed at Edina Minneapolis in 1956. Underhill says:

> The shopping center's innovation was to turn things around, so that the stores faced not the road but one another-a circling of the suburban wagons, so to speak, now surrounded by (rather than facing) the parking spots. It was a small step from there to placing a roof over the whole thing. That history, and the fateful turning away from the eyes of the outside world, steered the mall to the state in which we find it. (2004: 19)

In its basic form, then, the enclosed shopping centre is a concrete island turned inside out. It presents an uncompromising exterior. As Underhill describes it:

> Next time you're at a mall...stroll around the perimeter of the place. It will be one of the most joyless promenades you will ever make. You'll be very alone out there, on a narrow strip of sidewalk, assuming there is a sidewalk...with maybe a security guard to keep you campany....nobody is going to pay much attention to a mall parking lot. All the action is on the inside. (2004: 21)

Unlike Trostre Park, the enclosed shopping centre will generally make little or no allowance for external appearances (see also Goss 1993; Morris 1988). Although some of the larger 'super malls' such as the Trafford Centre outside Manchester do make some considerable effort in their external architecture (see Morrison 2003: 290) the essential point is that such places have put the outside on the inside. Like the Nazi cosmology of the hollow Earth, the shopping mall is conceptually a closed universe in an infinity of nothingness (see Moorcock 1969; Symmes 1887; Teed and Morrow 1899).

In this situation the informal landscape of the open shopping centre gives way to a formality which probably owes its origins to the fabled hanging gardens of Babylon and more particularly to the courtyard gardens of Persia and the Arabic world. Although in some cases the internal 'universe' is more elaborated – as at the West Edmonton Mall in Canada (the world's largest), which includes the 'Submarine Lake' (complete with a full sized sailing ship), the 'World Water Park' and the 'Galaxyland Amusement Park'. This centre, along with Mall of America, Bloomington, Minnesota, takes the shopping centre to the beyond, as a tourist attraction in its own right – the shopping equivalent of Disneyland (Goss 1993; Sorkin 1992). In other cases, formality can go to extremes. The King Centre in Watts, Los Angeles was explicitly designed by architects Haagen Development on the principles of Bentham's Panopticon (Davis 1992).

Transgression

As the earlier quote from Underhill suggests, even walking around the outside of a shopping mall may be perceived as a transgressive act. Similarly, the 'wild' landscapes distributed around the outdoor shopping centre deter the shopper from entering. Yet, as discussed above, the pedestrian cannot even enter the Trostre site without walking on the grass, since, as with Underhill's mall, there are no pavements to walk on. Moreover, as I have described, the original Trostre centre features two

Figure 32. Parc Tawe Two seen from Parc Tawe One. Note the erosion on the central reservation.

separate 'islets' adjacent to the main bulk: the nearest consists of a drive thru McDonald's, the most distant a Blockbuster video store. Anyone shopping at Tesco is left with a conundrum. In order to visit McDonald's s/he must either cross a landscaped area, cross the main access road and then find a gap in McDonald's hedge, or get back in the car to travel a mere 50m. To get to Blockbuster yet another road must be crossed and Blockbuster's hedge and flowerbeds have to be breached; or get in the car, return to the main road junction and thence to Blockbuster.

Clearly this arrangement has all the appearance of being unplanned. In the absence of hard evidence one assumes that these polyps grew onto the body of the existing site. Yet observation shows that many people will indeed transgress the site boundaries to get between one sub-site and another (see Figure 31). I have heard many similar accounts of shopping centres where the customers started to make their own paths through the landscape, often despite the fact that on occasion site management would deliberately block these transgressive routes.

My favourite example of this phenomenon can be found at Parc Tawe, in nearby Swansea. This centre, largely constructed on the site of Swansea's defunct North Dock, came in two phases. Parc Tawe One, dating from the early 1990s, includes a multiplex cinema, bowling alley and a variety of shops. Parc Tawe Two, added in the late 1990s, is dominated by a Homebase hardware store. The two phases of the centre are divided by a dual carriageway that serves both as access to Parc Tawe Two and to the city centre. Parc Tawe Two boasts a vaguely Neo-classical arch that gives pedestrian access from the car park to the pavement. Yet pedestrian access to Parc Tawe One is on the opposite side of the busy road and some 30–50m away. To complicate matters, the pedestrian crossing of the road is some 30–50m in the opposite direction. Here again shoppers have developed their own *ad hoc* road crossing, in the process wearing a distinct path through the carefully planted vegetation of the central reservation (see Figure 32).

Here it is tempting to follow Ribeiro (a) in quoting Deleuze (1999[1980]: 19):

> The weed exists only to fill the waste spaces left by cultivated areas. It grows between, the poppy is maddening – but the weed is rank growth…: it points a moral.

These examples represent, albeit a limited way, what Ribeiro (1997; b) calls 'informal spaces'. His examples are drawn from the shanty towns of Brasilia and Bangkok, in particular the *ad hoc* uses of space to build homes, or sell wares in the street, which occupy the interstices of planned development in these cities (see also Edensor's 2002 account of roads in India). By contrast, in the developed North/West, the opportunities for informal use of space are limited and resisted by authority: think of the hysterical reactions to free festivals and travellers that characterised the period from the mid '80s to mid '90s.

In both my examples the informal use of space arises not from some desire to confront authority, but rather from the need to circumvent the shortcomings of the planned environment (which presumably also applies in the case of shanty towns). In wishing to get from A to B people appropriate what their environment affords (*sensu* Gibson 1979). Normally speaking we tacitly accept the many boundaries and non-spaces that are created in the urban landscape, but when the sanction of these barriers becomes inconvenient we overcome our tendency to conform. This seems to cohere with Merleau-Ponty's (1964: 82) account of the phenomenology of perception – non-spaces are always there but remain peripheral to us until they 'arouse…thoughts and volitions'.

Ephemerality and change

What characterises the transgressive routes and paths discussed in the last section is their ephemerality, especially when those responsible for that formal space undo what has been created informally. Of course, as Ribeiro (b) suggests with respect to the development of Bangkok, the planners *could* recognise the sense of the

Figure 33. B&Q at Trostre Park South merges seamlessly into the Corus Steel Works (on the left of picture).

informal crossing between the two halves of Parc Tawe and turn it into a proper crossing. But they do not. Yet, as Ribeiro (1997) describes in the case of Vila Paranoa, Brasilia, what starts as an informal use of space *can* harden into a more formal arrangement. If we think of the City of London, for example, its pattern of streets developed in an *ad hoc* fashion that has 'fossilised'. Despite Wren's desire to institute a planned layout in the aftermath of the Great Fire, this informal pattern has prevailed.

But what is interesting in a contrary way is the extent to which the formal, planned space can itself be ephemeral. Some structures in the modern world are intended to be ephemeral: scaffolding, cranes or hoardings. In some cases, structures intended to be ephemeral become more permanent: the Crystal Palace or the Eiffel Tower, for example. Although Trostre has an air of permanence, the whole development has a social liminality, which makes it expendable and liable to arbitrary change. As noted above, the 'market cross' at Trostre is no more; it was demolished as part of an expansion and remodelling of the Trostre site, which now boasts KFC and Pizza Hut restaurants, new stores and some new roundabouts. Given the apparent impossibility of finding any documentation of the site, this article represents perhaps the only record of some of its former features.

Moreover, the destruction of the 'market cross' is, as I see it, a metaphor for changing attitudes to the out of town shopping centre. In the expansion and remodelling of Tesco, the removal of some of the previous landscaping and in the architecture of some of the new stores of Trostre Park South, we see a move away from the bucolic of the 'Essex Barn' to a starker approach. In effect a kind of postmodern take on modernity, a trend that reverses that observed by Miller *et al* (1998). The new B&Q superstore is almost indistinguishable from the adjacent Corus Steel Works (see Figure 33). This seems to epitomise much of recent superstore design and represents, I suggest, the fact that developers no longer feel the need to soften the impact

of their buildings with a veneer of tradition. The world of postmodernity is now so familiar, not to say passé, that there is no longer a need to disguise the glass and steel warehouses as anything but what they are.

Conclusion: privatisation and the illusion of control

As I argue elsewhere (Graves-Brown 2000; forthcoming b), the car culture that underpins the modern shopping centre is part of a larger process of privatisation of experience. Activities that used to be social/communal are increasingly practiced in private, either alone or with family and friends. But this privatisation extends eerily into the public domain; think, for example, of how mobile phone users assume a kind of virtual privacy around them when discussing their private lives in public. Shopping is similar. Since the development of self-service stores in the 1960s (in the UK at least) shoppers need hardly communicate with anyone, except to grunt at the till operator when handing over a credit card. This is archetypally the 'mixing without meeting' described by Lefebvre (1971) or Berman (1988). Hardly surprising then that the car park and its environs are liminal and or peripheral spaces fraught with the social dangers of such spaces. We want to shop without the bother of interacting with strangers. And, as I have argued, the designers of shopping centres deliberately or tacitly conspire with this goal.

As is the case with car culture (Graves-Brown 2000), the corollary of privatisation is what I call the 'illusion of control'. The tacit ideology of individualism leads us to believe that we act entirely independently of others and are entirely in control of what happens to us. Again, I would argue, the shopping experience underlines this belief – we park, collect our shopping and depart without needing to interact with others – a kind of 'drive thru' life. Ironically, I suggest it is only when the neatly planned world we live in thwarts us that we *really* take control. For it is at this point that we informally appropriate our surroundings to our own ends, in spite of whatever they were originally intended for. It might be a little far fetched to see this as a communal or social activity in the cases I have described here: nobody planned to create the worn path on the central reservation between Parc Tawe One and Two. Yet, like the development of shanty dwellings and their networks of paths and alleys described by Ribeiro (1997), there may be a sense in which the actions of others, either directly observed or tacitly assumed from a worn path, embolden us to 'follow suit'. In other words these may be seen as social acts mediated through a material, constructed affordance.

Again such things are highly ephemeral, but their ephemerality lies in an inverse relationship to their use. If enough people choose to cross between the halves of Parc Tawe at this point, if this persists and if the City Council is provoked by the odd road accident, it might just get round to creating an official crossing at this point. Moreover, one might also argue that the recent changes in the formal design and layout of the Trostre site also represent a response to informal social action and changing public perception. In the traditional town centre, the external appearance of shops was an important indicator. But perhaps the semiotics have changed to the extent that shoppers are only interested in what is inside, as epitomised by the enclosed universe of the larger mall. In a virtualised existence this is Underhill's (2004: 19) 'fateful turning away from the eyes of the outside world' to one where only enclosed spaces continue to exist.

Acknowledgements

Thanks to Carolyn Graves-Brown for comments on the text. Also to Jenny Hall (formerly SMR Officer, Cambria Archaeology), John Schofield and Kathryn Morrison for their help and advice.

References

Ballard, J.G. 1973. *Crash*. London: Cape.

Ballard, J.G. 1974. *The Concrete Island*. London: Cape.

Ballard, J.G. 1975. *High-Rise*. London: Cape.

Benjamin, W. 1970. Thoughts on the Philosophy of History. In Arendt, H (ed.), *Illuminations*. London: Cape.

Berman, M. 1982. *All that is Solid Mets into Air: The Experience of Modernity*. London: Verso.

Boddy, T. 1992. Underground and overhead. In Sorkin, M. (ed.), *Variations on a Theme Park: The New American City and the End of Public Space*, 123–53. New York: Noonday Press.

Davis, M. 1992. Fortress Los Angeles. In Sorkin, M. (ed) *Variations on a Theme Park: The New American City and the End of Public Space*, 154–80. New York: Noonday Press.

Deleuze, G. 1999[1980]. *A Thousand Plateaus: Capitalim and Schizophrenia*. London: Athlone Press.

Douglas, M. 1966. *Purity and Danger*. London: Routledge and Kegan Paul.

Edensor, T. 2002. *National Identity, Popular Culture and Everyday Life*. London: Berg.

Gibson, J.J. 1979. *The Ecological Approach to Visual Perception*. Boston: Houghton Mifflin.

Goss, J. 1993. The 'magic of the mall': An analysis of form, function and meaning in the contemporary retail built environment. *Annals of the American Association of Geographers*. 83 (1), 18–47.

Gould, S.J. and Lewontin, R.C. 1979. The spandrels of San Marco and the Panglossian paradigm: a critique of the adaptationist programme. *Proceedings of the Royal Society of London*, Series B, 205(1161), 581–89.

Graves-Brown, P.M. 2000. Always Crashing in the Same Car. In P Graves-Brown (ed.), *Matter, Materiality and Modern Culture*, 153–65. London: Routledge.

Graves-Brown, P.M. forthcoming a. Soft Machines: The virtualisation of music.

Graves-Brown, P.M. forthcoming b. The Privatisation of Experience. In C. Holtorf and A. Piccini (eds), *Contemporary Archaeologies: Excavating Now*. London: UCL Press.

Institute of Field Archaeologists. 2001. *Standard and Guidance for Desk-Based Assessment*.

Lefebvre, H. 1971. *Everyday Life in the Modern World*. Harmondsworth: Allen Lane.

McLuhan, M. 1967. *The Medium is the Message*. London: Bantam.

Marx, K. and Engels, F. 1848. *The Communist Manifesto*.

Merleau-Ponty, M. 1964. *The Primacy of Perception* (translated by Carleton Dallery) Seattle: Northwestern University Press.

Miller, D. 1998. *A Theory of Shopping*. New York: Cornell University Press.

Miller, D. *et al* 1998. *Shopping, Place and Identity*. London: Routledge.

Moorcock, M. 1969. *The Final Programme*. London: Alison and Busby.

Morris, M. 1988. Things to Do with Shopping Centres. In Sherridan, S. (ed.), *Grafts: Feminist Cultural Criticism*, 193–226. London: Verso.

Morrison, K.A. 2003. *English Shops and Shopping* Yale University Press: London.

Ribeiro, G. 1997. An ecological approach to the study of urban spaces. *Journal of Architectural and Planning Research* 14 (4), 289–300.

Ribeiro, G. a. *Urban Makings: Formalisation of Informal Settlements in Thailand*. Unpublished paper presented at the workshop 'Debating Participation: Actors Shaping Sustainable Development. A Case-Oriented Workshop'. at Royal Danish Academy of Fine Arts, School of Architecture, Denmark. 22–23 November 2003.

Ribeiro, G. b. *Bangkok: Informal Space*. Unpublished pdf document www.karch.dk/udgivelser/publikationer/content/88/ribiero_uk.pdf (10 May 2006)

Sorkin, M. (ed.) 1992. *Variations on a Theme Park: The New American City and the End of Public Space*. New York: Noonday Press.

Symmes, J.C. 1878. *The Symmes theory of concentric spheres, demonstrating that the earth is hollow, habitable within, and widely open about the poles. Compiled by Americus Symmes from the writings of his father, Capt. John Cleves Symmes*. Louisville, Kentucky: Bradley & Gilbert.

Teed, C.R. and Morrow. U.G. 1899. *The Cellular Cosmogony; or, The Earth a Concave Sphere*. Chicago: Guiding Star.

Underhill, P. 2004. *The Call of the Mall: How We Shop*. London: Profile.

Winston, B. 1986. *Misunderstanding Media*. London: Routledge.

THE CONTEMPORARY AND FUTURE LANDSCAPE: CHANGE AND CREATION IN THE LATER TWENTIETH CENTURY

Graham Fairclough

Introduction

Was the English landscape transformed dramatically during the later twentieth century? People often claim it was a period of the greatest and most rapid change ever. The most interesting aspect of this, however, might be the changes that took place not to the material fabric of landscape but in how landscape is perceived and by whom.

There were of course substantial material changes to the English landscape in the twentieth century, for instance new forms of urbanisation or new-style agriculture, roads and wind turbines. There were also, and still are, important non-material factors: how peoples' relationships with the past and with the environment – that is, with landscape – evolved during the twentieth century, and it is this area with which this chapter is most concerned. Its starting point is the definition of 'landscape' as a matter of present-day perception rather than of materiality that is offered by the European Landscape Convention (Council of Europe 2000). Most current reference points for perceiving landscape (ie, ideologies or aesthetics), whether labelled, for example, as conservation, tourism, heritage, biodiversity, natural beauty, or countryside, have a tendency to be conservative as well as conservationist (Fairclough and Sarlov Herlin 2005; Fairclough 2006). These ways of seeing lament recent change at the same time as they celebrate equally far-reaching older changes such as Enclosure or Industrialisation; in an act of denial they condemn modern change as being destructive of landscapes that are 'traditional' and 'natural' but which themselves were of course destructive of what came before.

This chapter describes an English Heritage-sponsored programme called *Change and Creation* (C&C) (Bradley *et al* 2004) that seeks to explore some consequences of this position. The chapter's main perspective is that of archaeological resource management and heritage conservation, with its main frame of reference being landscape. It considers that landscape change, whether or not its outcomes are welcomed, should be seen as an act of creation as well as of loss, and that recent, current and future changes need to be understood in their own right and – insofar as it is possible – on their own terms. 'Contemporary archaeology' is taken to be not a date range or a period but a state of mind, intimately linked to how people live in the world (ie, to landscape), and to the resource management of all periods of the past as they contribute to the here-and-now.

Contemporary archaeology, landscape and heritage

Landscape archaeology often limits itself to studying the past at landscape scale (see Muir 1999). Its recovery of past landscapes, however, overlooks the historic and archaeological dimensions of the *present-day* landscape, the landscape that people live with, the only one we have. This concept of 'landscape' emphasises the relevance of the past to the present (ie, 'heritage') and should therefore be a principal field of contemporary archaeology. Through peoples' perceptions, it allows the remains of all periods of the past to be a real and significant presence in the contemporary world. In this sense, contemporary does not only include current (or very recent) material culture but also all older material culture that makes a contribution to contemporary perceptions of the world. Archaeological material and practice is always contemporary: the surviving past is within the present, and landscape is simply a particularly clear and accessible demonstration of this: yesterday's world becomes tomorrow's landscape, so to speak (Fairclough *et al* 1999; Fairclough 2003a).

Issues of public engagement with heritage also underlie *Change and Creation*. Public definitions of heritage are often personal, imported as well as 'locally-derived'. What matters most to people most of the time seems to be heritage that is relevant to 'their' place and that is recent, perhaps no further back than grandparents. Public opinion about heritage is also relatively generalised and (selectively) comprehensive, because it seems that non-specialists tend to see bigger pictures more than details. Inclusive and generalised 'umbrella' terms such as countryside, 'nature', biodiversity, or indeed (for all its problematic aspects) heritage score higher recognition rates in opinion polls – such as that carried out for the *Power of Place* review (HER 2000) – than more particular specialist attributes drawn from ecology or archaeology. One question posed by *Change and Creation*, therefore, is whether a focus on landscape, and on recent periods, might achieve greater levels of public engagement and participation in archaeological matters, and thereby perhaps make it easier to influence those who will create future landscapes.

The idea of landscape used in this chapter follows the European Landscape Convention: landscape is, quite simply, an area, whether rural or urban, ordinary or 'degraded', special or mundane, that is 'as perceived by people' and 'whose character is the result of the action and interaction of natural and/or human factors' (Council of Europe 2000, article 1(a); see also Fairclough and Rippon 2002: chapters 2 and 3). As a unifying concept, drawing together many aspects of the environment into manageable (but multiple) perceptions, this definition embraces the full span of human interactions with nature. It puts perception to the fore – landscape as a construct, an idea not a thing, that is not a synonym for 'environment'. Clearly, landscape is constructed to a greater or lesser extent from elements of the physical environment (archaeologists' material culture), but it is not in itself a material thing.

Defined in this way as perception, landscape only exists as a contemporary phenomenon, however deep its time depth. Some landscape-archaeological methods seek to recover past peoples' perceptions of their own contemporary environment, but an area of 'relict bronze age' field systems is of course no longer a bronze age landscape today; it is a contemporary landscape with (for some people) a dominant bronze age component. The present day provides a frame for all previous periods, and offers the potential to draw on the remains of all periods. In other words, landscape provides a context for recognising that the remains of all parts of the past are present in our own time. A recent British TV drama for example (*Life on Mars*, BBC1, Jan – March 2006) used the conceit of dreams within a coma to explore how far the past and the present co-exist in consciousness. Concepts such as that (or that in the *Dominic Hyde* 1980 TV films recently repeated – BBC3, May 2006 – and thus renewed in the present day at a time already past one of 'its' futures) can act as a metaphor for what the concept of landscape allows us to do with the past.

Landscape's dynamism and predisposition to change tells us that change is an attribute of landscape, not just an impact on it. A perhaps over-stated position on this is that landscape character cannot be destroyed but only changed, and that it is therefore neither finite nor irreplaceable. If it is accepted, for instance, that landscape character in some place is a combination of an eighteenth-century enclosure pattern over less visible or legible medieval remains (and so on, backwards, even if into an unknown past), then we cannot argue that change after any particular date (whether 1950 or 2000) does not also contribute to historic landscape character. The 'weight' of that contribution might be at issue (as a matter of personal perception), but not its existence. 'Landscape' has no original starting date, and no end: the late twenty-first-century landscape will be incomplete without a late twentieth-century layer. The process of apparently destroying landscape character is also an act of renewal, so that managing change and planning 'new' landscapes is as important as protection.

Change and Creation is concerned with how modern change is seen to impact on older aspects of historic landscape character, and with how people react and respond to this impact. Modern development is often automatically categorised by (for example) countryside conservationists and ecologists, tourism and heritage proponents, or politicians and commentators, as purely destructive to the inherited landscape, as 'loss' not 'creation'. There are notable small-scale exceptions such as actions supposed to enhance biodiversity (eg, pond-digging and tree-planting) which change inherited landscape character but which are usually presented positively, but these exceptions only serve to underline that for many disciplines – against all the evidence – landscape is a 'natural' thing that human action can only pollute.

Such generally negative responses to landscape change might be said to be based on two assumptions: first, that landscape was 'finished' at some point in the past and that this state can be preserved or retrieved. Perhaps this is why the problematic word 'traditional' is used so much in discussion about landscape protection. In the UNESCO criteria for World Heritage Cultural Landscapes, for example, traditional 'forms of land use' or 'ways of life' are important defining characteristics (except for very old landscapes – 'relict' or fossil' – which are apparently deemed to be pre- or non-traditional). A second assumption is a belief that in the past – usually just beyond living memory (Lowenthal 1985: 4-10, 23–24, 371) – the landscape was somehow better, and the human-nature interactions more harmonious. Thus landscape is romanticised.

Both of these largely unexamined assumptions deny landscape's flexibility and dynamism, and make difficult the acceptance of new layers to landscape. This is scarcely a tenable position if landscape is seen as an always-contemporary construct, and not only in the sense of the European Landscape Convention (see Olwig 2005). Whether deliberately or not, and whether recognised at the time or only with hindsight, change not only causes loss but also creates new landscape character. The *Change and Creation* programme asks that 'modern' landscape change be viewed positively as well as negatively. Nostalgic (or overly 'nature'-centred) approaches, seeing only loss within change, sets landscape apart as merely an inherited thing, not as something that is created anew every day in the multiple, shifting perceptions of all citizens or subjects.

From this perspective of continual renewal, two aspects of change need consideration here: changes in peoples' perceptions resulting from physical change in the world, and changes in how landscape is seen through cultural trends such as fashions in aesthetic appreciation, lifestyle changes, new knowledge, or revised priorities for use or preservation. Physical changes (new roads, changing agricultural practices, or wind farms) are commonly opposed by conservationists, but the ways in which a perception of landscape is constructed and changed are given little attention. It is these, however, that determine the impact of change on social values, on how future landscapes are created and whether they are accepted, and on how major issues such as 'quality of life' or common 'ownership' of heritage are debated.

Heritage management is often treated as a monolithic, unchallengeable set of principles but it is in fact always changing. Over the past two decades alone there have been significant shifts in political, public and institutional thinking and practice. New directions in England, for instance, include growing acceptance that values are attributed to things by people rather than being intrinsic to the things themselves; the idea of local distinctiveness and the work of groups like Common Ground; increased emphasis on people as well as place, especially since *Power of Place* (HER 2000) but originating in earlier discussions of what sustainable development meant for the heritage sector (EH 1997; Fairclough 1999 and 2003b); and the growing use of 'characterisation' as well as 'protection' as ways to respond to change in the historic environment (EH 2005; Fairclough forthcoming). The youngest member of the Council of Europe's 'family' of heritage conventions 'on the Social Value of Heritage' (Council of Europe 2005) offers new democratic ideas on why things are valued, whilst the Landscape Convention links landscape to the democratic agenda of the Council of Europe: landscape as the material aspects of human rights, which can be used to create new narratives of heritage and being. These narratives will in future include additions to landscape made during the late twentieth century as 'modern' layers begin to offer stories about the recent past just as it starts to slip into memory. Landscape also introduces a powerful cross-disciplinary imperative (eg, Palang and Fry 2003). Contemporary archaeology is potentially another pathway to a new heritage paradigm suited to the twenty-first century.

The Change and Creation programme and the late twentieth century

One aim of the *Change and Creation* programme, therefore, was to remind people that what is new will become old (unless swept away) and that as time passes attitudes change, as they have successively over the past few decades for Victorian, modernist and early post-war architecture. Three simple questions were posed: what did the later twentieth century add to present landscape character; what parts of that are already valued; and can the future significance of twentieth-century landscape be predicted in any way?

These are of course questions about a period of time that still lives vividly in memory and lived experience. It does not necessarily live accurately, consistently or impartially, however. Why should it? The novelist Sarah Waters, in describing the difficulties she found when beginning to write a novel about the 1940s, concisely summarised the problems. She tells how she was

> disconcerted by the sheer amount of material available ... books ... films, photographs, sound recordings, civil defence records, the physical ephemera of war, and – since so many people in the 1940s felt compelled to make a record of the startling events they saw unfolding around them – a staggering selection of diaries and memoirs. On top of that ... the period (was) still very firmly within living memory. ... the unnerving experience of looking around the room and realising that many members of my audience were old enough to recall the decade for themselves. In one way, this was exciting; ... it was also frightening. ..... I felt that the 1940s somehow belonged to the people who remembered living through them, and that I had a responsibility to them to get things right. .... Then again, memory is a funny thing, and experience is necessarily partial. .... I found myself relying less on oral history and anecdote than on the journals, letters, and novels written (at the time) (Waters 2006).

Most of all, Waters felt it had been safe for her to re-invent the later Victorian period for her first novels because it was 'to a certain extent like a stage set, already mythicised by its own extravagant fictions and by a century's worth of period novels and nostalgia'. But it was less easy for her to deal with the more proximate 1940s. Indeed, she reverted to the 1940s only after failing to write about the 1950s: her own emerging narrative had drawn her back into the slightly more distant, easier to re-imagine, war years. 'Knowing' what happened in the later twentieth century – recognising what has been added to landscape – is unlikely to be straightforward.

Nor is it straightforward to decide what is significant among recent heritage. This is why the Listing process for designating historic buildings (unlike scheduling for archaeological sites) has traditionally respected a 30-year cut-off date to allow time to lend a more objective distance. At the time of writing, there is supposedly a public consensus that the 1960s and 1970s produced thoroughly 'bad' architecture and urban planning (the 1950s are currently in the process of being rehabilitated). This is a less positive side to the innate British conservatism that has buoyed up the conservation movement since the 1960s. Town centre redevelopments from the 1960s are labelled as 'tears' in the urban fabric that need to be mended (were the urban conservationists who coined the term conscious of its alternative lachrymose meaning?). Television viewers are asked in an interactive programme called 'Demolition' to disapprove of modern architecture; one English Heritage member withdrew her subscription because a member of staff championed a 1960s building on the programme. The Government's 'Sustainable Communities' programme is opposed because it is seen to be repeating perceived planning mistakes of the 1960s: its proposals to demolish Victorian terraces are fought but the demolition of 1960s housing is deemed appropriate. New farming landscapes of the 1960s and 1970s have few defenders, though they have a certain charm and are paradoxically reminiscent of long-lost medieval open fields.

One common response to the architecture of the 1960s and 70s is that it was misguided, poorly conceived and badly executed. Aesthetic arguments are adduced ('these buildings are ugly'). They are said to be un-British, un-traditional. This is an essentially nostalgic viewpoint, however, and 'traditional' (in the context of new housing) increasingly turns out to be a sub-Poundbury faux-vernacular in the wrong place at the wrong time. Critics also sometimes speak as though architecture in the 1960s and 1970s happened by chance, an unfortunate accident whose consequences need to be dealt with, whereas archaeologists and anthropologists can speak of the social and political processes that lie behind twentieth-century material culture, thus underscoring its evidential value. Architecture of this period derived from a political consensus that has faded since the late 1970s and to many people now seems impossibly quaint. The terms of abuse routinely used for such buildings include 'Stalinist', 'communistic' and 'socialist', which suggests that these buildings are being seen through a post-Thatcherite lens and through the filter of the Cold War 'victory'. This allows development of the 1950s and 1970s to be labelled as the product of alien and inappropriate ideas, categorised as 'good' or 'bad' on ideological grounds alone.

There are frequent calls in conservation circles to 'restore' towns and cities to their 'traditional' forms by removing major additions of this period. An example is the Portsmouth Tricorn centre, categorised as a 'monstrosity'. These are classic examples of seeing change only as the loss of what went before. These mega-buildings can also be seen as new landscape types, interesting or illuminating products of a historically specific set of actions that signify what the past was like, and therefore why the present is as it is. Such buildings can also become valued because additional layers of meaning accrue to them, whether simply as familiar places full of personal memories, or through wider cultural significance: the demolition of the Gateshead multi-story carpark used in the film *Get Carter* (1971) met significant local opposition.

A debate about the future heritage of this period, about its significance to us today and about what it tells us about our recent past is therefore desirable. The *Change and Creation* thesis is that while we should not necessarily protect what we predict will be valued in future, we ought to recognise that attitudes will change, and that even things that are not valued today might come to be cherished. It might be predicted that in 50 years' time the last English towns to retain their Arndale Shopping Centres (or their Toys 'r' Us retail parks) will wish to preserve them simply because they have become rare as well as old. Creations of the 1950s–1970s may by then be a largely invisible or illegible layer in the landscape. 'Here today, gone tomorrow' and 'despised today, cherished tomorrow' are mutually exclusive axioms that represent the balance of heritage valuation and govern the future degree of legibility of recent landscape change. We cannot know where that balance will lie with respect to the past few decades, but given that conservation of the past is now a highly self-conscious activity it is logical to offer options to the future.

Conventional approaches to protecting heritage using designation based on national criteria might help to achieve this, particularly where they operate thematically, although they understate the local context at the heart of landscape. Much recent work by EH, for example, is wholly or partly concerned with this period (eg, Stocker 1995; Cranstone 1995; Cocroft and Thomas 2003; Fairclough forthcoming). More relevant, however, will be alternative or complementary methods such as Historic Landscape Characterisation and other types of characterisation (English Heritage 2005; Clark *et al* 2004; Fairclough 2006; forthcoming), which produce contextual interpretations of the influence of the past without necessarily prejudging what is to be kept.

Characterisation's ability to draw a bigger picture offers a way of coping with the extensive scale of late twentieth-century heritage. The social, economic and physical processes that created landscape change in the past few decades operated at national, if not global, scale. The mechanisms of change were large scale, both conceptually (eg, state planning, world markets) and physically (technology and capacity), whilst the completeness of survival because of proximity to our own times causes practical problems too. The sheer weight of remains means that they have to be understood in generalised terms; a big picture is necessary to see past the detail.

Reflecting on Archaeological Resource Management

The *Change and Creation* programme's interest in late twentieth-century material culture alone is a sufficient justification for the programme. The programme, however, also uses the landscape creation of the past few decades to reflect critically on the theory and practice of archaeological resource management more generally, as part of long-standing attempts to further theorise the sub-discipline. Contemporary landscape character can act as a laboratory for testing ideas or methods that are often taken for granted when dealing with 'simpler' periods.

The quantity, ubiquity, proximity and contested nature of recent material culture can make it easier to see fundamental issues, and can allow existing practice, both of method and objective, to be re-visited. This is especially so, it could be contended, in the realm of landscape character, with its issues of scale and perception as well as recentness. Like Historic Landscape Characterisation, *Change and Creation* leads us not only to recognise but to act upon the notion that all aspects of the archaeological record exist in and form part of the present. This is what 'survival' means.

The proximity of the past few decades does of course raise questions. The recent past remains in memory, and is often well documented. It may, therefore, be thought to be already 'known'. So what role can archaeology have? Memories and records do not always coincide, however, as Sarah Waters reminded us earlier, and the overlay of hindsight and ideology needs to be acknowledged. History does not really exist until it is written and re-written, usually by victors or at least survivors, and the contemporary past is likely to be more, rather than less, contested than the more remote past. We should neither expect nor desire to have interpretative closure on the period.

The *Change and Creation* programme invites us to challenge widely held assumptions: that old things are inherently more valuable; that things are valued mainly when they are threatened and when they become rare; that only things still in use should be regarded as part of the present not of the past. There is also the question, especially given the vast amount of data, of the role of interpretation and synthesis. Contemporary archaeology seems to concentrate, much more than traditional archaeology, on interpretation rather than on data. There is an analogy with how archaeology was practiced in the 'data-starved' 1930s, 1950s or even 1970s: the practices we have today were designed for different circumstances and are not always appropriate in a world where we have an embarrassment of data.

Looking after 'modern things' seems mainly, however, to call for a new accommodation to change, in the same way that new approaches were needed when the conservation focus shifted from a site to a landscape scale. There is,

however, simply too much late twentieth-century material for traditional heritage methods to cope with, because, explicitly or not, they depend heavily for their practicality (and social and political acceptance) on the selectivity offered by attributes of rarity and special-ness which, like objective distance, require the passage of time. Thresholds of quality or importance have been set at a level that allows a more or less manageable (and small) proportion of the older historic resource to cross it. Conveniently, for the earliest periods (eg, prehistoric monuments, medieval churches, monastic or castle ruins, or Georgian terraces) this proportion often roughly coincides with what has survived. The balance becomes harder to maintain as the mid twentieth century is approached, and is indeed only maintained by excluding the ordinary (such as the ubiquitous 1930s suburbs). *Change and Creation* asks us to re-examine this balance. Do we raise the 'quality' thresholds to retain a selectively preservationist approach or do we widen our goals to achieve less everywhere?

The latter side of the balance concerns attitudes to change. The historic changes to the environment that have created today's heritage have been sanitised by the passage of time, and are accepted as *part* of heritage (the patina of age on a building, the palimpsest of landscape etc). Current changes, however, remain controversial even though refusal to accept recent change as a *part* of landscape denies aspects of the concept of landscape and the notion that the past is part of the present, not just 'history' (EH 1997: 1). A question here is whether archaeologists and members of analogous disciplines are simply witnesses or actors, spectators or players? Do we only study and react against threatened loss, or do we try to act with others to influence or even cause the creation of future landscape? Influencing change positively, not just mitigating change to preserve the remains of the past, may be a more appropriate goal for twenty-first-century archaeological resource management. In particular, we might seek a trade-off in expanding from protecting relatively few special places to dealing in some other way with all aspects of the dense and ubiquitous complex of material culture that is contemporary archaeology. The other way might be to manage change and shape the future rather than trying only to preserve historic fabric.

This reflexive aspect of the *Change and Creation* programme is perhaps its most interesting feature. The scale and recentness of late twentieth-century heritage, which give it its complex and contested nature, challenges archaeological resource management by suggesting that traditional habits, such as waiting for 30 years until the later twentieth century is not so 'contemporary', is not an answer but an avoidance. There will always be a contemporary archaeology of the previous few decades however far into the future we look. We need continuously to re-set our sights, which is why the original *Change and Creation* end date of 2000 needs constant updating.

Characterising the late twentieth- / early twenty-first-century landscape in England

This chapter is not the place to attempt a characterisation or definition of landscape of the late twentieth century. A first step towards that is being taken by *Change and Creation* in preparing a first 'field guide' to late twentieth-century landscape with an accompanying thesaurus in the National Monuments Record (EH forthcoming). Another approach is already contained within EH's county-by-county HLC programme (Clark *et al* 2004), which demonstrates some of the time depth that resides within landscape in a modern-day context that frames the 'past in the present' approach. It is already providing GIS-based analysis of recent and current change. So, too, is the Countryside Quality Counts project, which is monitoring landscape-scale change for the Government by using trends rather than loss as its analytical tool (www.countryside-qualty-counts.org.uk, 10 February 2006).

It is worthwhile to conclude this chapter with a brief look at higher-level models that might help to define what makes the early twenty-first-century landscape different from what came before and to free it a little from the stigma of destruction.

One noticeable trend over the past few decades is that the rural landscape appears to have become simplified, and homogenised, through industrialised agriculture, notably through the market forces encouraged by the European Common Agricultural Policy. Urban townscapes too, particularly the High Streets and the housing estates, are deemed to have become too homogenous, increasingly devoid of local character, 'banalised' as the French might say. There are paradoxes as well: the roads are full of people, but the fields are depopulated; the 'wildernesses' are increasingly artificially maintained and full of people during holidays; the clear distinction between town and country is blurred as exurbs, not suburbs, are built, and as urban lifestyles re-invent rural-ness.

Post-industrialisation and new industries create extensive new landscape types. Service and leisure industries (often related to heritage) in particular use people as their raw materials where the 'old industries' used cotton, coal or steel. There are also new types of landscape that are not those of work or settlement but of play and mobility: landscapes of travel (the very distinctive but so-called 'non-places' of motorway service stations and airports, the almost beautiful sky-scape of vapour trails) and landscapes created by mobility that allow new modes of consumption in out-of-town mega shopping malls or 'shed-parks', retail distribution centres and even the 'use' of motorways as 'storerooms' as an increasingly large proportion of stock is on the move before at-need delivery to the supermarkets.

At the same time, the late twentieth-century landscape is also partly defined by areas where certain types of change are kept at bay: for instance, nature reserves or National Parks. These 'old' landscapes owe their relatively unchanging existence to policies and law that are distinctively late twentieth century, and should therefore be seen as modern landscape types – or perhaps 'non'-landscapes, if change and dynamism really is an attribute of landscape. The processes that created these 'old' landscapes are becoming merely a means to an end not the end in itself, which is now simply a beautiful, attractive, publicly accessible and socially acceptable landscape. In such areas, the experience of 'no change' and a display of mythic continuity and stability are the defining characteristics of late twentieth-century landscape character. The same is true of the stability created by other types of more-or-less conscious decision such as post-industrial economic and social stagnation, or military training and 'defence' exclusion zones.

Whilst the homogenising effects of globalisation are everywhere noted, new regional distinctions are at the same time emerging that sometimes reflect and at other times subvert long-standing patterns. South-eastern England is becoming fully (sub)urbanised, even before the high levels of house-building envisaged by the Government's latest mass housing initiative. There is in the South-east a growing perception that more wild birds now live in domestic gardens than in farmland. Large parts of the west and north of England – in the latter case despite the Government programme know as the 'Northern Way' designed to create renewed economic growth and vitality

– are slowly turning into a leisure landscape. Such trends also cloak a shift of landscape aesthetic from working landscape to lifestyle landscape, another area for research into late twentieth-century landscape change.

After-word / Future fore-word

Several recent projects, notably the Countryside Character map (Countryside Commission and Agency 1998–99), have characterised the present-day landscape. Their underlying tendency, however, is to characterise the past few decades as a period of erosion, loss and destruction, a decline from a mythical golden age of 'natural', perfect landscape. In the books just cited, the captions of photographs that include 'all those modern things' such as motorways, pylons, power stations or new urban fringes almost invariably mention them as intruding or destructive elements. In contrast, the *Change and Creation* project will attempt to look at the period constructively as a historic phase its own right, and to take change itself, 'good or bad', as the object of study. Its mode and scope of working will hopefully be as dynamic and open to change as the landscape itself.

Although framed to cover the English situation, *Change and Creation* also raises questions about national and regional differences across Europe. The Welsh, Northern Irish and Scottish experiences of de-industrialisation and demographic change are very different for example, as are those of the Netherlands and Belgium. Eastern and central Europe has different cultures, attitudes to change and chronologies. Its Soviet-era collective farms and landscapes are understood in terms of transience and not as heritage, because, after all, they were not 'traditional'. Yet they shaped (and continue to shape) a new landscape that in its turn is changing as they are replaced by market-led agricultural change (Fairclough 2002). Different cultural attitudes to the creation, use and, in some cases, removal of post-war social housing projects, specifically in Northern and Scandinavian Europe, would also benefit from trans-national study. Finally, attitudes to conservation and cultural heritage, to modern change and to ownership both legal and metaphorical, nevertheless reflect deep cultural differences, for which the *Change and Creation* 'brand' could offer a comparative framework.

Change and Creation is not a unitary programme but a context for many separate areas of work. We hope that the programme's characteristics will mimic some of the attributes of the late twentieth-century landscape itself, such as open-ness to multiple interpretations, multi-disciplinary appeal and its contested nature. It is a project in progress. It may have no conclusion but merely stimulate new ways of seeing. Yet it is more than simply the archaeological study of the recent past. It poses significant questions about attitudes to change and modernity in twenty-first-century England and whether the archaeological and heritage approaches to the past so usefully bequeathed to us from the nineteenth and twentieth centuries are fully suited to the ongoing construction of landscape as a way of being in the world.

Acknowledgements

This paper grew from papers at the first (where *Change and Creation* was previewed) and second (where the leaflet was launched) CHAT conferences, and at the joint SHA/SPMA meeting in York in January 2005 (in a session about new agendas for Post-Medieval Archaeology). It also draws on a paper about heritage conservation in a session called 'Defining Moments of the twentieth Century' organised by John Schofield at 1999s Theoretical Archaeology Group conference. It also reflects discussions over several years with many colleagues in EH and beyond on resource management, landscape and characterisation. It owes most, however, to my friends in the small collaborative group that produced the *Change and Creation* leaflet and that continues to steer the programme (Andrea Bradley and Janet Miller, WS Atkins Heritage; Victor Buchli, University College London; Dan Hicks, University of Bristol; and John Schofield, English Heritage). But I hope they do not agree with everything I have written because multiple and contested viewpoints are central to the spirit of our programme.

References

Bradley, A., Buchli, V., Fairclough, G.J., Hicks, D., Miller, J. and Schofield, J. 2004. *Change and Creation: Historic Landscape Character 1950–2000*, London: English Heritage, www.changeandcreation.org (7 July 2005).

Clark, J., Darlington, J., and Fairclough G.J. 2004. *Using Historic Landscape Characterisation, English Heritage Review of HLC Applications, 2002–3*. Preston: English Heritage and Lancashire County Council.

Cocroft, W.D. and Thomas, R.J.C. 2003. *Cold War: Building for Nuclear Confrontation*. English Heritage.

Council of Europe. 2000. *European Landscape Convention*, Florence, European Treaty Series, No. 176, www.coe.int/T/E/cultural-co-operation/Environment/Landscape (7 July 2005).

Council of Europe. 2005. *Convention on the Social Value of Heritage*, Faro, European Treaty Series, No. 176, www.coe.int/T/E/cultural-co-operation/Environment/Landscape (7 July 2005).

Countryside Commission and Countryside Agency. 1998–99. *Countryside Character* Volumes 1–8, Cheltenham, www.countryside.gov.uk/cci (7 July 2005).

Cranstone, D. 1995. Step 2 and 3 in the Monuments Protection Programme: A Consultant's View. In M. Palmer and P. Neaverson (eds), *Managing the Industrial Heritage*, 115–7. Leicester Archaeology Monograph No 2.

English Heritage. 1997. *Sustaining the Historic Environment*. London.

English Heritage. 2005. *Conservation Bulletin* 47 Winter 2004/05, www.english-heritage.org.uk/characterisation (7 July 2005).

English Heritage. forthcoming. *Images of Change – Field Guide to Late Twentieth-century Landscape.*

Fairclough, G.J. 1999. The S-word: Sustaining Conservation. In K. Clark (ed.), *Conservation Plans in Action: Proceedings of the Oxford Conference*, 127–31. London: English Heritage.

Fairclough, G.J. 2002. Europe's Landscape – Archaeology, Sustainability and Agriculture. in G.J. Fairclough and S.J. Rippon (eds), *Europe's Cultural Landscape: Archaeologists and the Management of Change*, EAC Occasional Paper no 2, 1–12. Brussels and London: Europae Archaeologiae Consilium and English Heritage.

Fairclough, G.J. 2003a. The Long Chain: Archaeology, Historical Landscape Characterisation and Time Depth in the Landscape. In G. Fry and H. Palang (eds), *Landscape Interfaces: Cultural Heritage in Changing Landscapes*, Landscape Series 1, 295–317. Dordrecht: Kluwer Academic Publishers.

Fairclough, G.J. 2003b. Cultural Landscape, Sustainability and Living with Change? In J.M. Teutonico and F. Matero (eds), *Managing Change: Sustainable Approaches to the Conservation of the Built Environment*, Procs 4th US/ICOMOS International Symposium, 23–46. Los Angeles: The Getty Conservation Institute.

Fairclough, G.J. 2006. A New Landscape for Cultural Heritage Management: Characterisation as a Management Tool. In L. Lozny (ed.), *Landscapes Under Pressure: Theory and Practice of Cultural Heritage Research and Preservation*, 55–74. New York: Springer.

Fairclough, G.J. forthcoming. From Assessment to Characterisation. In J. Hunter, J. and I. Ralston, I. (eds), *Archaeological Resource Management in the UK*, 2nd Ed.

Fairclough, G.J., Lambrick, G. and McNab, A. 1999. *Yesterday's World, Tomorrow's Landscape - the EH Historic Landscape Project 1992–94*. London: English Heritage.

Fairclough, G.J. and Sarlov-Herlin, I. 2005. The Meaning of Countryside: What Are We Trying to Sustain? In D. McCollin and J.J. Jackson, *Planning, People and Practice – The Landscape Ecology of Sustainable Landscapes*, Procs of 13th IALE(UK) Conference, 11– 19. Northampton: IALE(UK).

Fairclough, G.J. and Rippon, S.J. (eds). 2002. *Europe's Cultural Landscape: Archaeologists and the Management of Change*, EAC Occasional Paper no 2. Brussels and London: Europae Archaeologiae Consilium and English Heritage.

HER 2000. Historic Environment Review. *Power of Place, A Future for the Historic Environment*. London: English Heritage.

Lowenthal, D. 1985. *The Past is a Foreign Country*. Cambridge: Cambridge University Press.

Muir, R. 1999. *Approaches to Landscape*. London.

Olwig, K.R. 2005. Editorial. *Landscape Research* 30 (3), 294–95.

Palang H. and Fry G. (eds). 2003. *Landscape Interfaces: Cultural Heritage in Changing Landscapes*, Landscape Series 1. Dordrecht: Kluwer Academic Publishers.

Stocker, D. 1995. Industrial Archaeology and the Monuments Protection Programme in England. In M. Palmer and P. Neaverson (eds), *Managing the Industrial Heritage*, 105–13. Leicester: Leicester University Press.

Waters, S. 2006. Romance among the ruins. *Guardian Review*, 28 January 2006, http://books.guardian.co.uk/review/

Titbits Revisited: Towards a Respectable Archaeology of Strait Street, Valletta (Malta)

John Schofield and Emily Morrissey

There is something fascinating about closure and denial: closure in the physical and archaeological sense of locked doors and sealed deposits, and denial in psychological terms, describing things people have either forgotten or simply choose not to talk about; places associated with a shameful past for example, or with atrocity (Dolff-Bonekaemper nd). Memories then, like places, can remain inaccessible until such time as the correct key is found, the right question asked, a correspondence that reflects the close connections that exist between archaeological and psychoanalytic enquiry (eg, Holtorf 2005: 31). Faced with an entire street of locked doors, and people who would seemingly rather forget, with stories of drunken sailors, cross-dressers, music hall and cabaret and – above all – sex, closure and denial become all the more intriguing. When all of this exists in the heart of a World Heritage city (Valletta), and in a country that identifies strongly with the Catholic faith (Malta), the intrigue is greater still.

These are the characteristics and questions that attracted us to Strait Street. Why was it the way it was – abandoned, and seemingly without the support or interest of the local community? Was there really an 'Egyptian Queen' who had danced naked on the tables in the bar of the same name, as was once suggested to us? Was this a red light district as well as being a street of bars and music halls? What importance do people attach to this place today, over 40 years since Malta's independence? How can these stories of Strait Street be told in a way that is accurate yet respectful? Here we address some of these questions, arguing that it is largely archaeology – a 'mode of enquiry into the relationship between people and their material pasts' (Hodder 2003: 2) – that enables the story to be told in this way.

Inspiration for this project exists in two films, without which the ideas behind the project, and the sense of place we have sought to convey, would not have been the same. We were both struck in the film *Cinema Paradiso* (Director Giuseppe Tornatore 1989) by the strong sense of attachment felt by the main characters – the old projectionist and his apprentice – to the building in which they worked. The eventual demolition of that building was inevitable, but the reaction of the apprentice (now middle-aged) said much about attachment, social significance and meaning (Byrne *et al* 2001), as well as inspiritment and loss (Read 1996). *The Buena Vista Social Club* (Director Wim Wenders with Ry Cooder 1999) had similar resonance, again based around buildings that had been the focus of social gathering and interaction, reflected in the creative energy of the music performed there. In both films the buildings (mostly now either abandoned or in poor repair) were invested with social values. These may not be palaces, churches or the great houses designed by renowned architects, the sorts of buildings typically afforded protection for their cultural significance; these are places of the people, and the types of places – ordinary and mundane – that give people their sense of attachment, of belonging. It is here too that the ghosts of place are most likely to be found (Bell 1997). It

is these buildings that contain the potential – in their fabric, their material culture, their very existence – to enable the recollection and re-evaluation of memory.

The place

Malta is Catholic for the most part. Centrally and strategically placed in the Mediterranean, between Europe and North Africa, its location was heavily influential on its history, culture and language (Boissevain 1993; Mitchell 2002). From 1680 Malta was a British colony with naval ships and servicemen visiting regularly until independence was declared in 1964. Since then the number of servicemen has declined sharply, coincident with an increase in tourism, from 65,000 visitors in 1965, to over one million in the mid 1990s (Boissevain and Theuma 1998: 97). Malta's capital city, Valetta, absorbed most service personnel visiting Malta, though some also visited Sliema, across the harbour, and Floriana, outside the walled city of Valletta. Now Valletta is a magnet for cruise passengers. It is a World Heritage Site, its architecture an impressive and striking legacy of the Knights of St John. And through this fabulous city, in the unlikeliest of settings, runs Malta's 'street of shame' – Strait Street, or simply 'the Gut' (Saxon 1965).

Strait Street today is effectively two streets (Figure 34): a rather ordinary street of businesses and shops at the top (south) end, closer to the city gate; and what has the appearance of an abandoned alleyway at the bottom (north) end. Here it is narrower and unkempt with fewer buildings altered or renovated. Of the 60–70 bars that originally lined Strait Street, most that remain visible, through the voids of neon signage, the few bar names remaining above doorways, and painted walls, lettering and graffiti, are at this end of the street. Table 1 shows the distribution of bars according to the eight blocks of Strait Street, including those that have either opened in Strait Street recently, or which have remained open for business over the course of the last 40 years. A contradiction exists here. Taking the mid-way point (Old Theatre Street) as a division, five of the six bars (83%) that remain or have opened recently are at the upper end of the street; 48 of the 60 former bars (80%), recorded in our study, are at the lower end. The distribution of bars today is a mirror image, therefore, of what existed previously.

In 1965, *Titbits* magazine included the following description of Strait Street, under the title 'The street that shames Hero Island':

> British tourists should steer clear of Malta
> till the island's government take this advice;
> Stamp out the vice in a street that is the
> shame of Malta – Straight Street (*sic*).
>
> This is an area of vice and prostitution that
> ranks with the world's most notorious sin
> spots. …

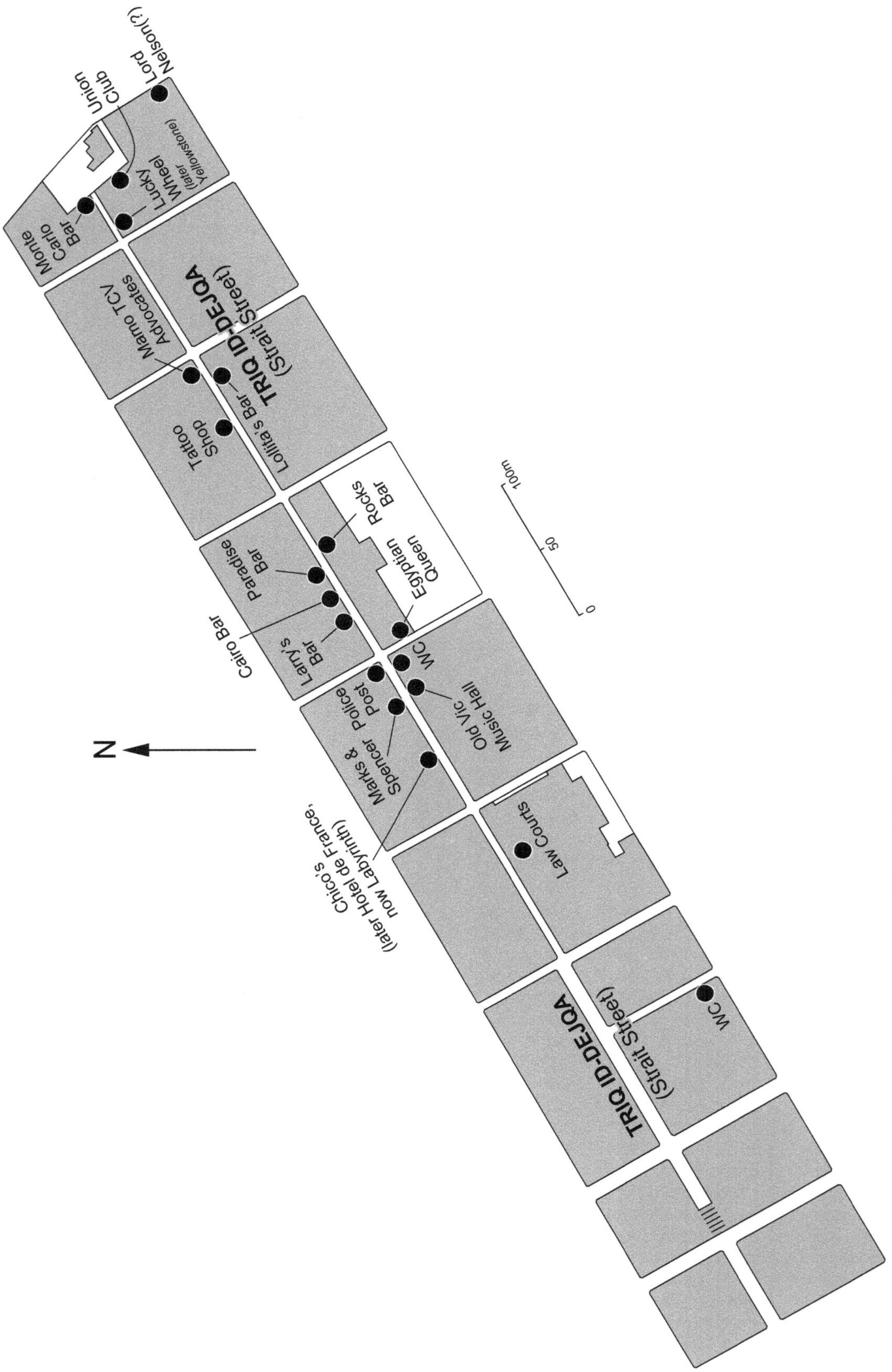

Figure 34. Map of Strait Street

Distribution of bars and music halls in Strait Street, arranged by block from south to north

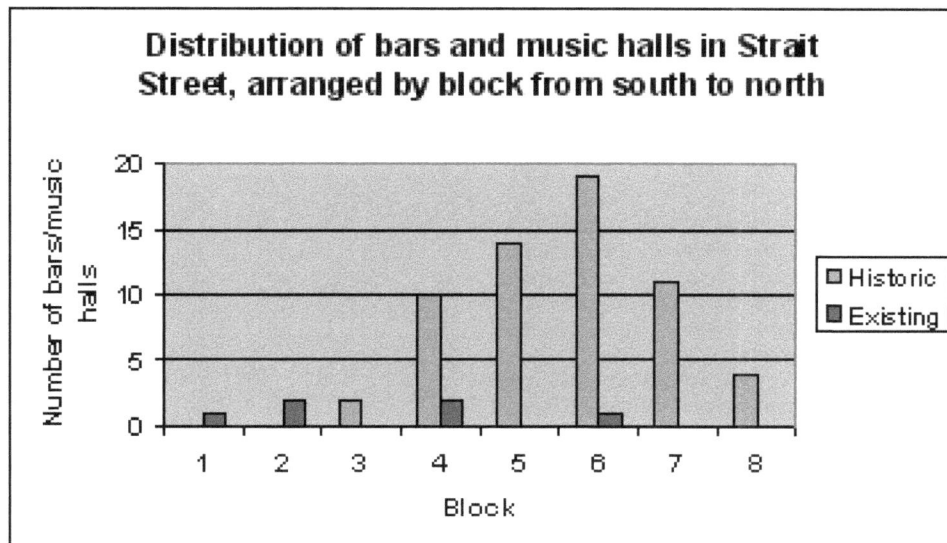

Table 1. Distribution of bars on Strait Street

Officially, the problem does not exist. The Gut is not mentioned in the newspapers, on radio, TV, by parliament or even in polite conversation. ...

The Maltese police turn a blind eye to what goes on in The Gut. The only effective control comes from the naval police who intervene when one of their sailors is involved in a fight.

The author goes on:

[The Gut] is a dirty, squalid alley that is packed from noon to early morning with prostitutes who sell themselves for the price of a drink. ...

A street where teenage British sailors are accosted by women old enough to be their grandmothers ... (Saxon 1965).

Dench (1975: 109) has assessed the impact of this article, exploring further the contradiction between Malta's strong identification with the Catholic faith, and the activities associated with Strait Street. To Maltese priests, Dench explains, deviant sexual behaviour and vice are almost unmentionable (1975: 109) – even uttering immoral words is unacceptable, with 58 men committed to prison for doing so as recently as 1960–65. Recourse to a prostitute is a mortal sin, like other sexual acts outside of marriage, for which absolution is necessary. Open reference to vice is considered utterly offensive and respectable Maltese try to close their eyes and ears to the topic (ibid: 109).

Local response to the *Titbits* article was perhaps unsurprising therefore, exciting 'a curious sensitivity in which evident consternation combines with half-hearted and equivocal denial that such a thing might be possible – in Malta at any rate' (Dench 1975: 109). The magazine was banned in Malta, but a few copies circulated. Local people were incensed, to the extent that public comment became necessary. Clearly a vigorous denial would have been a nonsense, as the article's allegations were true. Yet passive acceptance would have been painful and offensive to many, and would have led to calls for Malta to be 'cleaned up'. So the issue was fudged, stating that it did

not merit public scrutiny: '[E]yes were averted, and the vague belief entertained that the authorities have matters under satisfactory control' (ibid: 111).

Against this background our letter to the *Times of Malta*, requesting information about Strait Street for this project, received this anonymous reply:

If you have some respect for the G[eorge] C[ross] Island, skip the idea of shedding light on Strait Street. ... Yours truly, A.D. (anon letter nd).

A map included with this reply directed us towards researching Fort St Elmo where – we later discovered – various attacks on tourists had recently occurred! At least one local resident thought this was no coincidence.

History

Valletta was designed and built by the Knights of St John following the Great Siege of 1565. It was built on a regular grid plan, with blocks defined by straight streets of varying width. The main streets were wider for processional and ceremonial use; other streets were narrower, and some little more than alleyways. As in other planned cities, width reflected status and Strait Street was at the bottom of the pile. This and the lower end of Valletta in general was designed to house the poor and the needy, and thus it was here that poverty, petty crime and prostitution would be concentrated. Cassar describes the early history of Maltese prostitution and its restriction under the Knights to some 'remote part of the city' (1964: 224), presumably this bottom end around Fort St Elmo and furthest from the main city gate where a hospital for fallen women was also established. A map showing instances of plague in 1813, including deaths by household, highlights this area as the worst affected.

According to Denaro (1963: 25) Strait Street was residential through to the early 18th century, when hotels began to appear at least at its upper southern end (eg, the Hotel et Restaurant D'Australia was founded in 1840). The establishment of bars and music halls came a little later, as we can assume from the Old Vic Music Hall, which in 1920 advertised itself as 'The Oldest Established and most

Up-to-Date Music Hall in Malta. Established 1881'. Other bars began opening soon after this. However, when and how Strait Street became 'the Gut' is unclear. Was 'Gut' a derivation of ghetto, relating to the Jewish community that occupied part of this area, or did it refer to the gutter that Strait Street resembled, narrow and high sided? Or is there a more anatomical explanation? To date the answer has alluded us.

Strait Street has its place in literature. Nicholas Rinaldi's novel *The Jukebox Queen of Malta* (1999) takes Strait Street as its principal backdrop for a love story set during the Second World War. A secondary theme of this novel is the preponderance of jukeboxes in Malta's bars, causing the decline of live music here as elsewhere in the 1940s–60s. But Thomas Pynchon's *V* (1961) is the better known example, his use of Malta and Strait Street being the subject of critical assessment, for example by Cassola (1995). There is enough in Pynchon's descriptions of bars and 'whore-houses', says Cassola, 'to prove he was in Malta, but also to fix his presence on the island within a certain period of time' – that is, 1956 (1995: 25). This makes the novel a valuable source of information, especially passages such as those which describe the character of the street and social interaction within it. For example:

> Strait Street – the Gut – was crowded as Kingsway but more poorly lit. First familiar face they saw was Leman the red-headed water-king, who came reeling out the swinging doors of a pub called the Four Aces, minus a white hat. Leman was a bad drunk, so Pappy and Clyde ducked down behind a potted palm in front to watch. Sure enough, Leman started searching in the gutter, bent over at a 90° angle. 'Rocks', whispered Clyde. 'He always looks for rocks.' The water-king found a rock and prepared to heave it through the front window of the Four Aces. The U.S. Cavalry, in the form of the one Tourneur, the ship's barber, arrived also by way of the swinging doors and grabbed Leman's arm. The two fell to the street and began wrestling around in the dust. A passing band of Royal Marines looked at them curiously for a moment, then went by, laughing, a little embarrassed. (Pynchon 2000 [1961]: 430)

Now, after 40 years of neglect and inactivity, Strait Street is changing. Much of the street's bottom northern end feels empty, the sense of abandonment challenged only by the sounds and smells from the flats above, which we know from conversations with residents are typically damp and in poor repair. There are a small number of conversions at this end of the street, notably an advocate's office (previously the White Star), but these are exceptional. The southern end, however, is gradually being returned to use, but for retail and business. Some continuity of use can be seen: the bar and nightclub known as Labyrinth was previously the Hotel de France and Chico's; Papanni's nearby was previously the Happy Return Bar and before that Angels; and the clock-maker J.P. Caruana at 46 Strait Street remains, having been established in 1904. Three new bars have also recently opened at this end of the street. New businesses and retail outlets have opened also, notably Marks and Spencer, which occupies the former sites of Laddy's Bar, Max Refreshments and the Dowling Dance Hall (previously Hotel et Restaurant L'Australie). Here the decision to locate an annex to the main Marks and Spencer store on a street that carries such stigma was contentious, the argument being that customers would not walk down Strait Street, even for Marks and Spencer!

The novel solution was to construct a retractable bridge, from the main store to the annex, meaning that customers could avoid Strait Street altogether, passing over rather than through it. Just off Strait Street, the building occupied by the Egyptian Queen has recently also been bought for conversion to retail.

Given this background, our interest in Strait Street was twofold. First, we wished to construct an alternative archaeology of Valletta (after Schadla Hall 2004). Valletta is changing: planning policies have been drawn up and a transport strategy is in place to restrict vehicular access to the city. This is a World Heritage Site. For now Strait Street is largely forgotten and its heritage and history not realised or understood – self-guided tours of the city avoid Strait Street altogether. We believe this street has a place amongst the multiple narratives that exist for Valletta. Second, and related to this, we want to feed the interest and enthusiasm of residents of this and neighbouring streets, those that sit on their doorsteps and who congregate in the square in the evening; those who worked in the street, for whom this place was their lives, their hopes and ambitions. Many are proud of their association with the street. Equally, former sailors revisit and show their families the bars they frequented. They try to remember where the bars were, and we have tried to help them. People want to know, and contemporary landscape archaeology, as opposed to oral and social history alone, can provide answers.

Methods

Our approach to Strait Street is a simple one: we record what we see and what people tell us. But things are complicated, not least because most doors are firmly locked, and have remained so for many years. In most cases the owner is not known, or the keys cannot be located, the building is structurally unsound, or the owner is suspicious of our motives and will not permit access. When we do gain access it is usually for a few minutes only. These constraints have caused us to develop a very particular methodology. There are three stages to our approach, each of which requires explanation:

Stage 1 – 'Being seen'

It became obvious to us in the initial stages of the project that we needed to be seen in Strait Street – which is a rare thing: few people are seen wandering here, and being around for sustained periods was key. Our excuse was to record house numbers, names and signage, then – in detail and digitally – to photograph the doors, the locks, any physical traces of the buildings' former use, as well as all signage and graffiti. We also recorded the character of the street and how it changed from block to block: how noisy was it, how smelly? In all we must have spent three to four hours in Strait Street every day, and to everyone that witnessed the fieldwork our interest must have appeared deep and quite genuine. Once, early in the project, we walked up Strait Street with Victor Scerri, a friend who we had met on our first day in Valletta. Victor is a historian (eg, Scerri nd), a former town councillor, and our 'man of the streets'. Everyone seemed to know Victor; he commanded obvious respect. Victor was also researching aspects of Strait Street and presenting it as peoples' history, published in short semi-biographical essays in the Maltese language left-wing newspaper *it-TORĊA* (eg, Scerri 2004a; 2004b; 2005). Being seen in Strait Street with Victor changed things for us; it gave us credibility, and contacts were much easier to make and became more frequent thereafter.

Stage 2 – 'Bimbling'

How to conduct the oral historical research presented us with a dilemma. The few who knew about Strait Street had spoken already with Victor and we had their accounts through the pages of *it-TORĊA* (translated for us, fortuitously by a journalist using this material as the basis for similar articles in the *Times of Malta*). Victor had interviewed former barmaids, musicians, cabaret artists, cross-dressers and prostitutes. There was little more that we could ask substantively that had not been asked already. But most people we met in Strait Street had memories that would contribute to the multiple narratives we hoped to compile. We considered formal, structured interviews and a questionnaire to gather this information, but both approaches seemed inappropriate, given that meetings were necessarily of short duration, and appeared to benefit from their informality. We considered conducting the interviews informally over a coffee. However, experience elsewhere persuaded us to take greater account of situating these interviews in Strait Street, and especially while passing through the place: in Jon Anderson's words, 'to generate a collage of collaborative knowledge' (2004: 254). Sin describes the significance of *in situ* interviews for gathering information about the way participants construct their individual and social identities (2003; see also Collins 1998). She also notes that one can read wider social geographies from a single interview conducted at a single site, thus giving greater and broader relevance to the views expressed there. However, given the typically short duration of meetings, a slightly modified approach was required, and 'bimbling' seemed the obvious answer, a practice defined as walking or wandering aimlessly, a bit like ambling (Evans 1998: 205). Anderson has discussed

Figure 35. Joseph Buttigieg and his mother in the late 1960s.

this novel approach to fieldwork, following Casey's view that 'places [can] possess us – in perception as in memory ... insinuating themselves into our lives' (2000: 199). He borrows Kate Evans' (1998) idea that one can use 'bimbling' to both let off steam and escape the rigours and routines of daily life, and importantly in this context to reconnect with one's environment (Anderson 2004: 257). Anderson goes on to describe the philosophical and physiological potential of 'bimbling', giving people the opportunity to re-experience their connections with landscape, and to reminisce prompting, 'other life-course memories associated with that individual's relationship with place' (ibid.: 258). So, we bimbled – walking up and down Strait Street, talking with those we met, making notes and using the digital video camera where it felt appropriate. We were told what bars were where, and we began to gain an impression of what many of these places were like. Bimbling will remain a part of this project as it progresses.

Stage 3 – 'Seeing'

Through being seen, and by bimbling, some contacts were made that ultimately provided access to buildings. Rather frustratingly, access was generally for only a few moments, and so the detailed recording of space, and objects within it (such as that conducted by Buchli and Lucas [2001] at an abandoned council flat in England) proved impossible. Rather like the informality of bimbling, a rapid field recording exercise was required, and one that allowed us to remain in conversation with the owner while observing the space and objects that lay within. This was achieved by using the digital camera to photograph, at high resolution, everything in sight, and to keep the digital video camera running, to record both the place and the dialogue conducted therein (at least beyond the point at which we had the owner's consent to do so). We then reviewed the film and photographs and used these as the basis for note taking as a secondary stage. We will certainly have missed things. We were clearly influenced by what the owner wanted us to see (coat-hooks, the cash register), and therefore things that he did not may have been lost to us. This introduced a political dimension to our interaction with these places; however intentional, the owners or informants effectively decided what we should not be shown.

Results

Bars

Our fieldwork has included access to eleven bars, most of which are on Strait Street itself (those described in the text are shown in Figure 34). Some are now empty and unused; others have been adapted to new uses while retaining components of the bar that existed before. The Monte-Carlo Bar for example, at the lower (north) end of the street, was established as a bar by the father of the present owner and occupant. He took the decision to open a bar here, designed and built the furnishings (including a fabulous art-deco bar with rear mirror), and decided ultimately to close when business declined following Independence. His son later adapted this as an engineering workshop, though he retained as much of the original design as possible, including beading, the bar and cash-till, and a bell at the front entrance, which the doorman used out-of-hours to warn those inside that police were approaching. The present owner speaks with passion and enthusiasm for the bar, his regret at its closure, and of his decision to retain fabric in deference and honour of his father. While 'bimbling', he gave us a photograph of himself, with his mother standing in front of the bar

Figure 36. Trellis ceiling of Rocks Bar.

(Figure 35). It is a wonderful proud and intimate image that we are pleased to include here.

Opposite the Monte-Carlo is the Yellowstone (formerly the Lucky Wheel), which has a low window by the steps of Strait Street. Here a musician played to passers-by. Inside what is now a workshop, where window- and picture-frames are made, are traces of the internal (again art-deco) wall decoration and the recess with shelves where – an employee of the workshop told us – the underage girls who worked here as barmaids were 'hidden' when the police inspected.

A block away, to the south, are smaller bars; these are tight, claustrophobic and intimate spaces, which must originally have been people's sitting rooms, but which opened as bars to benefit from the lucrative passing trade. Paradise Bar was such a space, no more than four metres square, as was Lollita's Bar, now occupied by the bar owner's son as a recording studio, This bar was the first in Malta to have sound proofing installed. The present owner keeps the sign in his back room. Further up the street are Rocks Bar and the Roy Bar, almost next door to it. Behind the tattered door of the Roy Bar is a modern telephone exchange: light and air-conditioned. We were not allowed access to the interior. Rocks Bar is closer in character to how this must once have appeared: dark and claustrophobic. Here the original owners remain, though they live elsewhere, using the space as a kind of urban beach hut, with sitting area, and kitchen; their beach is the street where they sit out, watching the passing scene. Graffiti remains where the loos once were, and the owner told us that keeping the graffiti was a deliberate choice. The bar also remains, along with mirrors and glass shelves behind it. They also have memorabilia – lots of it. Most of the customers here were American sailors who often sent framed and signed photographs of

their ships, and even a flag, which is kept neatly folded and was opened for us with great ceremony. The owners took many photographs when the bar was active and busy, and we spent time looking at these. The decoration fascinated us, a blue and red patterned wallpaper with an elaborate trellis covered with artificial flowers hugging the ceiling down the narrow entrance passage (Figure 36). This was in 2004. When we revisited in 2005 the owner was taking this trellis down: 'too dark and dusty', he said.

Larry's Bar was a puzzle. It was a bar that looked like it had been used yesterday but the owner insisted that it had been empty and unused for 'years'. There were fluorescent lights that still worked (strobing blue and red in the half-light), ceiling and wall-mounted fans, the shadows where commemorative plaques from naval ships had hung on the walls, and bottles (some not empty) behind the bar. The owner was once a bouncer here. After showing us Larry's Bar he took us round the corner to the Egyptian Queen, where he was until recently part-owner. This was empty, and clearly unused. There was a sense of abandonment here which we had not experienced elsewhere. Artefacts included crates, bottles, a stool, tables, one with a draped portrait of Queen Mary (Figure 37), a rack for pool cues, and a photograph on the wall of the Maltese and Italian football teams when they played each other some time in the 1970s. Of all the buildings this was the one with real architectural merit, and obvious aesthetic appeal. This is also the bar most visitors remember. Sailors told of pub crawls that started here, and it is here that folk memories are concentrated, including that of an 'Egyptian queen' dancing naked on the tables (op cit.). This also became the home of the Liverpool Football Club Supporters Club in Malta.

Figure 37. Queen Mary at the Egyptian Queen.

Brothels

Prostitution existed here, both historically and recently, of that there seems no doubt. Former prostitutes have been interviewed (eg, Scerri 2004b); histories give definitive accounts (eg, Cassar 1964), as do sociological (eg, Dench 1975) and anthropological studies (eg, Walz 2004) and surveys of crime and criminality (eg, Linnane 2003). However, archaeologically there is as yet no evidence. Brothels have been the subject of significant archaeological enquiry in recent years (eg, Gilfoyle 1999, 2005), and the types of associated material culture are now better understood. One future direction might be to study the buildings in and around Strait Street. *Cityspaces* – a recent exhibition showing work by eleven of Malta's artists – was housed in a tenement building in Old Bakery Street (www.studio-international.co.uk/painting/malta. htm, consulted 20 June 2005). In it were 10 empty rooms across five floors, all resembling one another and each containing only a tiny sink with a bucket propped underneath. At the back of each room was the smallest of lavatories. Rumour suggests this was built as a brothel, and the artistic installations reflected this fact and its location in a Catholic cultural context. How many more of these buildings exist? Are they concentrated in a particular part of Valletta? And were they really designed and built to serve as brothels? These are questions we will investigate as our project continues.

Lodgings and a music hall

Our fieldwork has taken us to places that were hotels or lodgings, and also one music hall, the 'Old Vic', which was centrally located and mentioned by most people we spoke with as a central place, socially as well as physically. The Old Vic was hard to get into. We had to be patient, and when we did gain access we were disappointed. The building is now used to store statues used in religious festivals, and is packed to the extent that very little can be seen of the building. The statues are only removed once a year, so fieldwork will have to coincide with the festival if we are to fully appreciate and record the space.

Hotels that existed previously are now occupied by the Labyrinth restaurant and Marks and Spencer (op cit.). In both cases significant alterations have been made. However, while the Marks and Spencer store conversion included a complete rebuilding, the character of the original structure remains. The central atrium of the store, for example, represents the central stairwell of the hotel.

Beyond these obvious traces are references to lodging houses in Pynchon's novel *V*, and signage, including a threshold with the word 'Splendid', indicating the location of this much talked-about guest house.

Artefacts

In addition to the objects seen in places such as the Egyptian Queen, we have been shown and given some artefacts that contribute to the narrative. Victor Scerri gave us a small metal token, or check, engraved with NL (for the New Life Music Hall); the owner of Monte-Carlo gave us some from his cash till. Also known as *landa*, these

Figure 38. Artists, including on the left a cross-dresser called Bobby

Figure 39. Artists on stage in Strait Street.

tokens were accumulated by barmaids during the evening, one for each drink she persuaded a sailor to buy. At the end of the evening the *landa* would be exchanged for money (Lyall 1999: 3). Barmaids were licensed to work by the Malta Police, and had to wear a round, metal badge, with their licence number and the initials MP (for Malta Police). Tokens of this kind also existed in business and are now very collectable.

Other artefacts include the documents and written sources that exist describing the business of Strait Street. While many of these will remain in private hands, and most have no doubt been destroyed, we were allowed access to one set of papers by the son of a bar and music hall owner. Letters described the way breweries and bar owners conducted their business and the rivalries that existed between the main competitors. Whilst the real significance of these letters is unlikely to be realised without an understanding of their wider economic and political contexts, they do provide interesting insights into business practices and social relations of the time.

We also have photographs of bar interiors and the cabaret artists that performed there (eg, Figures 38 and 39). There must be more of these, but no doubt widely dispersed and, again, very collectable.

Conclusions

There are various themes that emerge from this study. There is the significance of retaining bar names, signage and lettering for example; the stories people tell; and the ways in which art and music can contribute to the production of multiple narratives in such a contentious place as Strait Street.

Take the bar names, and the signs over the doors which give those names – and the memories they invoke – their physical manifestation. Social anthropologist Jon Mitchell

describes their significance in a passage outlining his growing acquaintance with Valletta:

> Peter [the author's tutor] told me of his childhood on a walking tour of Valletta, during which he also alluded to the lively entertainments in The Gut. Like all children of respectable families, he had been forbidden from going into The Gut … He described how he used to sneak into the street with his friends, to observe the drunken goings-on of sailors and their paid escorts. As we walked up the gently sloping street, he told me to write down the names of the various establishments – The Cotton Club, Cape Town, The Garden of Eden – all names he associated with his childhood, with home and with the erstwhile vibrancy of this now defunct red light area of a declining city. (2002: 59–60)

There are several examples where bar names remain, but where the building is now owned by a different family, and where the original owner (or at least their descendents) want 'their' signs back. They regard these signs as their personal heritage, and the act of removal is seen not as theft or vandalism but rescue and reclamation. The bar sign for the Smiling Prince Bar, for instance, is a wonderful example of its kind (Figure 40) – its elaborate use of silver, gold and red showing a creative flair unmatched in other surviving signs. However, the son of the one-time owner wants 'his' sign, and intends to take it and put it on private display. To those who walk up Strait Street, and who can use The Smiling Prince as a geographical reference, this will be a significant loss. In our view the signs should stay where they are; pride of (former) ownership can still be felt, arguably more so, with the signs *in situ*. There is perhaps even an argument for giving these few frontages where signs remain legal protection, as is afforded to 48 'historic'

Figure 40. The Smiling Prince sign (a) and detail (b).

timber shop fronts in Valletta (Magro Conti and Darmanin 2003). With increased local interest in Strait Street, most residents are likely to be receptive to this idea.

Signage, lettering and graffiti are other components of Strait Street that contribute to its character and interpretation. Although now faint, examples can be deciphered at various points along the street, whether the ghosts and voids where signs were attached to the walls ('Farsons' beer for example), names of places, or graffiti. The focus for lettering appears to have been street corners, places that have always had significance in Valletta, originating with the location of niches on every major intersection in the city (de Giorgio 1985; Scerri nd). Lettering points the way to 'Ye Old Vic Dancing and Cabaret' for example; brands of beer, stout, whiskey and cigarettes are promoted; and, in one case, the building now occupied by a firm of advocates, has seen conservation of the corner wall and the signage it contains. In addition to this 'official' signage, graffiti is also significant, marking individual actions and interventions over time. The graffiti themselves – individually – are not so significant; it is the cumulative effect that matters, and how that conveys sense of purpose amongst those that used the street.

Much has been written recently about those who worked in Strait Street. Victor Scerri's essays in *it-TORĊA* (op cit.) tell us of cross-dressers, prostitutes, musicians and barmaids. It is through Scerri's patient cultivation of good relations that these insights have been possible. But other stories remain to be told, including that of Tony the tattoo artist, who runs a tattoo parlour in Strait Street, as his father and grandfather did before him. Some of Tony's clients are former sailors, clients of his father and grandfather, who return today to have their original tattoos 'refreshed'.

Finally, and unexpectedly, we have now *heard* Strait Street, and seen it in full swing. A BBC *Tonight Special* documentary from 1964, on Independence night, included a visit to Strait Street and the packed Splendid Bar, where sailors mixed with girls, and sang *Allouette* for the cameras. The journalist described The Gut as a 'narrow, odorous alleyway'. He continued: 'Only the air is free in this sleazy reeking ditch, and no one would want to breathe more of that than necessary'. Recently Dominic Galea, a composer and musician, has drawn together recordings made by musicians working in the bars and music halls of Strait Street (Galea 2004). The recordings appeared as a double-CD: one a re-recording of songs played in Strait Street, by the original artists; and the other the original recordings. Although finding this soundtrack was not a direct result of our work, hearing it was perhaps the most exhilarating moment of all – hearing for the first time the sounds of the street, making the intangible tangible, and instilling a degree of the positivity and purpose back into Strait Street that *Titbits* – of all publications – did so much to remove.

Acknowledgements

Our involvement with Strait Street has been dependent upon the many friendships made and offers of help received during our time in Valletta, and subsequently. In particular we'd like to thank: Malcolm Borg, Victor Buchli, Joseph Buttigieg, Andrew Calascioni, Mark Casha, Joseph Chetcuti, Dennis Dowling, Dominic Galea, Reuben Grima, Joe Magro-Conti, Lolly Muscat, Anna and Tony Pace, Oliver Phillips, Joe Piccinino, Rachel Radmilli, Jim Sims and Clotilde Mifsud, and Leah Walz for advice and help of various kinds. Our very particular thanks however are to our 'man-of-the-streets', Victor Scerri, for boundless generosity and friendship, and without whom many of our contacts would never have been made, and several ambitions never realised. Victor also supplied Figures 38 and 39 from his private collection. We are also grateful to Vince Griffin of English Heritage for producing Figure 34, and Joseph Buttigieg for Figure 35. This project was supported by a small research grant by the British Academy.

References

Anderson, J. 2004. Talking whilst walking: a geographical archaeology of knowledge. *Area* 36 (3), 254–61.

Bell, M. 1997. The ghosts of place. *Theory and Society* 26, 813–36.

Boissevain, J. 1993. *Saints and Fireworks: Religion and Politics in Rural Malta*. Valletta: Progress Press,.

Boissevain, J. and Theuma, N. 1998. Contested Space: Planners, Tourists, Developers and Environmentalists in Malta. In S. Abram and J. Waldren (eds), *Anthropological Perspectives on Local Development: Knowledge and Sentiments in Conflict*, 96–119. London and New York: Routledge.

Buchli, V. and Lucas, G. 2001. The Archaeology of Alienation: a Late Twentieth-century British Council House. In V. Buchli and G. Lucas (eds), *Archaeologies of the Contemporary Past*, 158–68. London and New York: Routledge.

Byrne, D., Brayshaw, H. and Ireland, T. 2001. *Social Significance: a Discussion paper*. New South Wales National Parks and Wildlife Service.

Casey, E. 2000. *Remembering: a Phenomenological Study*. 2nd edn. Bloomington: Indiana University Press.

Cassar, P. 1964. *Medical History of Malta*. London: Wellcome Historical Medical Library.

Cassola, A. 1995. Pynchon, V., and the Malta Connection. In P. Bianchi, A. Cassola and P. Serracino Inglott (eds), *Pynchon, Malta and Wittgenstein*, 15–38. Malta University Publishers.

Collins, P. 1998. Negotiating selves: reflections on unstructured interviewing. *Sociological Research Online* 3, www.socresonline.org.uk/socresonline/3/3/2.html (1 May 2006).

de Giorgio, R. 1985. *A City by an Order*. Valletta: Progress Press.

Denaro, V.F. 1963. Yet more houses in Valletta. *Melita Historica* 3 (4), 15–32. www.geocities.com/melitahistorica/files/1963yetm.html?200520 (1 May 2006).

Dench, G. 1975. *Maltese in London: a Case-study in the Erosion of Ethnic Consciousness*. London and Boston: Routledge and Kegan Paul.

Dolff-Bonekaemper, G. nd. Sites of Memory and Sites of Discord: Historic Monuments as a Medium for Discussing Conflict in Europe. In G. Dolff-Bonekaemper (ed.), *Forward Planning: the Function of Cultural Heritage in a Changing Europe*, 53–58. Council of Europe.

Evans, K. 1998. *Copse: the Cartoon Book of Tree Protesting*. Biddestone: Orange Dog Publications.

Galea, D. 2004 (prod.). *Tribute to the swinging pioneers of Malta* (audio CD). Malta: Heritage.

Gilfoyle, T.J. 1999. Prostitutes in history: from parables of pornography to metaphors of modernity. *American Historical Review* 104 (1), 117–41.

Gilfoyle, T.J. 2005. Archaeologists in the brothel: 'Sin City', historical archaeology and prostitution. *Historical Archaeology* 39 (1), 133–41.

Hodder, I. 2003. *Archaeology Beyond Dialogue*. Salt Lake City: University of Utah Press.

Holtorf, C. 2005. *From Stonehenge to Las Vegas: Archaeology as Popular Culture*. Walnut Creek: AltaMira Press.

Linnane, F. 2003. *London's Underworld: Three Centuries of Vice and Crime*. London: Robson Books.

Lyall, B. 1999. *The Tokens and Checks of Malta*. Lolly Barrett, Timperley (England).

Magro Conti J. and Darmanin, D. 2003. *Scheduled Property Monitoring, Timber Shopfronts and Kiosks in Valletta (1995)*. Draft unpublished internal report. Malta: Malta Environment and Planning Authority.

Mitchell, J.P. 2002. *Ambivalent Europeans: Ritual, Memory and the Public Sphere in Malta*. London and New York: Routledge.

Pynchon, T. 2000 [1961]. *V.* London: Vintage.

Read, P. 1996. *Returning to Nothing: the Meaning of Lost Places*. Cambridge: Cambridge University Press.

Rinaldi, N. 1999. *The Jukebox Queen of Malta*. London: Bantam Press.

Saxon, E. 1965. The street that shames Hero Island. *Titbits* February.

Scerri, V. nd *Niches and Statues in Valletta*. Valletta Local Council, Malta.

Scerri, V. 2004a. Dwellijiet … u briedel. *it-TORĊA* 3135, 28–29.

Scerri, V. 2004b. Nitkellmu ma' Nonny-l'*barmaid*. *it-TORĊA* 19 September, 20–21.

Scerri, V. 2005. Dejjem ħareġ ta' raġel … bil-ħwejjeġ ta' mara! *it-TORĊA* 3165, 26–27.

Schadla Hall, T. 2004. The Comforts of Unreason: the Importance and Relevance of Alternative Archaeology. In Merriman, N. (ed.), *Public Archaeology*, 255–71. London and New York: Routledge.

Sin, C.H. 2003. Interviewing in 'place': the socio-spatial construction of interview data. *Area* 35 (3), 305–12.

Tornatore, G. 1989. *Cinema Paradiso*. Arrow Films.

Walz, L. 2004. 'A necessary evil': clandestine prostitutes, soldiers and venereal disease in early 20th century Malta. Conference abstract. www.crwh.org/events/gsrd2005.php (19 June 2005)

Wenders, W. with Cooder, R. 1999. *Buena Vista Social Club*. FilmFour.

CULTURAL IDENTITY AND PERCEPTIONS OF SLAVERY IN THE CLOVE PLANTATIONS OF ZANZIBAR

Sarah Croucher

Introduction

Clove plantations were a major social institution on nineteenth-century Zanzibar. At present, written histories draw on the accounts of European travellers, missionaries and colonial officers (Cooper 1977; Sheriff 1987). This is despite the fact that clove plantations were distinctly non-European institutions: they were run by Arab plantation owners who used the labour of African slaves. Contemporary presentations of clove plantations to Western tourists on Zanzibar also largely reinforce the Eurocentric image of the islands. This image has been constructed and negotiated from the nineteenth century and continues to be so today.

Within this paper archaeological data from the Zanzibar Clove Plantation Survey 2003 (hereafter ZCPS03) presents a contrasting view to both historical and tourist understandings of clove plantations. Two islands actually comprise the political area of 'Zanzibar' (see Figure 41); the southern island of Zanzibar (also called Unguja) and the northern island of Pemba. Four areas in total across the two islands were surveyed by the ZCPS03. Rather than simply supporting historical representations the results from the ZCPS03 provide an alternative interpretation of clove plantations. Archaeologies such as this that focus upon later historical periods of the East African coast are few at present. Yet whist they exist alongside alternative historical narratives they are crucial in enabling us to broaden our understandings of the East African coast during the nineteenth century.

Previous archaeological research on the East African coast has focussed primarily on the 'Swahili', an urban Islamic civilisation that developed from the first millennium AD. Settlements fitting within this cultural grouping exist from Somalia in the north to Mozambique in the south, and are also found on many offshore islands, including Zanzibar, Mafia, the Comoros and Madagascar (Horton and Middleton 2000: 5). Research on Swahili stonetown sites means that the East African coast is one of the few areas within sub-Saharan Africa where there has been concentrated archaeological research.

Most archaeological research conducted on the coast has focussed on these stone town settlements. It is intimately woven within the history of European colonialism on the coast, with archaeologists first drawn to investigate towns that textual history suggested were the product of Arab invaders (Reid and Lane 2004b: 11). Despite these beginnings the focus of such archaeological investigations has now shifted to investigate the African origins of the Swahili (eg, Chami 1998; Horton 1996). More recently there has been a new focus within archaeological research on the coast to understand the growth of urbanism and to situate the stone towns within their wider non-urban settlement patterns (Fleisher 2003; Fleisher and LaViolette 1999; LaViolette *et al* 1999; Wynne-Jones 2005). Most of this archaeology has been loosely categorised as 'historical archaeology', with Arabic texts available that document

some of the earliest towns on the coast (Freeman-Grenville 1962). Indeed, one of the earlier practitioners of coastal archaeology labelled his work explicitly as historical archaeology (Kirkman 1957). Although Swahili archaeology is certainly no longer reliant on Arabic texts in the same manner as this earlier generation of scholars, it is still seen as being a part of historical archaeology within Africa with chapters focussed on the Swahili appearing in a recent volume *African Historical Archaeologies* (LaViolette 2004; Reid and Lane 2004a).

In contrast to the relatively well-studied Swahili town sites, almost no archaeology has been carried out that examines sites postdating Portuguese contact with the coast from the sixteenth century. Notable exceptions to this are the excavations by James Kirkman at the Portuguese (and later Omani) Fort Jesus, located in the town of Mombasa, Kenya (Kirkman 1974). Work at this site was aimed primarily at locating remains associated with an elite colonial minority and not those of the majority of Mombasa's residents. In addition the project has been rightly critiqued as being part of the colonial milieu seeking to provide physical points for the longer history of colonialism in the area (Reid and Lane 2004b: 11).

Contrasting with this, the focus of my research is the archaeology of nineteenth-century Zanzibar on sites that offer a departure from both the stone towns and forts of the coast. Historically we know that the nineteenth century was a period of rapid social change for coastal residents in opposition to the seeming social stability often presented within Swahili town archaeology (although this static picture of Swahili town life has recently been critiqued; see Fleisher 2004). From the early sixteenth century Portuguese colonial power over the coast gradually expanded as part of their wider colonial rule over many Indian Ocean areas (Sheriff 1987: 16), although few Portuguese actually settled in East Africa. From the late seventeenth continuing into the early eighteenth century, Omani forces gradually wrested political control of the Swahili coast (Sheriff 1987: 17). This Omani control eventually centred on the port town of Zanzibar, causing rapid urban expansion here from the late eighteenth century (Sheriff 1995: 12). Concomitant with this was the expansion of the caravan trade in ivory and slaves to east and central mainland Africa, and the gradual incorporation of eastern Africa into global capitalist markets (Glassman 1995: 36; Sheriff 1987: 245).

Successful Omani merchants used profits from the caravan trade to invest in the agricultural sector. This resulted in the development of localised plantation economies on several areas of the East African coast; grain plantations around Malindi in Kenya (Cooper 1977: 80); sugar plantations around Pangani in mainland Tanzania (Glassman 1995: 82); and clove plantations on Zanzibar (Cooper 1977: 47; Sheriff 1987: 48). The establishment of these plantation areas occurred only within the early to mid nineteenth century – indeed the clove, as a crop, was not introduced

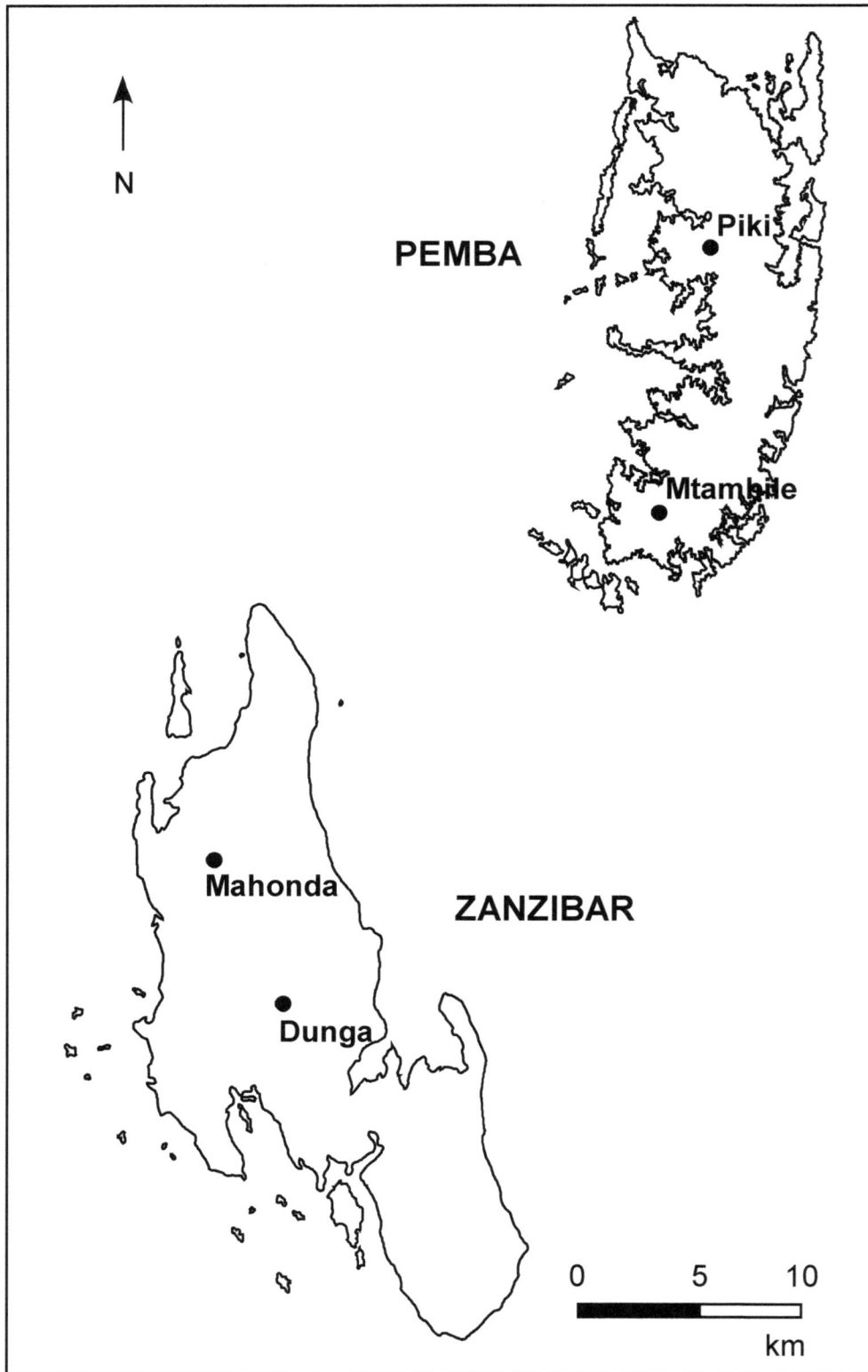

Figure 41. Map showing location of ZCPS03 survey areas on Zanzibar and Pemba

to Zanzibar until 1818 (Cooper 1977: 48). Furthermore, the establishment of clove plantations was mostly through the new Omani merchant class, particularly on Zanzibar (Sheriff 1987: 48), rather than the broader pre-existing Swahili patrician elites.

Immigration is a key theme of the history of nineteenth-century Zanzibar. This was due to both the commercial success of Zanzibar, which drew voluntary immigrants to the islands, and by clove plantations, which demanded high levels of slave labour. The majority of voluntary immigrants were concentrated in urban areas, particularly Indians, of whom about 3,000 were estimated to live on Zanzibar by the 1870s (Fair 2001: 13), and immigrants from the Hadramaut (a region on the Southern coast of the Arabian Peninsula) and the Comoro Islands. Omani immigrants formed the majority of voluntary migrants to the islands. Their pattern of residence changed over time; during the early nineteenth century many were drawn to urban areas in order to participate in mercantile activities. This changed with the growth of the plantation economy as more and more of them began to live on their plantations; by the 1840s 5,000 Omanis had migrated to Zanzibar (Unguja) alone (Burton 1872: 368; Fair 2001: 13).

By far the greatest numbers of (forced) immigrants to Zanzibar in the nineteenth century were agricultural slaves. Slaves were brought along the expanding caravan routes from a wide region of East Central Africa (stretching as far as the Congo on the western side of Lake Tanganyika) as a commodity alongside ivory (Iliffe 1979: 48), and were drawn from a wide variety of ethnic groups. Although slave-owning had been a feature of both Swahili and Omani society prior to the nineteenth century, clove plantations dramatically increased the number of slaves living on the islands. By the end of the century the majority of the population of Zanzibar consisted of slaves or recently manumitted slaves (Fair 2001: 13). The number of slaves ever present on the islands is debated, but is likely to have reached approximately 100,000 (Sheriff 1987: 60).

Current scholarly historical interpretations of clove plantations on nineteenth-century Zanzibar demonstrate that they comprised a radical new kind of social institution for the islands, forming an integral part of the transformative process of Omani colonialism. This physically transformed the geography of the islands as cloves were rapidly planted over the majority of Pemba and over the northeastern half of Zanzibar (Cooper 1977: 48; Sheriff 1987: 48–56). New social relations were created on plantations with a population who were in the majority immigrants: an Omani 'landed aristocracy' (Sheriff 1987: 53) and their slaves living alongside the indigenous Swahili population of Zanzibar. Before moving on to demonstrate the way in which archaeological evidence can provide an alternative history of clove plantations I shall first show the way in which historical interpretations of nineteenth-century Zanzibar are entwined with the presentation of Zanzibar's history to tourists.

Presentations of clove plantations

Zanzibar today is a popular holiday destination for both affluent tourists and backpackers from around the Western world. Tourists are drawn here by an image of Zanzibar as an exotic tropical island with a rich Oriental history, an image promoted by tour operators and guidebooks. Intimately tied to this history are clove plantations, and whilst they may not be an immediate image for tourists when they decide to travel to the islands, they form a part of their experience of Zanzibar. Tourist companies and restaurants alike peddle the image of the 'spice islands' in

both the history and the cuisine of Zanzibar. The exoticism of this is further enhanced by the majority of tourists' experiences in 'spice tours', suggested by one guidebook to the islands as 'virtually obligatory' (Finke 2002: 116).

Such tours take visitors around a plantation that mostly consists of clove trees, but in which visitors can also see a variety of other spices grown on the islands, such as black pepper, cardamom, cinnamon, nutmeg and lemongrass. Alongside the sensual experience of seeing, touching, smelling and tasting such spices most tours also take visitors to at least one nineteenth-century site associated with Omani colonial rule, such as the Kidichi Persian Baths or the slave caves at Mangapwani. The idea that such spices were grown by a rich elite with a large subjugated population of slaves is thus presented for tourist consumption as part of the exotic history of Zanzibar.

Such images, presented to tourists on a daily basis, reinforce the stereotypical images of Zanzibar that have been created in the Western imagination. Garth Myers (1996) has recently analysed popular British and American literary representations of Zanzibar from the 1870s to the 1990s. Within these he found that the complex geographical realities of Zanzibar were suppressed, with sexualised notions of veiled women and the 'sultriness' of the islands embedded in the Western psyche (Myers 1996: 419). The exoticism of the islands is further intertwined with the history of clove plantations, with cloves 'at the heart of this fragrant imagination' (Myers 1996: 416). Zanzibar is not alone in having such stereotypical images of an historical and archaeological past being presented through tourist images and popular culture. Archaeology is commonly used in presentations of heritage to tourists, another example in Africa being the Kalahari (Reid 2005: 351).

Such exotic images of Zanzibar's nineteenth-century history are at present uncontested by archaeological research. The only archaeological work to engage with post-sixteenth-century remains on the islands is the work of Clark and Horton (1985), who produced an inventory of archaeological sites and monuments on Zanzibar. Their survey work had a limited remit simply to record the major archaeological sites of the islands for the Zanzibari government. Both eighteenth- and nineteenth-century sites associated with Zanzibar's later colonial history were included in the survey alongside sites dating back to the ninth century AD. Later sites recorded were associated solely with the remains of Omani or British colonial palaces, grand houses or mosques. The only exception to these elite structures was the Mangapwani slave caves, which were used to conceal slaves as they were imported to Zanzibar after the abolition of slavery (Clark and Horton 1985: 15). This survey therefore recognised later elite sites as worthy of recording and preservation whilst not recording any of the lower status sites of the nineteenth century. In doing so the mainstream heritage presentation of Zanzibar's later colonial history was, and is, reinforced. Archaeology's potential to challenge stereotypical images of Zanzibar has so far not been utilised as no archaeologists have carried out any investigations of the archaeology of everyday life of the majority of nineteenth-century Zanzibari residents.

The archaeology of clove plantations

When directed at such questions, historical archaeology offers an opportunity to study the social changes that took place amongst the many immigrants arriving on Zanzibar and Pemba, and the changing social relations between slaves and their owners on plantations. It had been suggested that identities on nineteenth-century Zanzibar were 'multiple,

Figure 42. Stone built plantation owner's house, Mgoli.

fluid, strategic and situational' (Fair 2001: 55) – yet this is the limit of understandings so far. Historians openly admit that for this period of East African history they are hampered by a lack of historical documents relating to social histories (Cooper 1981). Unlike history however, historical archaeology offers an opportunity to transcend the constraints of historical documentation. My fieldwork research, the ZCPS03, was thus designed not only to provide a culture historical recording of clove plantation sites on Zanzibar, but also to explore the ways in which historical renderings of the exotic image of Zanzibar interacted with the realities of the archaeology of clove plantations and the oral histories associated with these.

The ZCPS03 was undertaken in May and June 2003 to locate archaeological sites relating to clove plantations on Zanzibar. The project employed a basic reconnaissance methodology, with local residents asked about the locations of such places. As well as recording archaeological remains oral histories relating to the archaeological sites and to the history of clove plantations on the islands were recorded. Four areas on the islands (see Figure 41 for a location map of these) around the villages of Dunga and Mahonda on Zanzibar (Unguja) and Mtambile and Piki on Pemba were investigated by the survey. Archaeological remains were recorded as site constituents with each of these representing related archaeological remains in any given location. Due to the large scale nature of some clove plantations this meant that more than one site constituent could be recorded which related to the same plantation. In total 64 site constituents were recorded by the survey, which represents a wide range of locales associated with clove plantations. I do not intend to present a detailed picture of the results of this survey here, as such results have been published elsewhere (Croucher 2004). Instead I intend to highlight the ways in which the overall findings of the survey can present us with a differing picture of clove plantations than that given by conventional histories.

All sites recorded by the ZCPS03 were associated with clove plantations in some way. In addition they show that as clove planting swept across the islands in the early- to mid-nineteenth century the settlement landscape of the island was also dramatically changed. None of the sites recorded showed traces of any occupation prior to the nineteenth century. Thus new settlements developed and changing areas became locations of social importance for islanders.

This different nineteenth-century landscape incorporated a variety of sites, in contrast to other archaeological surveys of the islands. Clark and Horton's survey (1985) has already been mentioned, and the results of the ZCPS03 differed from the characterisation of nineteenth-century Zanzibar resulting from this in reflecting a wider social range in the sites recorded. The results of the ZCPS03 were also markedly different to those produced by a survey of Pemba (Fleisher 2003) that had focussed on earlier periods, and which had recorded only one site with nineteenth-century occupation from a total of 35 sites overall (ibid: 133).

Within sites recorded on the ZCPS03, some were easy to place into basic categories of plantation owner or slave settlements. Yet within these very divisions great variation between sites was apparent. Some plantation owners did indeed live in grandiose stone houses as might be expected from their historical characterisation, and left archaeological traces that conform to the idea of an Omani 'landed aristocracy' (Sheriff 1987: 53). Such sites included site constituent 19 in the Mahonda survey region; this site comprised an artefact scatter, the ruins of a stone built house and a mound. The site had been the home of Udi Masoud, a rich nineteenth-century Omani plantation owner whom we were told owned so many *shambas* (farms or plantations) on Zanzibar and Pemba that he would say 'it cannot rain without raining on my *shamba*' due to his landholdings being spread over so wide an area.

Another such plantation owner's home was site constituent 51 (see Figure 42) in the Piki survey region, a site known as Mgoli. Several local residents informed us that the site had been owned by a man named Abdalla bin Jabir, from Oman, and that he had owned a large landholding, slaves and concubines. Substantial remains of a coral stone house could be seen at the site, including the remnants of a carved wooden lintel. The elaborate nature of the wooden lintel and the arched niches within the building's plaster work, coupled with the romantic ruined condition of the building, were evocative of stereotypical images of luxuriant Omani elites ruling over their plantations.

Many sites identified to us as having been the homes of plantation owners had not been elaborate stone buildings. Plantation owners also lived in more modest houses of wattle and daub. These houses generally left few archaeological traces: an artefact scatter and perhaps an earth mound were the standard archaeological remains recorded at such sites. We were fortunate to also record one such standing structure in the village of Bweni within the Mahonda survey region. This was the long-standing home of a plantation-owning family and as people were still living in the house it was not recorded as an archaeological site. Currently a large wattle and daub house stands here, separated from another wattle and daub building by a large, compacted earth and rubble floor that had been used for drying cloves. Our interviewee could recall a maximum of 20 people living in this house in the past.

Many Zanzibari residents today live in wattle and daub houses. However, the example found at Bweni was markedly different to the majority of such structures: the elaborateness of the door and the clove-drying floor set it apart. Although they lived in homes built of the same material as many poorer village residents, plantation owners may have still been able to differentiate these structures within a wide range of building styles. Such minor differences reflect the way in which a considerable spectrum of social differentiation between plantation owners themselves, and between plantation owners and other Zanzibaris who lived in wattle and daub houses, was shown through domestic architecture. This differentiation of social status, which was closely intertwined with both the available resources for house building and the ongoing presentation and use of the house, is similar to that which existed in the poorer neighbourhoods of Zanzibar town during the nineteenth century (Myers 1997).

Sites recorded within the survey also challenged the dominant gender stereotypes of plantation owners and alongside this the stereotype of the sexualised Arab veiled woman on Zanzibar, as identified by Myers (1996: 419). Two sites in the Mtambile survey region were identified as the homes of female plantation owners. One of these was site constituent 24, the home of Mwanaiki Nassor, shown to us by her son and grandson. The imported ceramics from the site suggested it dated to the late nineteenth and early twentieth centuries. Her home had been built of wattle and daub, with workers (it was not clear if these had once been slaves) living around her house in thatched houses. The remains of Mwanaiki Nassor's home could clearly be seen in the form of a small mound. In contrast no archaeological remains could be found of these thatched houses, despite an extensive search. Site constituent 24 represents an archaeological site that testifies both to the presence of less wealthy plantation owners' homes and those of female plantation owners as an integral part of the social landscape of nineteenth-century Zanzibar.

Sites associated with slaves were more difficult to identify than those associated with plantation owners. The traces of these within the Zanzibari landscape are ephemeral. Slave houses were commonly built from thatch, resulting in few obvious archaeological remains today. At several of the plantation owners' sites we visited we were told that there had been associated slave residences, but despite extensive searches in the areas these were rarely located. Of the total recorded sites only four specifically related to slaves. One

site consisted of a large artefact scatter, mostly of locally produced ceramics, in an area where we were informed that slaves had been living. Another was a graveyard for slaves, with coral rag (the local stone) grave markers in an Islamic style. This latter site supported both documentary and oral historical evidence that slaves had converted, at least in public practices, to Islam.

Despite the small number of slave sites recorded variance was obvious within this category. Both settlement sites and Muslim graveyards formed part of the recordings of the survey, but there is no clear pattern to the relationship between slave sites and those of plantation owners. As with the archaeology of plantation owners, the archaeology of slaves on clove plantation sites defied easy categorisation. This lack of obvious categorisation again complicates current historical understandings of clove plantation slaves as a simple monolithic social category. Their physical location in relation to plantations varied. The form of their houses (whether of wattle and daub or thatch) varied, and as with plantation owners' homes this has important ramifications for the overall social status of slaves within Zanzibari society. Their religious practices were obviously complex also: although they followed Islam like their owners, their graveyards were also clearly delineated from those of plantation owners. Although these four sites are only the beginning of an archaeology of clove plantation slavery on Zanzibar they already begin to add to and change historical interpretations.

The majority of sites recorded by the ZCPS03, 41 of the total, fell within the grouping of village sites. A large number of the residents of nineteenth-century Zanzibar were living in village sites and were neither plantation owners nor slaves. Their lives were very much tied to clove plantations; members of a village or household might undertake seasonal labour on a clove plantation (particularly in the early twentieth century) or might have a smallholding consisting of only one or two clove trees that they tended themselves. In all of these scenarios clove plantations were an essential part of the social interactions occurring within these areas on the islands, despite the marginalisation of such villagers in historical narratives.

The archaeological evidence shows that there is no simple schema of nineteenth-century settlement on Zanzibar. Although broad categorisations can be drawn of plantation owner sites, in slave sites and village sites great variation existed. Whilst the ZCPS03 demonstrated broad trends within clove plantation settlement on Zanzibar in the nineteenth century, which could fit with both the image of Zanzibar's luxuriant exotic elite and with the historical notion of an Omani 'landed aristocracy' creating their plantations with groups of slaves, the results also show significant disparities with such images. Plantation owners were not only very wealthy Arab men living in stone houses. There was variance in the wealth of plantation owners. Whilst they were perhaps not poor, those who lived in large wattle and daub houses were obviously much less wealthy than those (such as Udi Masoud) who lived in monumental stone houses. The site of Mwanaiki Nassor's plantation demonstrates that female plantation owners were an accepted part of Zanzibari society, forcing us to examine critically the role of gender in plantation-owner identities. Although slave sites are difficult to identify, the remains of these also allow for a more nuanced understanding of slaves on plantation sites. Archaeology also restores the importance of village sites within the wider nineteenth- and twentieth-century plantation landscape, providing a more balanced social interpretation of those who were involved in the daily routines and interactions of plantation life.

The recording of sites on the ZCPS03 drew largely on oral histories recorded from contemporary Zanzibari residents. No simple fusion of oral histories and archaeology can be applied, as demonstrated in an East African context by Helm (2004). Oral histories do, however, provide an alternative historical narrative to that of documentary history, and present an alternative dimension to aid in the interpretation of nineteenth-century archaeological sites on Zanzibar. Residents of clove plantation areas in Zanzibar today have a differing view of the nature of sites associated with plantations than the images created through Western discourse and histories, which largely rely on written documents. Such viewpoints allow the juxtaposition of archaeological sites alongside differing historical interpretations to provide a discordant image of clove plantations.

Conclusions – the importance of later historical archaeology on Zanzibar

The study of the nineteenth century has been marginalised within archaeological investigation of East Africa, with archaeologists content to allow history (and often histories that reflect European colonial discourse) to create interpretations of nineteenth-century coastal life. The results presented within this paper construct a compelling case for further research to be undertaken that relates to such later periods. This kind of archaeology does not simply create a culture history for the nineteenth century on Zanzibar, nor merely catalogue sites that provide a backdrop against which historical narratives can be placed. The recording of a wide range of archaeological sites that relate to clove plantations on Zanzibar reveal a much broader history than has been formerly discussed.

Clove plantations had an immense impact on all levels of society on nineteenth-century Zanzibar. In areas where clove plantations were founded they had a profound effect on the lives of all those around them. An archaeological perspective upon such a period can ask, and begin to answer, new and challenging questions. It questions the existence of a single plantation-owning elite during this period, and the relationship of gender roles in such elites. From the evidence presented here it would suggest that plantation owners represented a diverse section of society, including women. Questions are also raised relating to the role of slaves on plantations: whether they had a single role, and how straightforward their hierarchical relationship was to other plantation owners around the islands. Zanzibari villagers are also added in to the scope of enquiry, forcing a new set of questions to be asked as to their interactions with plantations.

By approaching these questions it is also possible to challenge some of the accepted images of gender roles and elites that may have been unquestioningly accepted by archaeologists focussing upon earlier periods of the coast. Interpretations of the social structure in place on the coast in the nineteenth and twentieth centuries are often projected back to interpret earlier Swahili archaeological remains. As archaeological investigations into later periods add complexity and alternative understandings to received historical interpretations, this will in turn raise questions about and problematise current interpretations of the social interactions taking place in earlier periods on the coast.

I often find that as an archaeologist who focuses upon the nineteenth century I am asked to justify my research both to other archaeologists, and to non-archaeologist friends and acquaintances: why do I not study prehistory? What can an archaeologist find out about the more recent past? It has been suggested in a recent volume on African historical archaeologies that archaeology 'can make an important contribution in its own right to the investigation of the creation of modern Africa, by using its own distinct range of sources to reach out to wider, more inclusive histories' (Reid and Lane 2004b: 3). Whilst the results of the ZCPS03 presented here certainly do not provide a conclusive narrative of life on nineteenth-century clove plantations, they amply challenge the normative image presented of these sites. Archaeology that focuses upon later historical sites clearly has a major role to play in locating sites that confront such stereotypical images and, crucially, also in presenting these to a wider audience.

Acknowledgements

The ZCPS03 was undertaken with grants from both The British Institute in Eastern Africa and the Zochonis Special Enterprise Awards of the University of Manchester. My grateful thanks go to The Department of Archives, Museums and Antiquities (DAMA), Zanzibar for their support of this research, particularly to Abdurahman Juma, whose support and advice was invaluable, and to Mr Hamad Omar, head of DAMA, who has been unfailingly supportive of my project. Many thanks also to Ali Abdalla Dade, Antiquities Officer and Ange Brennan of the University of Manchester for their invaluable help and support on the fieldwork itself. Residents of the survey areas on Zanzibar who gave both their information and support are too numerous to mention here, but the survey would not have been possible without them. Many thanks also to Karina Croucher, Keith Croucher and the editors of this volume for their comments and suggestions on earlier drafts of this paper.

References

Burton, R.F. 1872. *Zanzibar: City, Island and Coast* (2 Volumes). London: Tinsley Brothers.

Chami, F. 1998. A review of Swahili archaeology. *African Archaeological Review* 15 (3), 199–218.

Clark, C. and Horton, M. 1985. *Zanzibar Archaeological Survey 1984/5*. Unpublished report: The Ministry of Information, Culture and Sport, Zanzibar.

Cooper, F. 1977. *Plantation Slavery on the East Coast of Africa*. New Haven: Yale University Press.

Cooper, F. 1981. The Ideology of Slaveowners on the East African Coast. In P.E. Lovejoy (ed.), *The Ideology of Slavery in Africa*, 271–307. London: Sage.

Croucher, S. 2004. Zanzibar clove plantation survey 2003: some preliminary findings. *Nyame Akuma* 62, 65–69.

Fair, L. 2001. *Passtimes and Politics: Culture, Community and Identity in Post-Abolition Urban Zanzibar, 1890–1945*. Oxford: James Currey.

Finke, J. 2002. *The Rough Guide to Zanzibar*. London: Rough Guides.

Fleisher, J.B. 2003. *Viewing Stonetowns from the Countryside: An Archaeological Approach to Swahili Regions, AD 800–1500*. Unpublished PhD thesis, Department of Anthropology, University of Virginia.

Fleisher. J. 2004. Behind the Sultan of Kilwa's 'Rebellious Conduct': Local Perspectives on an International East African Town. In A.M. Reid and P.J. Lane (eds), *African Historical Archaeologies*, 91–124. New York: Kluwer/Plenum.

Fleisher, J. and LaViolette, A. 1999. Elusive wattle-and-daub: finding the hidden majority in the archaeology of the Swahili. *Azania* 34, 87–108.

Freeman-Grenville, G.S.P. 1962. *East African Coast; Select Documents*. Oxford: Clarendon Press.

Glassman, J. 1995. *Feasts and Riot: Revelry, Rebellion, and Popular Consciousness on the Swahili Coast, 1856–1888*. London: James Currey.

Helm, R. 2004. Re-Evaluating Traditional Histories on the Coast of Kenya: An Archaeological Perspective. In A.M. Reid and P.J. Lane (eds), *African Historical Archaeologies*, 59–90. New York: Kluwer/Plenum.

Horton, M. 1996. *Shanga: the Archaeology of a Muslim Trading Community on the Coast of East Africa*. London: British Institute in Eastern Africa.

Horton, M. and Middleton, J. 2000. *The Swahili: The Social Landscape of a Mercantile Society*. Oxford: Blackwell.

Iliffe, J. 1979. *A Modern History of Tanganyika*. Cambridge: Cambridge University Press.

Kirkman, J. 1957. Historical archaeology in Kenya 1948–56. *Antiquaries Journal* 37, 16–28.

Kirkman, J. 1974. *Fort Jesus: A Portuguese Fortress on the East African Coast*. Oxford: Clarendon Press.

LaViolette, A. 2004. Swahili Archaeology and History on Pemba, Tanzania: A Critique and Case Study of the Use of Written and Oral Sources in Archaeology. In A.M. Reid and P.J. Lane (eds), *African Historical Archaeologies*, 125–62. New York: Kluwer/Plenum.

LaViolette, A, W.B. Fawcett, N.J. Karoma and P.R. Schmidt. 1999. Survey and excavations between Dar es Salaam and Bagamoyo: University of Dar es Salaam Field School, 1988 (Part 2). *Nyame Akuma* 52, 74–78.

Myers, G.A. 1996. Isle of cloves, sea of discourses: writing about Zanzibar. *Ecumene* 3 (4), 408–26.

Myers, G.A. 1997. Sticks and stones: colonialism and Zanzibari housing. *Africa* 67(2), 252–272.

Reid, A. 2005. Interaction, Marginalization, and the Archaeology of the Kalahari. In A.B. Stahl (ed), *African Archaeology: A Critical Introduction*, 353–77. Oxford: Blackwell.

Reid, A.M. and P.J. Lane (eds). 2004a. *African Historical Archaeologies*. New York: Kluwer/Plenum.

Reid, A.M. and P.J. Lane. 2004b. African Historical Archaeologies: An Introductory Consideration of Scope and Potential. In A.M. Reid and P.J. Lane (eds), *African Historical Archaeologies*, 1–33. New York: Kluwer/Plenum.

Sheriff, A. 1987. *Slaves, Spices and Ivory in Zanzibar: Integration of an East African Commercial Empire into the World Economy, 1770–1873*. Oxford: James Currey.

Sheriff, A. 1995. An Outline History of Zanzibar Stone Town. In A. Sheriff (ed.), *The History and Conservation of Zanzibar Stone Town*, 8–29 Zanzibar: The Department of Archives, Museums and Antiquities (in association with James Currey, London).

Wynne-Jones, S. 2005. *Urbanisation at Kilwa, Tanzania, AD800 – 1400*. Unpublished PhD thesis, University of Cambridge

From Rhetoric to Research: the Bloody Meadows Project as a Pacifist Response to War

John Carman and Patricia Carman

We once received the following question from a colleague who had learned of our interest in studying historic battlefields: 'Do you like war, then?'. The short answer is 'No'. The longer answer is as follows...

The aim of our Bloody Meadows Project is to contribute to current debates on the place of war in the world by developing an understanding of changes in warfare practice and ideology over the long-term. In doing so we seek to overcome the limitations of the dominant discourse in the study of war, which derives particularly from military history.

Our project is an exercise in the comparative study of battlefields from all periods of history and in all parts of the world. We treat battlefields as landscapes, drawing upon recent approaches adopted in landscape archaeology. Battles, as single and unique events, are a main focus of military history in all periods, and battlefields are also increasingly being taken up as part of a nation's 'official' cultural heritage and as the focus of research by archaeologists and others who also seek to elucidate the sequence of events at such sites. By placing the focus upon the battle*field* itself, however – and by looking at those from all periods – it becomes possible to gain an insight into the underlying cultural imperatives guiding the practice of war, and to discover aspects of warmaking in the past that allow new understandings of war as a cultural phenomenon. From this standpoint there emerge challenges to modern perceptions and expectations.

The contribution of such a study to understanding war as a cultural activity lies in examining the assumptions underlying the choice of place in which to fight. Work from 1998 to 2002 (Carman and Carman 2006) has highlighted the range of different landscapes in which battles are fought: but while similar types of place may be chosen in one period of history, these will differ significantly and noticeably from those chosen in other periods (see Figure 41). The choice of battleground, we believe, therefore reflects unstated ideas about how war should be conducted, and these ideas vary across history. By studying the places where these acts took place we can develop an insight into the minds of soldiers in the past which challenge our own assumptions about the place of war in our society and force us to look again at our own assumptions and expectations.

The Project has its origin in some of the shared interests of the authors. One of these concerns the nature of heritage places of all kinds. Another concerns the place of war in human history. A third concerns the attempt to develop a specifically archaeological contribution to one of the important debates of our time (for an early and provisional statement of this, see Carman 1997b). The very specific focus of the project arose initially out of the interest of one of us in the way in which particular heritage objects are selected, categorised and given value (an issue addressed in terms of the legal frameworks available in Carman 1996). We wished to take this theme further – in particular to delve more deeply into specific categories

– and also to develop a fieldwork project that would allow some contact with fresh air rather than the stuffy gloom of the academic library. Accordingly, we sought a suitable category of heritage object for examination, and one that would also provide the opportunity to do more in the way of research than merely note its existence and the bureaucratic arrangements that exist for its treatment, or simply adding to its number by identifying new sites that fit the category. At the same time, and in order to avoid duplicating the work of others, the category needed to be one not yet being systematically addressed either in terms of heritage or some other research areas. It needed to be a category sufficiently large – and preferably with some international recognition – to allow a reasonable amount of specific fieldwork time, but not one so broad as to cover almost anything or any place marked as 'heritage'.

The happy accident of the production of the English Heritage *Register of Historic Battlefields* (English Heritage 1995) coincided with the period of this search for a focus of fieldwork. Its production tied in with both our interests in war as a contemporary and historical problem – especially in the context of the return of war to Europe after the end of the Cold War – and also with the simultaneous rise of battlefield archaeology as a distinct specialism (Freeman and Pollard 2001; Doyle and Bennett 2002). A focus on battlefields appeared to be a good way of meeting the needs of the desired fieldwork project and at the same time incorporating a concern with human violence. A project that expressly combined issues of heritage with research into an aspect of the past represented a new kind of project: we know of no others that combine these two aspects from the outset and where the two interact so closely.

The problem: the discourse of war studies

The study of war and, especially, battles has a particular trajectory of its own and a particular purpose: it is derived originally from professional military studies of war, the purpose of which is to assist the professional soldier in the performance of his duties (Keegan 1976: 15–22). The discourse of war – one shared in political and strategic studies – that has arisen out of this is quite distinctive and highly powerful. Much 'battlefield', 'combat' or 'conflict' archaeology also subscribes to it (Freeman and Pollard 2001; Doyle and Bennett 2002; Pollard and Banks 2006; Schofield 2005). The conventional discourse of war is one that can be understood in terms of incorporating three mutually supporting elements.

Linear narrative

The first element is a focus upon linear narrative (eg, Brodie 1973; Cline 2000; Fuller 1970; Weigley 1991), and especially upon the narrative of individual events. Military histories seize upon the violent encounters that make up the waging of war to consider them in terms of their level of 'decisiveness' to the general exclusion of other criteria

Discourses of battle

DATE

1000	1200	1400	1600	1800

LANDSCAPES

OPEN
Maldon 991
Assandun 1016

HILLTOP/URBAN
Stamford Bridge 1066
Bouvines 1214
Courtrai 1302
Tewkesbury 1471
Bosworth 1485
Stoke 1487

DEFENSIVE WORKS
Aljubarotta 1385
St Albans I 1455
Northampton 1460
St Albans II 1461

VALLEY
Roundway Down 1643
Cropredy Bridge 1644
Naseby 1645
The Dunes 1658
Sedgemoor 1685
Oudenaarde 1708

Linton 1648
Fontenoy 1745

FEATURED
Roliça 1808
Corunna 1809
Sorauren 1813

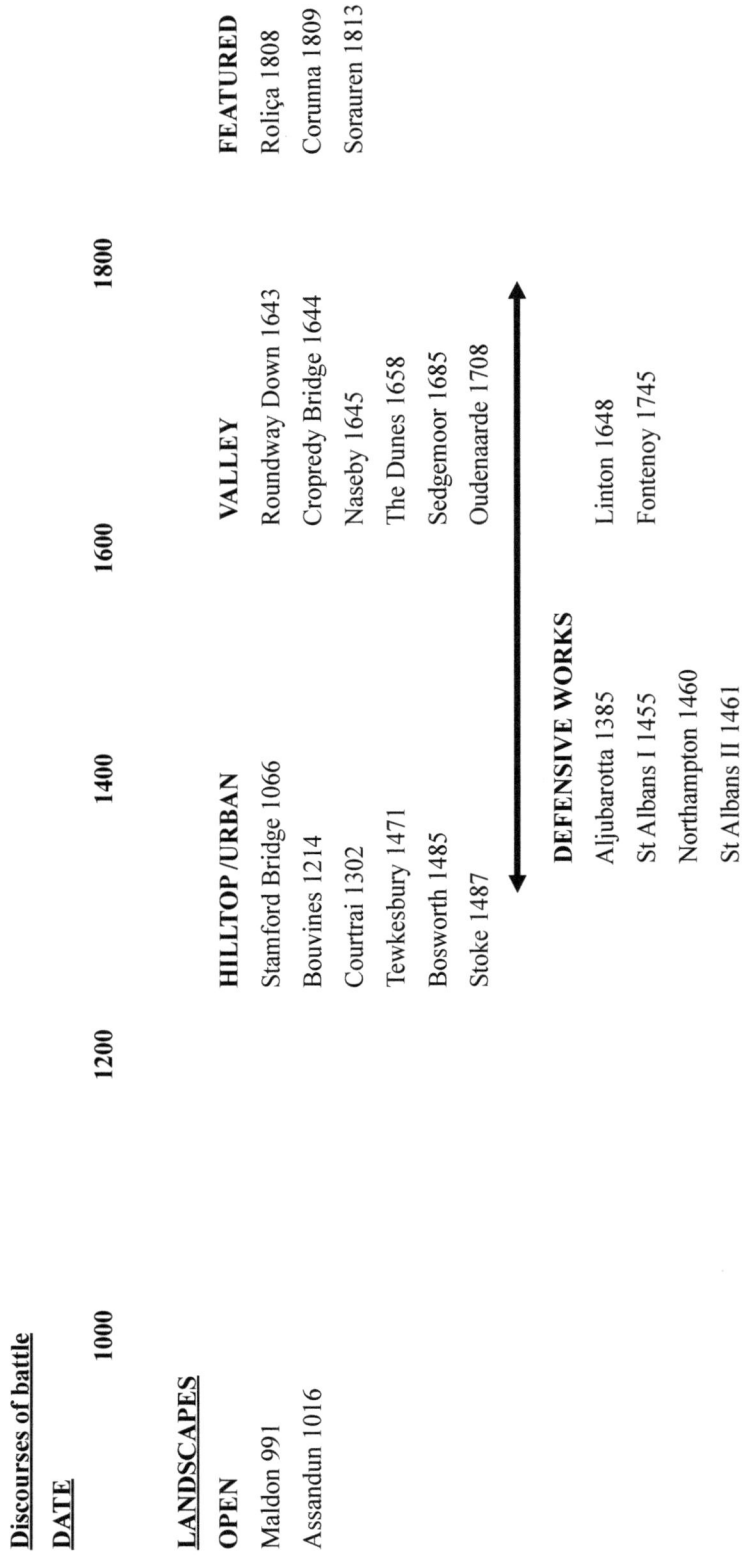

Figure 43. Discourses of Battle

(Creasy 1908; Fuller 1970; Weigley 1991). John Keegan – paradoxically also focussing on the single military event in his own work – points out that this approach has led

> whole squads of modern military historians [to indulge in] an endless, repetitive examination of battles that... can be said to have done nothing but make the world worse [and to ascribe to] strategically piffling, pointless bloodbaths... the cachet 'decisive' on the grounds that they must have decided something (Keegan 1976: 62).

Keegan is highly critical of the so-called 'battle piece', the traditional 'rhetoric of battle history' narrative (Keegan 1976: 36), composed of 'disjunctive movement... uniformity of behaviour... simplified characterization [and] simplified motivation' among large numbers of individuals (ibid: 65–66).

Wars, campaigns and battles can all be reduced to a story of the same basic form. Initial background information concerns the reasons for fighting, the forces available and their relative position in space. Movements to bring the forces closer together are then described and what happens at the point of contact. The third and final phase concerns the outcome: victory for one side, defeat for the other, and the consequences for victor and defeated. The focus is upon the *reasons* for conflict, the *means* applied, and the *outcome*: this is war as a rational means-ends relationship.

Functionalist interpretations

The second element derives from the first, since a focus on cause-and-effect relationships leads to a view of war and the practices of warfare as practical means to practical ends, and this in turn leads to a particular interpretive stance. The focus of attention is placed upon those who organise and lead in war, and who are assessed for their skills as commanders – especially in terms of how they mobilise resources to achieve ends (eg, Montgomery 1968). In the same vein, landscape features present on a battlefield are treated as having varying levels of functional utility: as objects that are useful to a soldier; as objects that have no utility to a soldier; and as objects that actively present threats to a soldier. The literature of the study of war is accordingly littered with commentary upon landscape representing threat or opportunity: classic theoretical writers such as Clausewitz (1976: 348–54) and Sun Tzu (Tao 2000: 116–23; Chaliand 1994: 221–38) refer to it as 'terrain'; while the more practically-oriented Montgomery (1968: 307) writes of 'obstacles'.

Such physical features play their part in the telling of the narrative. Major river valleys and passes through mountains become spaces through which armies are repeatedly drawn (Cline 2000) while other accessible spaces constitute 'blood alleys' through which armies repeatedly march and in which they repeatedly fight (eg, Hanson 1991: 254; Holmes 1996). The typical – and expected – shape of a battlefield is a space containing distinct features, such as watercourses to impede movement or mark the edges of territory, and bridges across them; roads and tracks to facilitate movement; buildings and other places in which to conceal troops and for which fighting must take place; and steep slopes and high ground on which to stand.

Warfare as a means-end relationship requires tools to achieve its object. Among these are the people who do the fighting, the strategies and tactics they apply, the equipment they carry, and the ground on which they stand or over which they march. In interpreting war in the past, all these have rational and functional roles to play. Their

presence and absence from the battlefield, their effects upon the fighting, the outcomes they produce – all can be explained in utilitarian terms. Among historians of war in the ancient world, Victor Hanson is critical of 'classical' military historians who have focussed on 'deployment, drill, weapons and tactics' (Hanson 1989: 24), taking a distanced viewpoint 'as if they were suspended above the killing on the battlefield in an observation balloon looking downward, detached from if not uninterested in the desperate individuals below' (ibid: 23).

'Ritual' versus 'real' war

This dominant 'functionalist' reading of warfare in the historic period reflects a deeper set of assumptions in the treatment of war that are particularly evident in studies of *pre*historic periods. Turney-High's (1949) distinction between 'primitive' and 'true' war (although adopted in part more recently by Keegan [1993]) has in general given way to a distinction between 'real' and 'ritual' war in the distant past (Halsall 1989; Carman and Carman 2005). This distinction is also evident in the influential *War Before Civilisation* (Keeley 1996). It challenges the general assumption of a 'peaceful' past, maintaining, for example, the highly functionalist 'defensive' purpose of large hilltop bank-and-ditch enclosures against those who argue for these constructions' more symbolic role. In considering what he calls *Postmodern War* Chris Hables Gray (1997) also argues for the maintenance of a distinction between 'ritual' war and 'ancient' war: the latter is more akin to our own highly organised and highly technological warfare. However, in his book *The Western Way of War: infantry battle in classical Greece*, Victor Hanson (1989) is at pains to point out that ancient Greek hoplite warfare was not a matter of the rational consideration of strategy and tactics but a brutal – and essentially irrational – ritual of community. Keegan (1993) brings the argument up to date, by suggesting that the modern Western form of war is the product of particular cultural factors, rather than being inherently 'natural' or rational.

Alternatives: some inspirational texts on war

John Keegan's *The Face of Battle* (1976) and Victor Hanson's *The Western Way of War* (1989) offer sustained critiques of the accepted manner of writing military history and examine in some detail the sequence of battlefield events from various periods of history in terms of their experiential aspects: the effects of particular weapons on the human frame; the means of keeping men in the fighting line or of urging them to the attack; and the aftermath. Instead of a distanced, 'general's eye view' and rationalistic account of battle, these books offer the possibility of constructing a view 'from the inside' and of understanding the experience of war at the sharp end. In terms of our interests, Keegan's work opened up the possibility of taking an overtly 'materialist' approach to battle (Carman 1997a) – in the simple sense of looking at its physical characteristics and consequences, rather than dealing with battle as the outcome of purely cerebral activity. Keegan's directly comparative approach across several centuries also strikes a chord with our own interest in taking a long-term perspective on battles (Carman 1997b).

Hanson went one step further in attempting to use his analysis as a window through which to consider the approach to war generally taken in the Western world. Arguing that the single, decisive clash of arms represented by Hoplite battle has been taken in the West as the model for how war ought to be, Hanson points up the inappropriateness of such an attitude in an age of long-range weapons of mass destruction. He thus uses an understanding of war in historical times as a means to critique our own age. Keegan develops this theme in his own *History of Warfare* (1993), which seeks to draw on history for alternative but subordinate models of war. These works thus contain the seeds of investigating the ideology of warfare by an examination of its specific form in particular historical periods.

Chris Hables Gray's *Postmodern War* (1997) and Michael Shapiro's *Violent Cartographies* (1997) are works originating from disciplines beyond and separate from both archaeology and military history. They represent the return to war as a topic in the social sciences and a new critical approach to the study and understanding of war in our own age. *Postmodern War* – like Keegan's *History of Warfare* – seeks to reveal the cultural basis for the modern project of making war appear a realm of rational decision-making and one subject to human control. Shapiro explains his own purpose in *Violent Cartographies*:

> I have had to mount a resistance to many familiar languages of analysis, in particular the rationalistic discourses that dominate 'security studies' [out of which Shapiro himself comes. The aim of his book] is to juxtapose such rationalism to a more ethnographic mode of thinking, to make rationalistic and logistical thinking appear to be a peculiar preoccupation rather than an edifying pedagogy (1997: xi).

Gray (1997) chooses to address the components of modern war systems, unpacking the illogic and untruth that lie at the heart of military organisation and planning. Shapiro (1997) addresses the rhetoric of military activity, mapping in a series of chapters the ways in which – at least in the American imagination – enemies have their humanity stripped from them, creating a moral space in which the military preference for violence can prevail. In thus taking a critical perspective upon war in our own time, these works – and others like them – inspire the possibility of a critical examination of war in the past, one not limited to the professional expectations of military history held by the soldier; nor to dominant traditions of enquiry. Instead, it opens up the possibility of examining aspects of war in the past in their own terms. It is this that the Bloody Meadows Project aims to do in relation to the places where military violence was carried out.

Our method: a 'phenomenological' approach to historic battlefields

Most archaeologies of war have adopted a military history approach to such matters. The possibility nonetheless exists of using archaeology to subvert these ideas and, in particular, to provide a framework within which individual battle-sites can be considered as places of cultural – rather than merely functional – significance. The purpose of such an approach is to find out what these places may be able to tell us about the people who went there in the past and those peoples' attitudes to each other and that place. For us, the key element is always the landscape of the battle itself, which we approach by drawing upon the recent application of ideas from phenomenology in archaeology.

As Tilley puts it in justifying such a 'phenomenological' approach to studying landscapes in archaeology:

> [What] is clear [from the ethnographic record] is the symbolic, ancestral, and temporal significance of landscape [to peoples]. The landscape is continually being encultured, bringing things into meaning as part of a symbolic process by which

human consciousness makes the physical reality of the natural environment into an intelligible and socialised form.... It [is accordingly] evident... that the significance of landscape for different populations cannot be simply read off from the local 'ecological' characteristics of a 'natural' environment (1994: 67).

And:

> Cultural markers [such as monuments are used] to create a new sense of place.... An already encultured landscape becomes refashioned, its meanings now controlled by the imposition of [a new] cultural form (ibid: 208).

We think the same can be said for the relationship of warriors in the past to the land in and over which they fought: there is more to it than mere 'terrain'. By fighting a battle – imposing this particular cultural form on the location – a new sense of that place is created, to be carried into the future. What we are interested in getting at is what sense of place was brought to that location and what change was wrought by fighting a battle there.

Tilley's remarks specifically refer to the relationship of prehistoric monuments to mostly 'empty' rural landscapes in Britain. Following his lead, a phenomenological approach to the study of landscapes as taken by archaeologists has therefore generally been limited to the monumental 'ritual' landscapes of later European prehistory. The approach is, however, also of more general relevance to any encultured space. The typical interpretive device in battlefield research is the battlefield plan – an objective view from above, divorced from the action – but as Tilley also emphasises, place is not something that can be understood 'objectively':

> Looking at the two-dimensional plane of the modern topographic map with sites [or artefact scatters] plotted on it, it is quite impossible to envisage the landscape in which these places are embedded. The representation fails, and cannot substitute for being there, being *in place*. [The] process of observation requires time and a feeling for the place (ibid: 75).

The same is true of the traditional battlefield plan: it cannot substitute for actually being there. Nor can it substitute for movement through the space. We therefore draw upon the ideas of prehistoric archaeologists who are developing ways of utilising the idea that the way of moving through particular kinds of spaces can be considered a form of ritual or performance (Barrett 1994; Carman 1999: 242; Pearson 1998; Thomas 1991). The often slow and deliberate movements of bodies of troops across the space of a battlefield – frequently in defiance of a natural desire to avoid danger – have obvious ritual connotations. So, too, do aspects such as drill, the proper use of equipment, standardised formations, and the focus on the capture of enemy standards and correctly worn regalia (Keeley 1996: 62–63). Accordingly, gaining a feeling for the place as a place and focussing on how one moves through it in performance, one can perhaps gain a sense of what a particular historic battlefield represents in terms of experience and meaning.

Research as political challenge

For those who 'like' war and for large numbers of those who study it (but who may not like it), warfare is seen as a rational activity carried out in a functionalist mode of thought. If this were so, however, it seems more likely that it would be a very last resort rather than an early one. It would not require that the enemy be demonised or transformed into figures of fun (and sometimes both simultaneously). Military organisations would not need to focus so heavily upon the trappings of their craft: uniforms, insignia, flags, rank and status. The problem for those of us who do not like war is in overcoming this very powerful and well-established understanding of the nature of war.

Our work goes some way towards that aim, we hope, by challenging the academic discourse that provides support to the military ideology of war and its popular perception. Our challenge to military history is a simple one: if war is a rational activity, then functionalist explanations can be made and sustained *in detail* for any aspect of warmaking over time. We have chosen to examine battlefields as landscapes and in Figure 43 we show battlefields we have investigated in terms of changes to the landscapes where they were fought (for a sustained discussion see Carman and Carman 2006). They group conveniently: medieval battles were generally fought on high open ground and near or visible from urban centres; early modern battles were generally fought on low, open ground away from urban centres; and later battles generally occupied ground that contained a range of different features both natural and built. In parallel there is also a subsidiary preference for places offering something like built defences, a preference that declines with the advent of the 'featured' battlespace. We have – and do so again here - challenged military historians to explain these changes in battlefield landscape preference, and so far we have failed to receive any detailed explanation of why technological changes (the usual explanation offered) affect choice of landscape. This supports our own belief that what dictates this choice is not a functionalist reading of ground but ideas about where it is appropriate and 'proper' to fight wars. In other words, that cultural – even ritualistic – factors are more important than a reasoned consideration of utility.

This is not, in the end, an earth-shattering finding. No military establishment will fall because of the work that we do, nor will it stop any particular war from happening. But what it will do, we suggest, is help to chip away at the intellectual supports for the convenient myths of warmakers that what they do is grounded in reason and sense. Our research is done with the aim of affecting people's attitudes and understandings about war and challenging what we believe to be one of the most powerful and dangerous discourses of our age. Our project began in rhetoric (Carman 1997b), developed as a search for a suitable object of study, and has gone on to produce a set of provisional statements about some of those factors that condition the practice of mass violence. We hope that it will mature into an approach to the study of war that causes people to think more deeply about those things that drive them to behave towards other people and communities in hostile ways, and the unstated assumptions we carry with us into our dealings with others. We hope that it will empower those of us who object to the use of violence in all its forms to reveal the lack of rationality that lies at its heart, whatever rhetoric may be used against us in defence of the military option.

Acknowledgements

Thanks are due to Angela Piccini and Dan Hicks for allowing us to present at CHAT 03 without being actually present, and to the reader of our paper. Some of the content of this version has also seen life elsewhere, especially at TAG 2001 in Dublin, and at the *Fields of Conflict* conferences in Glasgow, Åland and Nashville. Our gratitude also goes to the organisers of these events for allowing us to present our results to them. We are grateful too to the editors for their kindly handling of our text and their helpful advice on sharpening it.

References

Barrett, J. 1994. *Fragments from Antiquity: An Archaeology of Social Life in Britain 2900–1200 BC.* Oxford: Blackwell.

Brodie, B. 1973. *War and Politics.* London: Cassell.

Carman, J. 1996. *Valuing Ancient Things: Archaeology and Law.* London: Cassell.

Carman, J. (ed.) 1997a. *Material Harm. Archaeological Studies of War and Violence.* Glasgow: Cruithne Press.

Carman, J. 1997b. Introduction: Approaches to Violence. In J. Carman (ed.), *Material Harm. Archaeological Studies of War and Violence,* 1–23. Glasgow: Cruithne Press.

Carman, 1999. Bloody Meadows: The Places of Battle. In S. Tarlow and S. West (eds), *The Familiar Past? Archaeologies of Later Historical Britain,* 233–45. London: Routledge.

Carman, J. and Carman, P. 2005. War in Prehistoric Society: Modern Views of Ancient Violence. In M. Parker-Pearson and I. J. N. Thorpe (eds), *Warfare, Violence and Slavery in Prehistory: Proceedings of a Prehistoric Society Conference in Sheffield.* BAR International Series 1374, 217–24. Oxford: BAR Publishing.

Carman, J. and Carman, P. 2006. *Bloody Meadows: Investigating Landscapes of Battle.* Stroud: Sutton.

Chaliand, G. 1994. *The Art of War in World History From Antiquity to the Nuclear Age.* Berkeley and Los Angeles: University of California Press.

Clausewitz, C. von 1976 [1832]. *On War* (edited and translated M. Howard and P. Paret). Princeton NJ: Princeton University Press.

Cline, E.H. 2000. *The Battles of Armageddon: Megiddo and the Jezreel Valley from the Bronze Age to the Nuclear Age.* Ann Arbor MICH: University of Michigan Press.

Creasy, E. 1908 [1851]. *The Fifteen Decisive Battles of the World. From Marathon to Waterloo.* London: Macmillan.

Doyle, P. and Bennett, M.R. (eds) 2002. *Fields of Battle: Terrain in Military History.* Dordrecht: Kluwer.

English Heritage. 1995. *Register of Historic Battlefields.* London: English Heritage.

Freeman, T. and Pollard, A. (eds) 2001. *Fields of Conflict: Progress and Prospects in Battlefield Archaeology, Proceedings of a Conference Held in the Department of Archaeology, University of Glasgow, April 2000.* BAR International Series 958. Oxford: BAR Publishing.

Fuller, J.F.C. 1970. *The Decisive Battles of the Western World and Their Effect Upon History,* 2 vols, J. Terraine (ed.). London: Paladin.

Gray, C.H. 1997 *Postmodern War: the New Politics of Conflict.* London: Routledge.

Halsall, G. 1989. Anthropology and the Study of Pre-Conquest Warfare and Society: The Ritual War in Anglo-Saxon England. In S.C. Hawkes (ed.), *Weapons and Warfare in Anglo-Saxon England,* 155–177. Oxford University Committee for Archaeology Monograph 21. Oxford: Oxbow Books.

Hanson, V.D. 1989. *The Western Way of War. Infantry Battle in Classical Greece.* Oxford: Oxford University Press.

Hanson, V.D. (ed.) 1991. *Hoplites. The Classical Greek Battle Experience.* London: Routledge.

Holmes, R. 1996. *War Walks: from Agincourt to Normandy.* London: BBC Books.

Keegan, J. 1976. *The Face of Battle.* London: Hutchinson.

Keegan, J. 1993. *A History of Warfare*. London: Hutchinson.

Keeley, L.H. 1996. *War Before Civilization. The Myth of the Peaceful Savage*. Oxford and New York: Oxford University Press.

Montgomery, Field Marshall Viscount, of Alamein. 1968. *A History of Warfare*. London: Collins.

Pearson, M. 1998. Performance as Valuation: Early Bronze Age Burial as Theatrical Complexity. In D. Bailey (ed.) *The Archaeology of Value: Essays on Prestige and the Processes of Valuation*, 32–41. Oxford, BAR International Series 730. BAR Publishing.

Pollard, T. and I. Banks (eds). 2006. *Past Tense: Studies in the Archaeology of Conflict*. Leiden and Boston: Brill.

Schofield, J. 2005. *Combat Archaeology*. Duckworth Debates in Archaeology. London: Duckworth.

Shapiro, M.J. 1997. *Violent Cartographies: Mapping Cultures of War*. Minneapolis MI: University of Minnesota Press.

Tao Hanzhang. 2000. *Sun Tzu's Art of War: the Modern Chinese Interpretation*. New York: Sterling Publishing Co.

Thomas, J. 1991. *Rethinking the Neolithic*. Cambridge: Cambridge University Press.

Tilley, C. 1994. *A Phenomenology of Landscape*. London: Berg.

Turney-High, H. 1949 [2nd ed. 1971]. *Primitive War: its Practice and Concepts*. Colombia: University of South Carolina Press.

Weigley, R.F. 1991. *The Age of Battles: the Quest for Decisive Warfare from Breitenfeld to Waterloo*. Bloomington and Indianapolis: Indiana University Press.

Afterword: Towards an Archaeology of the Contemporary Past

Victor Buchli

As the chapters in this volume testify there is clearly a new forum - the CHAT conference group - in which archaeologists can finally engage with issues related to the historic and contemporary past. Of course, this preoccupation with the contemporary and recent past is by any means a novelty within archaeology. The preoccupation with the contemporary can be traced at least as far back as one of the discipline's early practitioners, Pitt-Rivers. His initial interest in archaeology emerged from his studies of contemporary rifles while a military officer. Similarly Alfred Kroeber performed one of the key studies of the archaeology of the contemporary at the beginning of the twentieth century with his study of the evolution of contemporary women's dress lengths, entitled *On the Principle of Order in Civilization as Exemplified by Changes of Fashion* (Kreober 1919). The interest in the contemporary proceeded intermittently with occasional work emerging, such as Kidders' unpublished excavation of a town dump in the 1920s (Rathje 1979: 3). However, it was not until the advent of the New Archaeology and the development of ethnoarchaeology that the contemporary become an established concern within the field. Although the intellectual motives differed, the contemporary was clearly the focus of archaeological work. With Schiffer and Gould's *Archaeology of Us* (Gould and Schiffer 1981), Rathje's Garbology (Rathje 1979), Hodder's study of the material culture of an English pet food factory (Hodder 1987) and Shanks and Tilley's analysis of beer cans (Shanks and Tilley 1987), the study of contemporary material culture has gained in interest and significance. The archaeological concern with the contemporary is by no means new but it has certainly been marginal. This publication and the activities hosted by the CHAT group mark in many ways the end of this marginality as they strive to move the archaeological study of the present and recent past into the center of the discipline's intellectual debates.

Much of the debate concerning the study of the contemporary past has, appropriately, been about timing. At times rather arbitrary cut-off dates have been imposed to distinguish the work of the archaeologist from the historian. These of course have shifted considerably over the past century as historical archaeology and the periods it covers extends closer and closer to the present, to the point where now we do not feel inclined to make these distinctions as vigorously as we once did. Much of the concern over these distinctions over time and area can be attributed to a concern over increasing professionalisation, specialisation and the maintenance of disciplinary boundaries – something our nineteenth-century forebears were not too preoccupied with in the early days of anthropology.

But the appropriateness of these temporal boundaries and timing in general is not, I would say, a misplaced concern. One of the dominant concerns of mid nineteenth-century anthropology and archaeology was the establishment of what Pitt-Rivers described as a 'philosophy of progress'. In short it was the impact of modernity and rapid industrialisation and the creation of global and colonial economy and empire that necessitated such a philosophy. How could one explain the Australian aboriginal club and the steam engine occupying the same time and space of Empire? Similarly, the rapidity of technological change in arms manufacture in the lifetime of Pitt-Rivers (such as the replacement of smoothbore muskets with new rifles) necessitated an understanding of how such change could be understood and made sense of in the lifetime of one individual – hence the over-riding need of a 'philosophy of progress' to cope with the rapid pace and tumult of Victorian-era modernity. Within the imperial Victorian imaginary, the primitive and modern were not simply separated by chronological time but existed side by side in contemporary time and space. This was a context in which the distinctions of time, progress and geographic distance were rapidly being overcome and converging, while simultaneously receding were the traditions and peoples who stood as a gloss for the past and the primitive. Thus a philosophy of progress found use for a recently emerging conceptual tool: material culture as a new super-artefact and category of analysis with which to reckon lineal notions of progress, to negotiate these newly emerging conflations of time, culture and space.

In a similar vein, Gavin Lucas and I observed that the archaeology of the contemporary past upsets these distances that archaeology traditionally negotiates – making the strange familiar (Buchli and Lucas 2001). But in the case of the contemporary past it does the opposite. It makes the familiar strange. We suggested that the moment we are now in, at the beginning of the twenty-first century, is characterised by a particular set of affairs that make this period distinct from others for the archaeologist – not only in terms of the sheer overabundance of information but also in terms of the material culture in which we are enveloped. This is a state of overwhelming superfluity that renders many aspects of human experience silent and invisible. Though distinct, these conditions are not unlike the more traditional settings of archaeological work, where the dearth of data has rendered whole realms of human activity mute and invisible. Archaeology, as a consequence, has developed a very sophisticated body of technical and conceptual tools with which to presence these absences under these conditions.

What might be at stake then with absences we attempt to presence through the archaeological act in the present? Of course a 'philosophy of progress' is a notion that has seen its time, but at another level there is something else that I think might connect these two moments: a certain emotional quality that I would identify as melancholy.

The nineteenth-century ethnologists and archaeologists were often motivated by a certain melancholic urge to stem the losses wrought by the march of time and progress. The rapid pace of cultural contact and industrialisation in both the imperial centers and their margins saw the rapid disappearance of ways of life, knowledges of the past, and vanishing indigenous traditions. This fuelled a melancholic preoccupation that produced folklore, ethnology and archaeology. This was a highly emotionally charged and desperate attempt to hold on to these disappearing worlds in time and place. To quote Pitt-Rivers, speaking on a June Friday in 1867:

> for there can be little doubt that in a few years all the barbarous races will have disappeared from the Earth, or will have ceased to preserve their native arts. The law which consigns to destruction all savage races when brought into contact with a civilization much higher than their own, is now operating with unrelenting fury in every part of the world (Pitt-Rivers 1867).

Much of archaeology and anthropology was devoted to this melancholic resistance to the inevitability of the march of time and progress. In the light of this, I would like to reconsider this melancholic quality surrounding the study of material culture and archaeology with reference to Sigmund Freud and Walter Benjamin. Recently, the literary scholars Eng and Kazanjian have refocused attention on the insights of these two thinkers and the radical potential of melancholy for historical understanding, particularly of the contemporary past (Eng and Kazanjian 2003).

Sigmund Freud suggested that melancholy is pathological, the sufferer resisting the resolution of mourning and refusing to let go of the lost object of desire. That refusal, Eng and Kazanjian suggest, has radical implications. They note how Benjamin later remarked in relation to the writing of history: '...to articulate the past historically... means to seize hold of a memory as it flashes up at a moment of danger...to retain that image of the past which unexpectedly appears to man singled out by history at a moment of danger' (Benjamin cited in Eng and Kazanjian 2003).

Archaeology serves Benjamin's purpose, as Pitt-Rivers understood so well the necessity of 'seizing hold of a memory as it flashes up at a moment of danger' when he described 'The law which consigns to destruction all savage races when brought into contact with a civilization much higher than their own...' (Pitt-Rivers 1867)

This urgent melancholic loss is by definition unfixable or objectifiable. It cannot be assuaged and is fundamentally inconsolable, implacable and resistant to the objectification and sublation that the integrative process of mourning allows. The resolution afforded by mourning may be therapeutic, but it is one that always favours the victor. As Forty observed '...the filling of a void, whose emptiness had exercised diverse collective memories, ends by excluding all but a single dominant one' (1999: 10). If we think of the victims of the Argentinean dictatorship, once the inconsolable demands of the mothers of 'the Disappeared' have been met and the bodies discovered, identified and buried, then the radical melancholic challenge the grief of these mothers represented is no more. Mourning sets in and social life is stabilized and we memorialise so that we might forget and move on.

This implacability is the source of melancholy's radical potential that Eng and Kazanjian describe. And it is this implacability that is at the heart of Benjamin's description of memory '... as it flashes up at a moment of danger.' Timing, strategy and appropriateness is everything if we think about the interventions archaeology performs whether it is in 'moments of danger' in Pitt-Rivers' days or ours.

This issue of timing brings me to the issue of social relevance in relation to contemporary archaeology and the archaeology of the recent past. It is of course obvious that the political dimension of this activity is great. One of the things Gavin Lucas and I were keenly aware of when we were considering the archaeology of the contemporary past was the fact that the archaeological act is almost always a political intervention within the prevailing unresolved and inconsolable traumas and conflicts characterising contemporary life. The chapters in this volume all engage with this political dimension. To do the archaeology of the contemporary past is to engage directly with its raw and extremely painful nerves – such as homelessness, social exclusion, war crimes, or reconciliation – to name just a few. These are, in effect, profoundly melancholic contexts that are unresolved and in which archaeology materialises those troubling absences and serves as a therapeutic device.

It is now taken for granted that archaeology in all its aspects is a contemporary practice taking place in the present, within living communities which are affected and shaped by these practices. Sometimes the interventions are successful, sometimes they fail, and one might add, arguably, rightly so: some of the problems encountered in the archaeology of Native American groups testify to this. Work occurs at certain historical moments and the materiality that is constituted is historically contingent. This is what happens when Nora describes how a lived, embodied community of memory becomes a static and material place of memory (Nora 1989). The realisation of this shift is what archaeologists and artists actually do to bring about their work, which, to quote Nora, 'relies on the materiality of the trace, the immediacy of the recording, the visibility of the image' (Nora 1989: 13). Ultimately the judges of these activities will not be us but the communities we serve who, in an archaeology of the present, are unavoidable and are in fact an integral part of the whole process, not unlike the communities of descendants produced by more traditional nationalist archaeologies. Timing here is everything. If the proper historic moment is not at hand to permit such interventions, we can get things very wrong. After all, not everything can be remembered; sometimes it is a question of timing, sometimes it is simply a question of sustaining manageable lives built upon strategic forgetting. Like the madness of Luria's patient, who could never forget anything that happened, we must forget in order to be able to pursue viable lives (Forty 1999), but this forgetting always has its social costs with which we must reckon.

There is, of course, a certain question of propriety at stake here, which traditional archaeologists have always felt intuitively, regarding the study of the contemporary past: whether and when it should or should not be done. By no means does anything go and by no means should the entirety of twentieth- and twenty-first-century experience be the object of our inquiries. We cannot and should not do the archaeology of everything – archaeologies of the contemporary past must prove their worth. The contexts of traditional archaeology are often dictated by the happenstance of post-depositional processes – which alone is usually enough to justify it – though as we know not always. This element of chance is less evident in the contemporary past. Technologies suggest that we have access to almost everything, if we want to, so we do have the freedom to be deliberate and strategic. It is the political, social and intellectual will that determines what we do and do not investigate and intervene within.

Relevance is critical here. This is of course a question of the responsibilities we have towards the communities, individuals, and institutions directly implicated and involved in the production of archaeologies of the contemporary past. After all, the archaeological act is an intervention into the fabric of social life that disrupts with eruptive force through its compelling empiricism, materialising that which is unseen and unheard, that which challenges prevailing settlements and that, at times, can be therapeutic and, at other times, unreasonable or simply irrelevant.

Empiricism's ability to reiterate presences and fix our identifications in reference to it constantly renegotiates that identification in every instance. This empiricism is relentless and does not permit us to get away. It always draws us back in and challenges our identifications and, in fact, produces them anew with every encounter. It collapses time and space, it produces a past in the present, and it relentlessly makes the obscure visible – good hard data is implacable, irrefutable and will not be denied. Such empiricism facilitates a merging of perceptual horizons that produces our identifications and challenges historically produced temporalities through the archaeological intervention.

The materialisations that our ever increasingly sophisticated empiricism affords are not all together straightforward. They range from the highly durable and monumental to the ephemeral. The kinds of materialisations we perform matter and as well as the way in which they are disseminated. As Rosemary Joyce observed a little while ago at the World Archaeology Conference in Washington DC (2003), this is a distinction between *monumental* materialities and other collectively organized durable projects, and *trace* materialities – the short-term ephemeral consequences of daily life usually at the scale of the individual, household and immediate community. These are the materialities at play between those recognised by UNESCO criteria for inclusion in the World Heritage List of cultural properties and nation-building projects, and the ephemeralities of daily life that speak of the mute and marginal activities of individuals and communities. Archaeology serves both. This is, of course, a question of the social effects of the materialities we constitute, the absences we presence.

However, the material terrain of our work – the constitution of material culture with its solid materialities that have served various social projects – are shifting. Projects such as a 'philosophy of progress', social revolution, nation-building enterprises and the reconstitution of oppressed communities that 'strategic' materialisations enable - the sort of traditional Foucauldian disciplinary and subject-producing enterprises that materialities of archaeology shape – are increasingly superseded by new materialities, considerably attenuated and ephemeral. I have in mind here, for instance, new forms of governmentality such as the actuarial practices described by Jonathan Simon that constitute subjects not according to some materially and spatially palpable subjectivity, but according to highly attenuated and ephemeral social aggregates (Simon 1988). That is, less and less are we constituted as corporeal members of a community with a specific body in a specific social space but by new categories. I, for instance, would be constituted as an unmarried, white, male, non-smoker in a London WC1E postal code. This unstable and rather banal social aggregate of which I am a part holds little ontological and corporeal relevance for me as an individual, yet it is according to such aggregates that, increasingly, the social terms of enfranchisement are allocated and managed. This is what Bauman describes as the shift to the unstable fluid modernity (Bauman 2000) of late capitalism as opposed to the solid modernity of Marx's and Pitt-Rivers' days. It inhibits any possibility of the sedimentation of a stable coherent subjectivity according to the materialities we archaeologists have traditionally been able to constitute. This is a shift from the highly material forms of traditional Foucauldian disciplines to the rather immaterial forms of late-capitalist management and governmentality.

Plural Materialities

Recently, in my own work on the construction of the new capital city, Astana, in the post-Soviet state of Kazakhstan, I find I have been confronted with a plurality of materialities at play that reckon differently: continuity, ethnic belonging and the terms of social exclusion and inclusion. Various groups, individuals and interests produce and manipulate these diverse materialities at key historical moments or 'moments of crises' to challenge settlements or enable enfranchisement. The heritage, the monument, the archaeological artefact are part of a plurality of materialities at play negotiating the instabilities of social life after the collapse of Communism. The archaeological intervention, and the peculiar materialities it constitutes, is just one of many different kinds that arise.

In the new capital Astana these various forms of materiality are simultaneously at play to portray continuity, when continuity is under threat amongst different competing ethnic groups or when a continuity needs to be constituted. These various materialities also facilitate different versions of the nation-building enterprise. Here the archaeology of the medieval past and contemporary past is being constituted at the same time within the building of the new capital. Archaeology and architecture are two sides of the same coin of nation building and the production of ethnic continuity and legitimacy (be it Kazakh or Russian). All of this is done with recourse to varying degrees of materiality and their different understandings to cope and manage with an unstable present and uncertain future. For instance, traditional Kazakh architectonic elements, once used to reckon geneological time, now claim national space in very different material modes. Continuity is reckoned in materially diverse ways ranging from the monumental to the ephemeral, depending on whether that continuity is to be reckoned prospectively or retrospectively and which way or both is to be more socially effective. Thus, different materialities are used at once to achieve this, in different contexts and at different moments in time, whether employing the materialising technologies of archaeology, urban planning, heritage management or the seemingly banal activities of DIY. I do not want to suggest here a western/non-western duality or any other dualism, but to suggest that there are material limits, means and social contingencies that suggest one form of materiality over another. They work in different ways with different social effects, and people avail themselves of these as need be and not in terms of some ethnically determined, or developmentally determined point of view. They are appropriate in terms of the material and ontological limitations in which they need to function.

The result is a material environment consisting of multiple and seemingly incompatible regimes of materiality that are unstable, and incoherent, but constantly reckoning and reconfiguring the contested social and material terms of life. The increasing inability to cohere in the Kazakhstani contexts, whose unstable social relations are so cogently visible in monumental building projects on the verge of collapse that they attempt to sustain, actually offers the possibility to counter and challenge various claims for legitimacy and power.

Under the terms of fluid modernity in which we find ourselves increasingly, we might be seeing a new sphere of micropowers, whose unstable fluidities can be worked to enable as well as disable. Rather than fruitlessly bemoaning this situation, we might choose to see and understand how this state of affairs is emerging and works – how it empowers as well as disempowers. That our conventional solid ontologies are in crisis is no reason not to try to understand the effects of other materialities that undermine them. If we accept the Foucauldian understanding that all forms of power are at once enabling and disabling, then we might consider how the archaeology of the contemporary past and its empiricist legacy can facilitate those 'eruptions' in the present within the superfluity of the information in which we are enveloped. This is not because of the reality effects such empiricism produces, but because of the means by which it facilitates identification and relevance for the individuals and communities our work might benefit. It is the empiricist tradition within the archaeology of the contemporary past that challenges things as they seem to be, through its eruptive effects. Our increasingly melancholic circumstances which mourn the loss of coherent subjectivities are also the circumstances whereby these melancholic impulses erupt to challenge the highly attenuated and ephemeral settlements about which power mercurially coheres in the present.

References

Bauman, Z. 2000. *Liquid Modernity*. Cambridge: Polity Press.

Buchli, V. and Lucas, G. 2001. *Archaeologies of the Contemporary Past*. London: Routledge.

Eng, D.L. and Kazanjian, D. 2003. *Loss*. Berkeley: University of California Press.

Forty, A. 1999. Introduction. In A. Forty and S. Kuechler (eds), *The Art of Forgetting*, Oxford: Berg.

Hodder, I. 1987. Bow Ties and Pet Foods: Material Culture and the Negotiation of Change in British Industry. In I. Hodder (ed.) *The Archaeology of Contextual Meanings*. Cambridge: Cambridge University Press, pp. 11-19.

Kroeber, A. 1919. On the principle of order in civilization as exemplified by changes of fashion. *American Anthropologist* 21 (3): 235–63.

Nora, P. 1989. Between memory and history: *Les Lieux de Mémoire*. *Representations* 26 (Spring): 7–25.

Pitt-Rivers, A.L.F. 1867. Primitive warfare: Illustrated by specimen from the Museum of the Institution (Section 1). *Journal of the Royal United Services Institution* 11: 612-645.

Pitt-Rivers, A.L.F. 1875. On the principles of classification. *Journal of the Anthropological Institute of Great Britain and Ireland* 4: 293-308.

Rathje, W. 1979. Modern material culture studies. *Advances in Archaeological Method and Theory* 2, 1–27.

Gould, R.A. and Schiffer, M.B. (eds). 1981. *Modern Material Culture Studies: The Archaeology of Us*. New York: Academic Press.

Shanks, M. and Tilley, C. 1987. Social Values, Social Constraints and Material Culture: The Design of Contemporary Beer Cans. In M. Shanks and C. Tilley, *Reconstructing Archaeology: Theory and Practice*. Cambridge: Cambridge University Press, pp. 172-240.

Simon, J. 1988. The ideological effects of actuarial practices. *Law and Society Review* 22 (4): 771-800.

www.ingramcontent.com/pod-product-compliance
Lightning Source LLC
Chambersburg PA
CBHW061002030426
42334CB00033B/3329